THE STUDENT'S COMPREHENSIVE GUIDE FOR COLLEGE

&

Other Life Lessons

"What to Expect & How to Succeed"

By

Valarie R. Austin

Vauboix Publishing LLC

The Student's Comprehensive Guide for College & Other Life Lessons
Copyright © 2018 by Valarie R. Austin

Published in the United States by Vauboix Publishing LLC, 15210 Dino Drive Unit 764, Burtonsville, MD 20866, info@vauboixpublishingllc.com

Publisher's Cataloging-in-Publication data

Names: Austin, Valarie R., author.
Title: The Student's comprehensive guide for college & other life lessons / by Valarie R. Austin.
Description: Includes bibliographical references and index. | Burtonsville, MD: Vauboix Publishing, LLC, 2018.
Identifiers: LCCN 2018908237 | ISBN 978-1-7325096-1-0 (pbk.) | 978-1-7325096-0-3 (Kindle)
Subjects: LCSH: College student orientation--United States--Handbooks, manuals, etc. | College students--Life skills guides. | Study skills. | Success. | College students--United States. | Universities and colleges--United States--Admission. | College freshmen. | College students--Psychology. | Academic achievement. | Young adults. | Adulthood. | Conduct of life. | BISAC: EDUCATION / Higher
Classification: LCC LB2343.3 .A97 2018 | DDC 378.1/98--dc23

Cover Design by germancreative, Fiverr.com and Interior Design by bongoneshian, Fiverr.com
Printed in the United States of America on acid-free paper
First printing edition 2018

10 9 8 7 6 5 4 3 2 1

ABOUT THE AUTHOR

In *The Student's Comprehensive Guide for College & Other Life Lessons,* author Lieutenant Colonel (Retired) Valarie Austin shares her knowledge about college from attending, graduating, and acquiring four college degrees from four different schools. LTC Austin earned her most recent Bachelor of Science degree at the University of Maryland-College Park. She also holds a Masters of Public Administration degree from the University of Wisconsin--Milwaukee, a Bachelor of Science degree from the United States Military Academy, West Point, New York, and an Associates of Applied Science degree in Network and Wireless Technologies from Montgomery College, Rockville, Maryland. In her distinguished career, LTC Austin also taught leadership and military science as an instructor in the Reserved Officer Training Corps (ROTC) program at Georgetown University, Washington D.C. From personal experience, she has unique insights into staying and graduating from college.

After her career of service in the Armed Forces including a combat tour during the Gulf War, LTC Austin retired with numerous military awards and decorations. She currently resides in Maryland.

ACKNOWLEDGMENTS

I would like to thank everyone who made this book possible. Without them, the book would have remained an idea. In all things, I thank the Lord for all of his blessings and then those who have been in my corner from the beginning. First, I would like to thank my parents, Albertha and Rayward. Although they have passed on, each laid the foundation for me to become the person who I am today. They showed me the importance of education, perseverance in achieving goals and having the confidence to reach them. Second, to my sisters of the heart, I want to express my thanks and gratitude to Dawn, Stephanie, Anna, Terrie, Nadine, Raffie, Melody, Robin, and Rachel for your input and advice. You gave me the insight to see concepts and behaviors in a different light for the better. Third, thank you to Ben, Jr., Ruth S., Deborah, Josephine, Florence, David, Sr. and Sylvia for your support and wisdom in all things. I appreciate the work of my beta readers: Maggie R., Ph.D. and teacher extraordinaire, Dawn, LaChara, Terrence, Anna, Terrie, Raffie, Melody, Deja, Kenneth, Ruth, Asia, Parker, and Carolyn. Your encouragement and editing of my book drafts were invaluable. To all of my readers, thank you for selecting this book to take your journey through college. I hope that you take pleasure in reading *The Student's Comprehensive Guide for College & Other Life Lessons* as much as I enjoyed writing it.

PREFACE

College is a wonderful experience for those who can attend; however, the trick is to stay and graduate. In writing this book, I wanted to pass along lessons learned from my experiences and knowledge about college. I am uniquely qualified to provide advice on college to the first time attendee. In my lifetime, I have obtained four advanced degrees: an associate's degree, two bachelor's degrees, and a master's degree. I graduated with an associate's degree from Montgomery College (MC) in Maryland; I attended and earned a bachelor's degree from the United States Military Academy (USMA or West Point) in New York; I obtained a second bachelor's degree from the University of Maryland-College Park (UMCP); and the University of Wisconsin-Milwaukee (UWM) conferred a master's degree on me. Therefore, I am not an armchair theorist. By attending each school, I have gained a greater understanding of the necessary tools vital for every student to graduate from college. My background as a college student provides a unique perspective in defining the keys to success in college.

While researching for this book, I noticed a lack of information that addressed the transition from high school to college, specifically, alternatives to college, preparing for college and completing college. Frequently, different books tackle the subject of getting into college, which include writing college essays, obtaining the appropriate Scholastic Aptitude Test (SAT)/SAT Subject Tests scores, and taking the proper courses in high school. A plethora of books discuss the financial aspects of college such as applying for Pell grants and loans. Thus, the dearth of comprehensive books about preparing for and staying in college through graduation is a disservice to current college students and future college-bound high school students.[1] When a student steps into his/her first college class, the clock starts ticking. Sadly, ignorance about the college culture and academic requirements prevent many students from walking across the graduation stage and receiving their diploma. I intend to sweep away the mystery and help students to understand the mechanics of college that are essential to success.

So, dear student, here is what I propose: I want you to think of me as a trusted friend or relative who wants the best for you and your future. Now, you will have access to my knowledge from attending, graduating and acquiring four college degrees from four different schools over the course of my life. Without a doubt, I understand the steps necessary to successfully earn a college diploma at a two-year or four-year institution. Although I focus on graduating from college, I also discuss whether a four-year college degree is the best choice for some people and explore alternatives. Nevertheless, college is necessary when you do not have marketable skills, knowledge, or talent. If you stay with this book till the very end, I promise that you will have many takeaway points and insights about college and yourself. I also want to highlight specific actions that you should consider in order for you to graduate from college on time.

Since every college is different, I cannot cover every topic within the scope of this book. Hence, you will encounter the "X-factor"- the unknowns about your specific school experience. In addition, every individual is different. I offer my advice based on the actions that have worked for me and these actions ought to work for you because you already have the desire to attend. As you read over the chapter titles, you can read some of the chapters or all of them in sequence based on where you are in your college journey. I hope that this book becomes a pocket guide that you read before college, read while in college, and pass along to friends and family who may attend college after you. High school graduates and current college students ought to gain a host of ideas and practical actions to make their college dream come true. As you pursue your college degree, you have the power to attain major achievements through hard work, financial wherewithal, a little luck, and hopefully many blessings. I offer my best wishes to you and your college success. College graduation on time is the goal. Now, let's reach it together.

TABLE OF CONTENTS

CHAPTER 1:
Is College for You?

College is not for or accessible to everyone. Regrettably, you may not see college as an option because you do not have the money, lack academic preparation, no desire to attend college, or lack time. In this chapter, I will explore those reasons why you may think college is not for you. I do not intend to judge your choice. In Chapter 2, I would like to offer valid arguments that college is necessary unless you have marketable specialized talent, knowledge, or skills. The problem with the current system of college attendance is that many students do not graduate on time within their two or four-year degree program. In addition, countless numbers also graduate with crushing student loan debt. In the U.S., the number of students attending colleges and universities annually is staggering. For instance, Fall 2014 statistics projected approximately 21 million students attended a higher education institution.[2] With millions of young adults enrolled in college, I would expect the U.S.'s highest level of educational attainment for its population 25 years or older to be 60% or more for bachelor's degrees. According to U.S. Census Bureau statistics, that is not the case. Statistics show that about 30.3% of the U.S.'s population obtained a bachelor's degree or higher in 2016 (see Figure 1).[3]

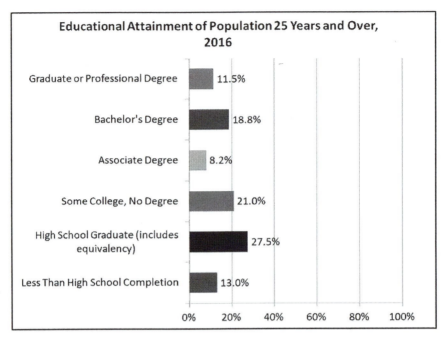

Figure 1: Educational Attainment of the Population 25 Years and Over, 2016
Source: U.S. Census Bureau. Public Domain. Data was derived from American Fact Finder table B15001 (*factfinder2.census.gov/*), a total population of 213,649,147 for 25 Years and Over with percentage margin of error of +/-.01.

Although rates are increasing incrementally, approximately 31% of the U.S. population consistently earns undergraduate and graduate degrees year-to-year.[4] As of 2014, 167.5 million were classified as working-age Americans from ages 25 to 64 years old. The levels of education for these individuals are shown below (see Figure 2).[5]

Levels of education for United States residents, ages 25-64

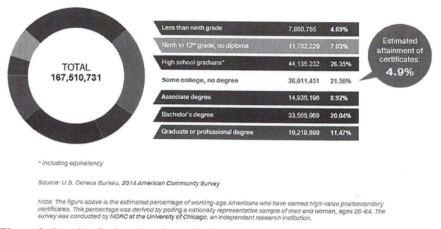

* including equivalency

Source: U.S. Census Bureau, 2014 American Community Survey

Note: The figure above is the estimated percentage of working-age Americans who have earned high-value postsecondary certificates. This percentage was derived by polling a nationally representative sample of men and women, ages 25-64. The survey was conducted by NORC at the University of Chicago, an independent research institution.

Figure 2: Levels of education for United States residents, ages 25-64
Source: A Stronger Nation 2016©2016. Lumina Foundation for Education, Inc. Reproduced with permission.

For 2014, about 31.5 % of the population obtained a bachelor's degree or higher. Despite this statistic, disparities in educational attainment of college degrees exist by race and ethnicity (see Figure 3).[6]

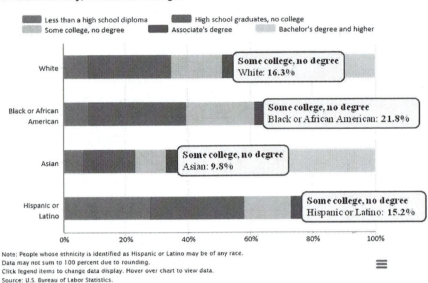

Educational attainment of the labor force age 25 and older by race and Hispanic or Latino ethnicity, 2014 annual averages

Figure 3: Educational attainment of the labor force age 25 and older by race and Hispanic or Latino ethnicity, 2014 annual averages
Source: U.S. Bureau of Labor Statistics. Public Domain.

The chart above highlights that 16.3% of Whites, 21.8% of African Americans, 9.8% of Asians and 15.2% of Latinos had some college but no degree. Students who drop out of college waste their time and money when they do not get their degrees. To graduate from college, every student requires a game plan that takes the necessary steps to achieve his/her graduation ambition. Otherwise, a student's college graduation goal is unattainable.

Section A: Cost

Many potential college undergraduates are stymied in the pursuit of their degree because of college costs. These college candidates just do not have the money to attend college or finish. College is expensive. The costs include tuition, room and board, meal plans, books and supplies, transportation, and other miscellaneous expenses.[7] Although expense should not be a deterrent, some people just cannot afford the costs associated with college over the course of four to six years. These individuals typically assess if college is worth it or even necessary. Encouraging the use of loans, some college administrators, loan officers, and others claim that students are investing in their future. The irony is that many graduates may not be able to find jobs after graduation. In his 2013 article, "Just Explain It: Is America's Middle Class Recovering?" Zelkadis Elvi claimed the average college graduate had $35,000 in total loan liability.[8] Undeniably, the consequences can be dire when a student takes out too many loans. College graduates with huge student loan debt may have to move back in with their parents, may be unable to afford a home purchase, may postpone starting their own families, or may miss other expected gates to adulthood. Just as subprime mortgage loans placed loan recipients' credit and financial future in jeopardy, outrageous student loans can destroy students' financial future.[9]

Another option is to delay or stretch out college for a few years if the money is not there. Unfortunately, numerous college undergraduates take longer than two years to graduate from community college and more than four years to obtain a bachelor's degree. In the interim, some students have personal/financial issues or other setbacks that prevent them from finishing school. In your best interest, you should want to graduate from college on the fast track at your two or four-year institution. You might wonder, "*Why?*" Saving money is the primary reason, specifically tuition, books, dorm fees, and other costs. Other benefits to graduating on time include:

- Decreasing student loan debt
- Maintaining eligibility for financial aid
- Applying saved undergraduate tuition towards a graduate degree
- Entering the workforce to receive a salary, or
- Gaining a competitive employment edge over those students still in school.

Hence, the lack of money to pay for college will have a profound impact on your ability to immediately pursue your college degree after high school graduation.

Section B: High School Academic Performance

When determining if college is the right choice, you should assess your academic performance in high school. You ought to consider if college will be a two to a four-year extension of your high school misery. In high school, grades reflect a student's ability to concentrate on the subject matter and successfully complete the coursework, indicating his/her potential to do well in a higher education environment. Every year, high school seniors with poor grades walk across the graduation stage and receive their high school diplomas. Some of them progressed without learning adequate reading, writing, or speaking skills. These students may have been bored, unchallenged, or just ready to go. Several may have undiagnosed learning disabilities such as a vision problem, hearing impairment, or dyslexia. Other high school students have terrible academic experiences and want to get out of school as soon as the ink dries on their high school diploma. Their neighborhood high school may have been terrible in the areas of instruction, climate, and standards. Today, some urban areas are modern day war zones with children dying from gunshots or drugs. Rural America also faces challenges in preparing students especially with rampant poverty, rising Opioid use/addiction, high unemployment and low median incomes.[10]

Parents or other family members may also create an untenable, volatile situation at home. Thus, many young adults may be exposed to a criminal lifestyle, sexual or physical abuse, human trafficking, neglect, food deprivation, alcohol/drug abuse, homelessness, familial gang involvement, or an absent unsupportive parent. Each of these factors influences a young person's ability to concentrate and cope within the school environment. They may feel that their lives are spiraling out of control with little choices. For many high school students, school takes a back seat to surviving. Students who have poor academic records in high school are likely unprepared to meet the academic challenges of college. In a highly competitive environment, college admissions administrators and scholarship boards also typically do not select poor high school performers for their undergraduate ranks. If you are living in such a situation, even graduating from high school can seem daunting. With the chaos of your environment, you may earn C's, D's, and F's in high school. You may feel that your family or the educational system has failed you. As a result, you may not want to set foot in another classroom after high school graduation.

Another issue may be that your high school may not have prepared you for college. You may not have had a high school counselor or adult guidance to ensure that you took appropriate college preparatory courses, especially in Math, English, and Science. In a 2012 article, for instance, author Annie Paul noted that most young adults with non-college attending parents came from low-income households.[11] She also stated that "more than a quarter of the young adults from low-income households leave school after the first year while 89% do not graduate within six years."[12] Without guidance and academic preparation, first-time college students must learn everything from scratch.[13] The students are basically unprepared for navigating interaction with professors, picking majors, scheduling a manageable level of classes and other practices necessary to graduate.

Despite the aforementioned obstacles, you have the capacity to overcome many challenges. I advise you to seek out a trusted adult role model to help you to channel your anger, frustration, or disappointment into a positive outlet. You can pick the brain of the mentor/role model about the requirements of college. If you have not identified a mentor, you must observe the adults in your life notably coaches, teachers, preachers, business owners, and others who have your best interest at heart. You ought to impart to him/her that you would like to attend and graduate from college. Hopefully, the guidance will not be a one-time interaction but will extend from high school through college and beyond. If college is not an option now, then you can ask for mentorship about entering a trade through an apprenticeship or attending vocational school.

I want to caution you to observe your potential mentor's interaction with you and other young adults. Human predators do exist. These individuals betray and exploit young people's trust. For instance, *no* teacher, preacher, coach, doctor, relative, college professor, teaching assistant, or any other authority figure should be in a sexual relationship with any young adult under 21 years of age. In addition, an authority figure who is in a position of power should not engage in any inappropriate or sexual relationship with his/her subordinate or student regardless of age. The relationship cannot be consensual because of the elements of power and influence. These types of breaches in propriety are unacceptable. Inappropriate behavior includes improper contact/touching, bullying, sexual harassment, sexual assault, rape, abusive language, or supplying alcohol/drugs to minors. If something like this happens, you must report the offender to your parents, a trusted adult, school administrators, medical personnel, or the police immediately. I want you to know that you are not at fault. When necessary, you ought to seek counseling to address the lingering effects of the abuse. In contrast, I know that there are many caring adults who willingly offer appropriate advice and support to teens and young adults. You ought to take the time to seek out suitable role models and mentors. Do not give up hope because your early life does not have to define your accomplishments as an adult. You have value and a choice to live a rich, productive life.

Section C: Specialized Talent, Knowledge or Skills

Each of us is different in our desire to attend college. When an individual has an inherent talent in arts, sports, technology, apparel design etc., he/she may thrive in a career without college. Some famous people namely John D. Rockefeller, Mario Andretti, Richard Branson,[14] First Lady Eleanor Roosevelt, and Thomas Edison followed their own path in life and did not obtain a college degree. Without a formal degree, Thomas Edison was a self-taught inventor who invented the light bulb, phonograph, and the prototype for modern movies. At the time, his inventions revolutionized the world and made him into a wealthy, famous and highly respected man. With creativity, ingenuity, and bravery, anyone can become a success in business, politics, or other sectors without college.

In high school, many young men and women train daily to become Olympic contenders or professional sports athletes in soccer, football, basketball, tennis, golf, gymnastics, competitive swimming, etc. When their talents produce the desired opportunity, these athletes put every effort into their profession. The shelf life for top athletic performance or high-paying careers may be only a few years. College may not seem like a priority while a professional athlete is at his/her peak. Or, a young man or woman may not immediately attend college because they have artistic talent and want to emulate the accomplishments of Aretha Franklin, Garth Brooks, Miles Davis, Ava DuVernay, Tom Hanks, Celine Dion, or Judith Jamison. In spite of the odds, these few select individuals have specialized talents that make them unique in music, dance, arts, or other areas. Shows similar to American Idol, The Voice, America's Top Chef and Showtime at the Apollo create many instant stars. The rewards can be fame, riches, and a place on the national or international stage. Other fame-seeking individuals constantly hustle, waiting for their big break into the business. These types always seek the next show, tour, or event to maintain artistic relevancy. Whatever the reason, many people with specialized talents may make a conscious decision to postpone or even skip college.

Despite any specialized talent, you ought to attend college at some point as an investment for the future. The tabloids are full of talented young men and women who declare bankruptcy or are financially broke after the fame runs out, retirement, or a career-ending injury. They never acquired the skills and knowledge to manage their money or careers. When you have the opportunity, you should at least get a college degree as a backup plan for your sports or arts career in areas such as Business Management, Business Administration, Theater, Culinary Science, Sport Management, Sport Merchandising, Finance, Law, or wherever your passion exists. In addition, you must become financially literate to preserve your wealth. Or else, lawyers, agents, business partners, managers, financial advisors, friends, family and countless others will exploit your ignorance. For role models who have successfully acquired unrelated fortunes beyond their sports or entertainment careers, you ought to research and imitate the business acumen of entrepreneurs in particular Earvin "Magic" Johnson, Serena Williams, Paul "Bono" Hewson, Sean "Diddy" Combs, Dolly Parton, Ion Tiriac, Kris Jenner, Ashton Kutcher, or Gloria and Emilio Estefan.

Section D: Working

Despite pressure from your parents, you are the one who will have to attend classes, live in the dorm, and immerse yourself in the college culture. If college is not your dream, then don't go. Instead, you can work. Working and a job well-done have immense importance to the community and you. To investigate the job opportunities in your town or city, you should review the classified ads for job announcements in your local newspaper, ask friends or family about employment openings, job hunt through your state employment office, or apply directly to the businesses that are hiring. Or, you might check online for available job opportunities on websites such as the Bureau of Labor Statistics, LinkedIn, Monster, or Indeed.com. When job openings are scarce locally, you should relocate within your state and/or nationally to exploit employment opportunities. Thus, you cannot let fear or complacency prevent you from relocating because the world is a huge place beyond your backyard. Your employment searches will also illustrate the salaries for specific jobs, the necessary qualifications, and any educational requirements. You will notice the monetary differences in those jobs available to high school graduates versus those jobs requiring a two or four-year college degree. One note of caution: you ought to start your search with reputable companies, limiting your exposure to work from home, commission-only, or other job scams. You should not have to pay money upfront or recruit friends to sell a low-quality product/service. Otherwise, you are probably the target of a scammer. Remember: If the pay is too good to be true for the type of work, it probably is.

Additionally, you should obtain a skill if you are going to enter the job market immediately after high school. You can obtain marketable specialized knowledge and skills by attending a high school technical/vocational program or becoming an apprentice while in high school. With this type of formal training, you may not need a four-year college degree. While getting on-the-job training, though, you can earn a living as a blue collar professional instead of racking up college student loan debt. Numerous high school, business and community partnerships like the Academies of Louisville in Kentucky sponsor student apprenticeships in an assortment of trades in order to meet local skilled labor needs.[15] You can research similar programs within your community or school system. In addition, you must investigate the future employment outlook, long-term job growth, and potential earnings for your occupation(s) of interest. A good source for information about diverse careers is the Bureau of Labor Statistics website, http://www.bls.gov/ooh/.

Thus, you ought to be able to translate work experience, knowledge, formal training, and certifications/licensing into high earnings within a blue collar career.[16] Such careers might include being a mechanic, welder, carpenter, electrician, claims adjuster, plumber, roofer, farmer, media camera operator, tower technician, funeral director, foley artist, film editor, audio engineer, computer repair person, cosmetologist, culinary chef, dental hygienist, land surveyor, or firefighter.[17] Most blue collar professionals in particular business owners have satisfying careers and earn more than some college graduates with four-year degrees. For example, experienced electricians make a great living, charging customers for home visits, and for parts and labor. For an entire project at a customer's home, an electrician can walk away with between $140 and $500. He/she can live comfortably, by working at four or five on-site jobs a day. Blue-collar professionals find most of their customers among college educated people who could not change their own car oil, remove viruses from their computers, or replace a ceiling fan to save their life.

Or, you might be able to start a business. With some capital, an industrious individual may turn an idea or product into a brand. For example, Leanna Archer started her business at nine years old, offering hair care products from her home and on her website.[18] She is the CEO of Leanna's Inc., which generates annual revenues of $110,000.[19] Like Leanna, your aspirations can turn into success with a great product, hard work, and perseverance. You can obtain guidance on starting a business from an online search of resources specifically the U.S. Small Business Administration or local high schools/colleges that offer summer camps, workshops, and business/entrepreneurship classes. If market gaps or problems exist within your community, you ought to identify effective solutions, products, or services that you can turn into a business.

Consequently, you can look for self-employment opportunities in lawn care, junk pick-up/disposal, house cleaning, childcare, shuttle services, storefront window cleaning, grocery pick-up/delivery, car customizing, or whatever. As needed, you ought to obtain the appropriate permits/licenses in accordance with your local government's requirements. Your business might even become a job creator by employing others. In truth, new business ventures can flourish in underserved communities specifically in urban and rural areas. You are only limited by your imagination. Your goal is to create a business that invests in your community and fills a need. To increase your clientele base over time, you must have a strong work ethic which translates into being on time, hard-working, trustworthy, proficient, reliable, organized, friendly, courteous and well groomed. Starting a business requires dedication, long hours, sacrifice and financial smarts. You can earn a living and reap the financial rewards of running a successful business. If college is not in your immediate future, you can work and be a leader in your community.

Section E: Lack of Time

Your time might be regularly devoted on a daily basis to other priorities. Then, you ought to carefully consider whether a two or four-year college is for you. You may be a full-time employee, a working parent, or a stay at home parent with small children. Although many do it, you have to determine if you have the time and money to attend college while juggling your busy life. As a returning adult college student, you may not have picked up a course textbook in five years or more. You also may be unsure of the demands and benefits of pursuing your associate's or

14

bachelor's degree. You can always ease into the college environment by taking online classes or taking one or two classes at your local community college. These small steps into the classroom will verify if you have the focus and time to devote to going back to school.

Before you decide to reenter the classroom, though, you must do your research. The most important information to find out is the availability and type of employment in your local job market; the major/degree of interest that will increase your earnings, and open up career opportunities for you; the prospective colleges that offer your major/degree; and the cost to obtain your degree. In addition, you ought to investigate methods to pay for college namely scholarships, grants, tuition assistance, or employer tuition reimbursement. To be clear, you want to earn a marketable college degree with the least amount or no debt. You do not want to spend money on a useless, expensive degree that does not improve your current standard of living. If you cannot use your new degree to find a local job, obtain a promotion in your existing job (ask your employer first), or increase your current earnings, then you might have to move out of your city, state, or region. If relocating to a new area or job is not in your future plans, you might have to rethink your potential major/degree of interest. So, do your research and exercise due diligence before you hit a college campus. Using cost-benefit analysis coupled with your personal introspection, you have to decide whether college is worth it to you.

Life lessons - Chapter 1: Is College for You?
- Cost may impact your ability to immediately pursue your college degree
  - College is expensive
  - Student loan debt without finishing college can have dire consequences
  - Save money by completing your degree within the required time for your two or four-year institution
- College admissions administrators and scholarship boards do not select high school performers who have poor academic credentials for their undergraduate ranks
  - Work to improve your grades
  - Seek out a trusted adult role model to help you if your grades are poor
- With a marketable specialized talent in sports, arts, or other areas, you may wait to enter college; eventually, you should attend college as a backup plan
- If college is not your dream, then don't go
  - Get a job or start a business
  - Attend a vocational school or become an apprentice to obtain marketable skills and knowledge
  - If job openings are scarce locally, then move to where the jobs are plentiful
- Ease into the college experience by taking on-line courses or a few courses at your local community college if you are juggling work, children, or other priorities
  - Research and exercise due diligence that a potential major/degree/certification will lead to a new job, promotion in an existing job, or higher earnings
  - Do not earn an expensive, useless college degree that will not improve your current standard of living
  - Investigate methods to pay for college specifically scholarships, grants, tuition assistance, or employer tuition reimbursement

CHAPTER 2:
Is College Graduation Your Goal?

Graduating from college should be your #1 goal. College is necessary for a stable financial lifestyle. Otherwise, you will need marketable specialized talent, knowledge, or skills in order to earn a substantial income to live comfortably. Before I graduated from high school, my mother gave me three options. I could go into the military, go to college, or move out. I could not stay at her house unless I had a game plan for my life. College was a foregone conclusion because my family expected it of me. However, I did not make a spur-of-the-moment decision. With early input from my parents and teachers, I took advanced placement and honors courses in high school. I also earned grades that looked attractive to college recruiters. I applied to and graduated from the United States Military Academy. College was one of the best decisions of my life.

In the U.S. economy, the job market is biased against both high school dropouts and graduates in unemployment rates and annual income. High school dropouts and graduates systematically had higher unemployment rates versus those individuals with some college or college graduates from April 2005 through April 2015 (see Figure 4).[20]

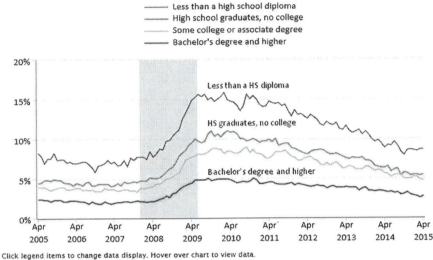

Unemployment rates for people age 25 and older, by educational attainment, seasonally adjusted, April 2005 to April 2015

Figure 4: Unemployment rates for people age 25 and older, by educational attainment seasonally adjusted, April 2005 to April 2015
Source: U.S. Bureau of Labor Statistics. Public Domain.

The disparity of unemployment rates is startling. Reinforcing the information about unemployment rates, U.S. Bureau of Labor statistics from October 2016 to October 2017 highlighted that high school dropouts who were 25 years old and over were almost three times as likely to be unemployed than those with a college degree.[21] From the statistics, a college degree lowered the likelihood of unemployment in the labor force.

Drum roll! Gasp! The hardship for high school dropouts and high school graduates extends to their median annual income and earnings. As of 2015, U.S. Census Bureau statistics showed that high school dropouts who were age 25 years and older earned annually a median income of roughly $27,200 and high school graduates earned approximately $36,800 (see Figure 5).[22]

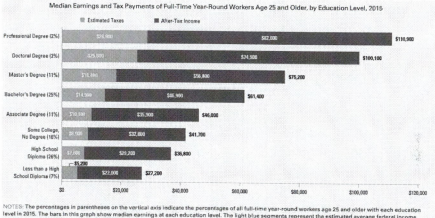

Figure 5: Median Earnings and Tax Payments of Full-Time Year-Round Workers Age 25 and Over, by Education Level, 2015
Source: Education Pays 2016 © 2016. The College Board. Data derived from U.S. Census Bureau, 2015, Table PINC-03; Internal Revenue Service, 2014; Davis et al., 2015; calculations by the authors. Reproduced with permission.

In contrast, a worker with a bachelor's degree earned a median income of about $61,400. For all, taxes reduced their take-home pay significantly. At any rate, non-degree holders in comparison to college degree holders have a humongous income gap to overcome. In an analysis, the Hamilton Project concluded that a typical college graduate with a bachelor's degree will earn on average $1.19 million.[23] This amount is twice as much as a typical high school graduate will earn ($580,000) over the course of his/her lifetime earnings. For example, according to a Georgetown University Center on Education and the Workforce study, nursing and home health aides with high school diplomas had lifetime earnings (2009 dollars) of $966,000.[24] In the same study, nursing and home health aides with some college/no degree had lifetime earnings (2009 dollars) of $1,030,000. In comparison, registered nurses with associate's and bachelor's degrees had lifetime earnings (2009 dollars) of $2,267,000 and $2,527,000, respectively. Thus, high school graduates and dropouts will find it hard to rise to the economic level of the baby boomer generation. The harsh facts of living and working on a minimum wage salary are indisputable. At minimum wage levels, a person who shells out rent; buys food; pays for utilities; spends money on a car payment with the associated insurance/gas; and pays state/local taxes will have nothing left for savings, entertainment, car maintenance, or general living. Therefore, you ought to decide as soon as possible the plan for your life after high school. Don't fall for the myth that you can make up for money shortfalls overtime or win the lottery. Living on minimum wage, you will always play catch up in lifetime earnings and saving for retirement.

I am providing these statistics to convince you that obtaining a college degree is in your best interest. Unless you have a great, recognized talent in the arts, sciences or sports; have knowledge, skill and experience in welding, auto repair, air conditioner repair, computer programming, or other trade; have an IQ over 140, making you a genius and a candidate for Mensa; have a couple of million dollars stashed away; are going to retreat from civilization to become a hermit; or plan to marry a rich spouse, you will be more marketable and valuable to employers with a college diploma in today's world. The above statistics demonstrates that a college degree namely an associate's or bachelor's degree provides a measure of insulation from unemployment and low pay. In your plans for the future, you ought to see more for your life than just hanging around the house after high school graduation.

Section A: College is required for Professional Careers

Despite all non-college options, college is important and beneficial in a unique way. If you aspire to join a specialized profession in medicine, law, engineering, computer science, etc., you will have to go to college and graduate with a bachelor's degree or higher. These professional degrees are highly prized within the business world. According to the BusinessDirectory.com, such professions indicate "mastery of a complex set of knowledge and advanced skills through formal education and practical experience."[25] A professional usually does not rely on physical or skilled labor to earn a living. Typically, a professional is a salaried earner who is paid for upholding the high standards of the profession as well as having acquired knowledge via an advanced degree. In addition, professional boards, notably state medical boards or bar associations, accredit, govern and enforce standards for individuals practicing within their professions. No one wants to hire a lawyer who never went to law school or was disbarred for stealing clients' money.

Many successful people who I admire have contributed to their community and the world. They are ambitious, innovative leaders. The few that come to mind are President Barack Obama, Governor LeRoy Collins, Warren Buffet, Ohio Congressman William M. McCulloch, Congresswoman Shirley Chisholm, Stephen Hawking, the National Aeronautics and Space Administration's Katherine G. Johnson, and Lowell High School teacher Flossie Lewis (as well as educators like her). Each earned a college degree. Given their professions and aspirations, they had to go to college. Actually, most employers select candidates for managerial, and a few entry-level positions based on their education. Depending on the career, human resources specialists will not even place a candidate's resume in the firm's interview pile if the candidate does not have the desired college degree. For many prospective employers, a college degree shows that you can integrate an onslaught of information, analyze and apply it to solve problems. You should not think of college as an extension of high school but an entrée into the business world.

Section B: College Preparation

As early as ninth grade, you should discuss your college options with your parents, guidance counselor and teachers. The competition for programs and colleges is fierce; so, you must start early. Your high school counselor, especially, should be able to assist you in developing a plan. This face-to-face meeting should not be a onetime meeting. At the start of each school year, you (and your parents) should meet with your counselor and ask questions to make sure you remain on track. Numerous high schools do not guide their students on how to prepare for college coursework and where to go to college. It is often left up to the parents and child. I want to emphasize that your classes and other extracurricular activities should make your academic transcripts more attractive to college admissions officers. Be proactive. Then, you can implement the necessary rigorous high school course load through your senior year that will prepare you academically for college.

While in high school, you must focus on studying and retaining the knowledge required to graduate from college. For that reason, you have to take challenging high school courses that will prepare you for college. For instance, the United States Military Academy (West Point) encourages every high school applicant to complete four years of English, four years of college preparatory math, two years of a foreign language, two years of a laboratory science, one year of history, and if possible a basic computing course.[26] Previously, you may have lacked guidance on which high school college preparatory classes to take. In spite of this, you ought to consider structuring your academic program to mirror the curriculum of the college that you would like to attend, starting in ninth grade. You should contact the college's admissions office to obtain that recommended high school curriculum.

If available, you should take academically rigorous advancement placement (AP) classes or International Baccalaureate (IB) Diploma Program courses. Both prepare you for college-level coursework and offer an opportunity to earn college credit.[27] Administered by the College Board, AP courses are designed to help U.S. high school students prepare for college. The College Board also publishes a course ledger that lists secondary schools that offer AP courses.[28] AP courses are more popular and widely recognized than IB courses in the U.S. Essentially, AP courses parallel freshman college courses, requiring the same course-work, class participation, and critical thinking. In contrast, IB courses were developed in Switzerland. IB students can earn a certificate of completion for each class. When a high school student completes all courses, he/she can earn an internationally recognized diploma, which is known as the IB Diploma Programme. The IB Diploma Programme is a two-year curriculum taken during the high school junior and senior years.[29] You should ask your counselor or teachers whether your high school offers AP or IB courses.

Another benefit of successfully completing AP or IB courses is preparation for AP or IB exams. Colleges use AP and IB exams to gauge a student's proficiency in various subject areas, including math, reading, and writing. For example, high school AP course curriculum covers academic areas tested on AP exams. In addition, AP and IB exams are not a pass or fail. A student can obtain an AP exam score ranging from the minimum of 1 to the maximum of 5.[30] A student can take AP exams without taking the associated AP courses. When a student takes AP exams, he/she can request that the College Board send the official AP exam scores to prospective colleges. In contrast, IB exams have a scoring range of 1 to a maximum of 7.[31] Students cannot take an IB exam unless they have taken the IB course. With the IB exam results, a student can request official transcripts be sent to six colleges.

The distinction between the AP and IB courses does not really matter. More importantly, college admissions officers look favorably on students who successfully complete either AP or IB courses. Many colleges may set minimum required AP or IB exam scores in which they may grant academic credit for selected introductory or general college courses in math, science, etc. When a student is granted academic credit for his/her exam results, he/she has "tested out." By testing out, the student can save tuition money because he/she does not have to take those specific college courses. The student receives the credit hours toward his/her degree. Some colleges do not give academic credit for AP or IB exam scores. Instead, these colleges allow the students to enter higher-level classes that place them beyond general freshman courses. The students are not stuck covering material that they already know. If you are interested in particular colleges, you ought to verify their policies about granting academic credit or advance placement for selected courses based on the minimum required AP or IB scores.

You may be reading this book, becoming overwhelmed or worried. As a high school junior or senior, you have time to study for advanced placement tests. Remember, you have the option of taking AP exams without taking AP courses. You can review practice exams in preparation for your college placement tests. Below are a few resources to check out practice AP exams:

- CollegeBoard.org website[32]
    - Provides practice AP tests, which is known as ACCUPLACER, in each test subject
- College(s)
    - May provide free AP exam workshops that cover the test format, topics covered and strategies on the best way to take the test
    - Provide practice exams/questions on the college's website
    - Community colleges excel in explaining the AP test process
        - Portland Community College's website has test examples within its review packet[33]
        - Grays Harbor College's Learning Links website lists useful exam preparation hyperlinks[34]
- EnglishTestScore.net website[35]
    - Provides good English grammar questions/practice exercises
- Math.com website[36]
    - Provides practice math questions
- The American Mathematical Society website[37]
    - Publishes mathematics help, summer programs, local math clubs, math competitions and other math related events

These resources ought to help your proficiency in various subject areas and prepare you for taking placement exams.

Unfortunately, countless high school graduates must take college remedial courses in subjects such as Math and English. These students are unprepared for college-level work. Some high school graduates cannot comprehend or perform basic math. They do not have the proficiency to pass college math courses that count towards their degree. Others are deficient in English sentence-structure, spelling and grammar. Statistics show that, frequently, high schools do not prepare their students for college-level courses. In her book, "Higher Ground: Preparing African-American Children for College," Leah Latimer found that African-American students attended remedial courses at a rate of 30% for four-year colleges, and 25% for two-year community college programs in 1999.[38] Depending on your placement exam results, your college or major may require you to take remedial college courses below the level that you expect. Although it will cost you time and tuition money, none of these remedial classes will count towards your degree. I do not want you to feel frustrated. You ought to view taking college remedial courses as a way to improve your knowledge and skills. Hopefully, the courses will get you to the level necessary to pass your more advanced required courses.

Beyond a doubt, you are best served by adhering to the placement exam's results. For example, a University of Maryland-College Park (UMCP) student who enrolled in a math course beyond his/her math placement test's recommendation was likely to withdraw or earn a "D" or "F" grade in the course.[39] At UMCP, I learned my lesson on this subject. My UMCP placement exam prescribed a math course below calculus II. Instead, I signed up for calculus II because I thought that I could walk into the class and excel. I took calculus I at the United States Military Academy. However, I had a gap of several years between that calculus I course and my UMCP calculus II course. The UMCP placement exam's results were right. After the first day, I dropped calculus II because I was completely lost. Later, I passed calculus I at UMCP and went on to pass calculus II. Advanced placement exams are good tools for determining a student's potential proficiency in college subjects. It is in your best interest to enroll in the corresponding courses based on your AP test results. You do not want your college transcripts to reflect failed grades because you were not prepared for the coursework.

Section C: Math

Math develops critical thinking and a sense of inquiry, which are vital to success in college and life. Critical thinking is important because no one should take answers at face value. Math forces students to understand the concepts behind obtaining the right answers to an equation. Also, math skills have a major impact on preparation for college and numerous future careers. If you plan on pursuing science, technology, engineering, or math (STEM) majors in college, you must take as many advanced high school math courses as possible to acquire and maintain proficiency. Math is the foundation for students to enter such fields as actuary (look it up, :O)), physics, bioinformatics, computer science, engineering, architecture, air traffic control, geospatial/geographic information systems, accounting, law, and medicine. Even if you major in English or another non-STEM subject, you will be required to take math courses in college. Additionally, many blue collar workers like avionics technicians, electricians, machinists, and construction workers must often have a strong background in math as well as certifications or associate's degrees for career progression. So, you should prepare in high school for your future career path by taking challenging math courses now.

Most high school students shy away from higher level math courses. That is a grave mistake for them and the nation. As a precursor to attending college, students and young adults ought to be skeptical and curious. To channel that curiosity, math develops problem-solving and procedures to answer questions in a methodical way. In the business world, every employer prizes employees who can solve problems effectively and efficiently. Also, these qualities make better voting citizens. When citizens are highly educated, involved, and not easily persuaded, they research issues and make decisions based on facts. They also hold those in power accountable for their actions and policies. An informed, questioning public is dangerous to demagogues and politicians.

If your high school does not offer honor, AP, or IB math courses, you should join or create a math club. Recruiting a competitive teacher, you and the other members can practice advanced math equations, compete in math competitions/events, or take part in college math summer outreach programs. Math is not like riding a bike after a large lapse in time. When you do not use your math skills, then you will lose them. A majority of students have to practice and practice at math in order to excel. Think about how many adults have forgotten the principals of geometry? Still, just as many highly paid individuals such as engineers, jewelers, car designers, game developers and architects use their knowledge of geometry every day. With the right motivation, I think you can master advanced math and have fun at the same time.

Section D: Final Thoughts

Honest, hard work never hurt anybody. Most U.S. citizens do not realize the chance for success that they have with access to free public education, gender equality, social mobility, a positive business climate and a diverse job market. Each person has to seek opportunity and grab it. In fact, opportunity is a concept that will not fall in your lap as you sit on the couch, watching television while eating potato chips. Instead, the U.S. is still the land of possibility; otherwise, people would not travel in harsh and violent conditions to get here. Every day immigrants from China, India, Haiti, Syria, El Salvador, and other countries migrate to the U.S. to attend college, find jobs and seek their fortune. Escaping prosecution, natural disaster, and economic crisis, some come to the U.S. with nothing: no money, family, or friends. Yet, they are able to thrive and contribute to their communities and new country. Thus, with initiative, skills, and knowledge, you can succeed by creating innovative ideas, products and/or services that your employer, and/or community will appreciate and need.

Without a college education, you may pursue a non-traditional path; however, statistics show that a person with a two or four-year degree will enjoy higher wages than a high school drop-out or graduate. Unless you have marketable specialized skills, knowledge, or talent, you must take responsibility for the path of your future life. In other words, you have to seize success: have a goal, envision how to achieve it and do it. Therefore, you should start early communication with your parents, teachers and guidance counselor to develop and plan for achieving your life's goals after high school graduation.

Life lessons - Chapter 2: Your Goal is Graduating from College on Time
- Graduating from college is your #1 goal
  - The job market is biased against high school dropouts and graduates in high unemployment rates and low life-time earnings
  - College graduates earn on average $1.19 million in lifetime earnings while high school graduates earn about $580,000
- You will need a college degree to enter a specialized profession in medicine, law, engineering, etc.
- Start as early as possible to decide if you want to attend college
  - The competition for colleges and programs is unreal
  - Talk to your parents, guidance counselor and teachers about college and the courses you should take in high school to prepare
  - Enroll and successfully pass Advancement Placement (AP) or International Baccalaureate (IB) Diploma Program courses if they are available
  - Take AP or IB exams to "test out" of college courses for academic credit or for placement into higher-level college courses
  - Study available resources to practice for advanced placement exams
  - Remedial college courses waste time and money but you may need them to acquire the knowledge to pass those selected college subjects
- Math is a problem-solving skill that you must master to prepare for college and apply to life
  - Take as many advanced math courses in high school as you can
  - Have fun!
- Unless you have marketable specialized skills, knowledge, or talent, you must take responsibility for the path of your future life and develop a plan to reach your college goals

CHAPTER 3:
College Selection

Searching for the right college is an annual rite of passage for high school students. If you attend the college that best meets your needs, you will more likely stay and graduate. You have to enjoy and feel comfortable where you attend school. During high school, you should start investigating colleges during your sophomore/junior year. Then, you will have at least nine months to a year to conduct a relaxed, thorough evaluation. By September, but no later than November of your senior year, you ought to know where you want to apply for college. In November, colleges and universities typically accept early admission applications to find their incoming crop of freshman for the next fall semester. Then, they accept regular admission applications between January and March.[40]

You can apply to as many potential colleges as you want. I propose that you apply to your heart's desire, a second, third, and fourth choice. Still, there are different types of colleges and universities, including community colleges, private universities, and public universities (see Figure 6).[41]

Types of colleges and universities	
College	An institution of higher education, particularly one that provides a general or liberal arts education rather than technical or professional training; sometimes called a four-year institution
Community college	A public institution that is funded by local, regional, or state tax dollars, providing both general and vocational/technical education and granting both certificates and associate degrees; sometimes called a two-year college or a junior college
Diploma mill	An organization that claims to be a college but exists only for profit and to distribute degrees
For-profit university	A college or university that is owned and managed by a private, profit-seeking entity and that has not achieved a not-for-profit tax status; some of the larger for-profit colleges that are regionally accredited include Capella University, University of Phoenix, DeVry University, Strayer University, Kaplan University, Walden University, American InterContinental University, New England College of Business and Finance, and Jones International University, among others
Junior college	An older term that refers to community colleges; a public institution that is funded by local, regional, or state tax dollars, providing both general and vocational/technical education and granting both certificates and associate degrees; sometimes called a two-year college.
Liberal arts college	A liberal arts college is one with a primary emphasis on undergraduate study aimed at imparting general knowledge and developing general intellectual capacities, in contrast to a professional, vocational, or technical curriculum
Post-secondary	Also called higher education; refers to any education following the completion of a high school diploma
Private university	A college or university that is not operated by a government entity; though, many receive public subsidies and are subject to government regulation; tuition and fees at private universities tend to be higher than at public universities
Public university	A college or university that is predominantly funded by public (local, state, or regional) tax dollars; tuition at public universities for in-state or in-region students tends to be lower than at private institutions
Proprietary school	A school organized as a profit-making venture primarily to teach vocational skills or self-improvement techniques
University	An institution of higher education that has several colleges within it, particularly a college of liberal arts and a program of graduate studies together with several professional schools, as of theology, law, medicine, and engineering, and authorized to confer both undergraduate and graduate degrees; sometimes called four-year institution
Vocational school	Generally a post-secondary school, sometimes the final year(s) of high school, providing preparation for specific jobs and/or technical education; can be public or private, non-profit, or for-profit.

Figure 6: Types of Colleges and Universities
Source: "A Consumer's Guide to Going to School," Chart, Types of colleges and universities. Chicago: Council for Experiential Learning, Susan Kannel, 2013. Reproduced with permission.

Then, the types of colleges may be even further divided into subcategories in particular single-gender colleges, military schools, faith-based colleges, or minority-serving institutions.[42] After selecting the type of college and/or subcategory that best meets your needs, you can start your search for specific college names. By narrowing the college choices to a select few, you will save money in online application fees. If you apply to five or more different schools, you will realize that the application fees quickly add up. In addition, you and your parents can visit as many schools as you would like, but these trips cost huge amounts of money in hotel bills, transportation, and meals. You should only spend money on those colleges that you really want to attend.

For instance, private, not-for-profit colleges and universities tend to have smaller student population and class sizes compared to public/state institutions. They receive funding from tuition and alumni endowments. Private, not-for-profit colleges, typically, cost much more to attend than public colleges. In contrast, public/state colleges may have sprawling campuses covering several satellite locations. Instead of endowments, public colleges primarily rely on local and state tax dollars to operate. A public institution's student population size can be immense. Public institutions also may offer a hugely diverse number of majors.

Even similar types of colleges/universities can be different in their sizes and environments. For example, the University of Maryland, College Park (UMCP) and the United States Military Academy (USMA) at West Point are both public, four-year institutions. Typically, UMCP has an undergraduate enrollment of about 29,000 students versus USMA's undergraduate student population of approximately 4,400. Truthfully, my first UMCP undergraduate math class was a little bit of a culture shock. I was prepared for small, undergraduate classes of 10 to 12 students comparable to those at the USMA. The reality was quite different. In contrast, over 250 students waited for the Calculus II instructor to begin class in an auditorium at UMCP. When he arrived, the math professor did not introduce himself. With his back to the class, he started writing from one end of the chalkboard to the other end. The board extended the length of the classroom. When we had a question, we had to call out his name to get his attention. Needless to say, I transferred out of that class after the first day. With larger schools, the professors might never learn your name or even recognize you on the street. If anonymity is an issue, you should verify a college's class sizes and faculty-student ratio.

In truth, you may be overwhelmed by the sheer number of colleges/universities and confused on which school to attend. Some students just apply to the top Ivy League schools with name recognition notably Harvard, Yale, Northwestern, Boston College, Columbia, Stanford, etc. The competition for acceptance at these schools is stiff. Individuals who plan to attend college ought to think outside the box of the well-known schools. You have to determine what you feel is important for your college experience. You can investigate colleges through books, the internet, or visits. At the time, you should note their available college majors, cost, location, amenities, student body composition, faculty-to-student ratio, admittance rates and any other factors that you value. These factors may affect whether you will thrive at college. Then, ask some basic questions:

- In what college environment will I be happy?
- Do I want to be close to a big city or a small town?
- Do I desire small class sizes?
- Do I want to attend a two-year or four-year institution?
- Does this school offer many diverse majors and degrees?
- Is transportation around campus and off-campus readily available?
- Is the local job market strong, and are different types of jobs plentiful if graduates remain locally after graduation?

Research and making a final decision to select a college are essential skills for you in life because these skills help you in choosing a college major, job, car, spouse, or any other item that is the best fit for you. As an analogy, your choice of a specific college is very similar to deciding your favorite Baskin Robbins™ ice cream flavor. During your first visit with your parents, they may select an ice cream flavor for you. More than likely, the flavor will be vanilla or chocolate. Of course, you love the coolness, texture and the newness of the ice cream. You might stay with that flavor until you hit your teens. When you have your own money to use, you will notice other flavors. You may try quite a few until you find the one that you like the best. In a similar fashion, you will listen to your family or friends about colleges. The suggested ones may be colleges that they attended or heard about. During your sophomore/junior year, you will have to research the colleges that interest you. You may even visit each college to test the fit. In the end, you must use your own judgment and preferences to select the best college or university for you to attend.

Section A: College Research

The college that you choose to attend may be one of the most important decisions of your life and a critical component of graduating. You must do as much research as possible before you hit the door of the college to determine if it is right for you. Otherwise, you may not have the incentive to stay and graduate if you hate where you attend college. You should pick a school that you will enjoy attending. In your sophomore/junior year, you should meet with your high school career/college guidance counselor to start researching colleges. He/she may have a few recommendations or direct you to review some college catalogs. Students are no longer limited to a few outdated, dusty college catalogs in a high school counselor's office. The internet provides huge amounts of *free* resources about college admissions, financing, college searches, etc. You and your parents do not necessarily have to pay sign-up fees to get college information because so much is available for *free* on the internet. Below are additional, useful resources that can help you in your college search.

- School or public library
  - Updated, free guides about colleges
  - Free internet access
  - E-readers such as the Nook or Kindle for check-out
  - Free publications or e-books available on subjects, including computer technology, foreign languages, science and study aids
- National Center for Education Statistics (NCES) College Navigator[43]
  - Supplies data on tuition, cost of attendance, accreditation, institution type, enrollment, financial aid and net price
  - Uses specific search criteria like programs/majors, test scores, school names, campus setting, or colleges by state to find information about colleges
- The Princeton Review website[44] (not affiliated with Princeton University)

- o Ranks 633 colleges based on each school's academic excellence and survey input from attending students
- o Provides basic information about each ranked college specifically academics, majors, admissions, student body, campus life/facilities, tuition costs and financial aid
- o Permits search for schools by a specific major, providing a sample college curriculum and suggested high school preparation
- Naviance.com[45]
  - o Software that helps students to match their interests with long-term goals and future career choices
  - o Offers method to identify college options based on interests and strengths
  - o Develops a course of study for college preparation
  - o Can only be purchased by a school or district but a student can check if the software is available at his/her school
- Forbes.com website[46]
  - o Provides an annual ranking of its top 100 colleges and universities
  - o Shows basic information namely the school's ranking on the Forbes' list, student population, undergraduate population, tuition information and contact information[47]
- U.S. News & World Report website[48]
  - o Publishes an online ranking of colleges and universities

- o Divides rankings into categories in particular national university rankings, liberal arts college rankings, best value schools, and other groupings
- Petersons' College Bound website[49]
  - o Offers free tools and articles about how to choose a college, how to get in, and how to pay for it
  - o Uses search criteria to identify colleges and offers a snapshot of the school, including its location
- YouUniversityTV website[50]
  - o Has an extensive library of college video tours/clips
  - o Must register on the site for access to all of the videos

Another part of college research is verifying each school's accreditation. An accredited school meets general standards in its overall mission, objectives and goals, admissions requirements, and faculty reputation according to 50States.com.[51] Notably, accredited colleges only accept students' transfer credits from other accredited colleges or universities. On its website, the Council for Higher Education Accreditation provides accreditation information for 19,000 programs, and 7,700 accredited vocational schools, colleges, and universities.[52] Although the U.S. Department of Education does not accredit educational institutions,[53] the Department's website allows a user to check a college's accreditation by an institution's name or by state.[54] Unlike accredited schools, diploma or degree mills award useless credentials and education.[55] The diploma mill school's academic rigor is questionable because students typically earn degrees within improbable amounts of time and for exorbitant tuition costs. In fact, no patient wants to go to a doctor who obtained his/her medical degree in a year from an online unaccredited school for

$2,000. In addition, companies' human resource personnel hire qualified college graduates based on their education from reputable, accredited colleges. College graduates must have a strong academic foundation to work in career fields such as science, technology, engineering, mathematical and law. The quality of the education is in question if the school is not accredited. After you have researched your choice of schools, you must exercise due diligence to verify their accreditation. If a college/university is not accredited, do yourself a favor and walk away. You do not want to spend your hard earned money on a degree that is worthless.

Section B: Local Colleges

Some students resist the notion of attending a local, state college or university. They think a local college is too close in proximity to their parents. Those students should rethink their aversion. Unless an undergraduate is set on a major at a specific college, he/she may be ignoring great local two and four-year schools. In-state colleges and universities offer many perks notably lower tuition than out-of-state college tuition, attending a hometown favorite, or saving on living expenses, if the student lives at home instead of on campus. Actually, when you want to live far away from home, you should still compare colleges and their offered programs throughout your state. For instance, Maryland has 16 community colleges according to the Maryland Association of Community College.[56] All offer in-state tuition to Maryland residents even if the residents live outside of their respective counties. Moving across your state, though, you will have to budget for added costs namely housing and transportation. As you consider potential colleges, you should investigate your local, state schools too. You might be pleasantly surprised at the quality and cost compared to out-of-state colleges/universities.

Another benefit of a local college specifically a community college is a student's ability to save money by completing general education courses and transferring those credits to a more expensive four-year college. Most of these required general subject classes overlap in Math, English, Humanities, Behavioral/Social Science, and non-lab or lab science. Since local colleges are typically cheaper to attend, you can stretch a scholarship, grant, or loan amount to cover more tuition costs.[57] Regardless of major, all two-year and four-year education institutions mandate that every student must complete general education or core courses in order to graduate. These required general subject courses ensure each student has the same academic foundation necessary to excel in college. For example, Montgomery College (MC)'s required general subject courses are known as General Education (Gen Ed) Courses while UMCP's required courses are called CORE courses.[58] MC students must take their Gen Ed courses in the required sequence by semester. A student's completion of MC's Gen Ed Program translates to 34 credits. If the MC student transfers to UMCP, he/she automatically acquires 34 credits for UMCP's required CORE courses.[59] In your situation, you should speak with your local college or community college's admissions office to ensure that you are taking appropriate general education courses. As a result, you may be able to transfer those credits and opt out of similar courses at a future four-year institution.

While completing courses toward your major at a community college, you may be guaranteed admission/transfer to selected four-year institutions. When considering a community college, you should ask the admissions officer if it is a member of a feeder or articulation program.[60] Articulation means one institution's courses for a program of study are recognized by another institution which then accepts the transfer of those associated credits. Typically, articulation programs facilitate student transfers from community colleges to four-year colleges. For instance, MC has transfer agreements with several four-year colleges namely American University, D.C.; Savannah College of Art & Design, GA; and University of Maryland-College Park, MD.[61] As a matter of fact, the National Student Clearinghouse Research Center claims that 20% of community college students transfer to a four-year institution.[62] Thus, community college transfers fill a large percentage of the student populations at local four-year colleges. Often, community college students have problems transferring credits toward their major to a four-year college.[63] Articulation programs help to ensure students receive admission as well as full credit for all general education and major specific classes. You should investigate if a feeder or articulation program exists at your prospective community college.

Essentially, when you earn 60 credit hours of coursework at your two-year or community college, you probably have enough credits to get your associate's degree/diploma.[64] Many students leave or transfer from community college but they never obtain their diploma. If eligible, you should research the process through your two-year or community college Registrar's Office and apply for your associate's degree/diploma. When your potential career only requires an associate's degree, then you have saved huge on tuition and costs because you are done. Otherwise, you can use your acquired credits to transfer to a four year school to complete your degree program. With your associate's degree, you are already half way towards your bachelor's degree. In this instance, your degree program should be a natural progression from associate's degree to bachelor's degree program. Remember, an associate's degree is 60 credit hours and a bachelor's degree is 120 credit hours.[65] You must do your research and coordination for the transfer of all 60 credits to the four-year institution. Then, you will transfer as a college junior instead of a freshman. Once more, think of the money that you will save! If you are unsure of a transfer strategy, you ought to check out CollegeTransfer.net.[66] This website offers free articles and transfer information like transfer friendly institutions and transfer profiles for specific schools in its database. In addition, Campus Explorer, Inc. is another excellent website that provides a step-by-step guide to transferring colleges.[67]

Section C: Community College

Although community colleges have a great deal in their favor, I want to address a few pitfalls of attending. The American Association of Community Colleges (AACC) database noted that 1,108 accredited community colleges granted associate's degrees in 2017.[68] Numerous community college students may not graduate on time or at all because of finances, poor academic preparation, family stresses, no clear graduation plan, work, or other reasons. For instance, many students from low performing high schools may have to take remedial academic courses. These courses lengthen the students' time in school and increase the costs. The students may not have the funds for the additional classes. Therefore, high school students must prepare financially and academically for community college just as rigorously as for a four-year institution in order to graduate from college on time.

Community colleges typically cater to local communities. Across the nation, students attend community college for many reasons in particular flexible class schedules, admittance to accredited technical/vocational programs, lower tuition costs, and proximity. Based on the AACC's Fall 2015 survey, the largest number of community college students attended part-time at 62% (4.5 million) versus full-time students at 38% (2.7 million).[69] In addition, most community colleges have open enrollment policies that accept almost anyone for admission as long as a student meets academic standards and pays tuition and fees. Some students' part-time status and open enrollment policies may create some retention and graduation rates issues. According to the National Student Clearinghouse Research Center, from Fall 2007 and to Spring 2013, two-year public schools or community colleges had the lowest percentage (26.5%) of students who obtained a degree within six years.[70] In contrast, four-year public and four-year private, nonprofit institutions had higher percentages of completion students at 50.6% and 59.0%, respectively.[71] Within six years, two-year private, for-profit institutions had a completion percentage of 57.4% for students.[72] For a second time, I emphasize to you that your goal is to acquire the required 60 credits toward your degree and graduate from community college as soon as possible. Stay focused!

After the military, I enrolled at MC, the largest community college in Maryland.[73] I valued my attendance there because my MC classes were challenging and interesting. The instructors were supportive and extremely knowledgeable in their fields. Most classes were small in size with about 25 to 30 students. So, students had more access and face-to-face time with their instructors. As a local community college, MC's student population consisted of returning adult students, military members, foreign students, single parents, homemakers, working students and a hodge-podge of first-time students. There was a vast amount of variety in life experiences among MC's students. In line with AACC's statistics, the ratio was more part-time students than full-time students. In 2016, MC had an undergraduate population of 23,916.[74] MC's undergraduate students divided into 63% who were part-time versus 37% who were full-time, first-time students.[75]

When I attended, though, I observed that the majority of full-time MC students were dedicated to cultivating an academic narrative of high grade point averages, excellent grades, and exemplary achievement to ensure ease of transferring to a four-year institution. I also witnessed that some of my younger classmates were not very focused. Many were teenage, part-time students who treated community college like an extension of high school. These part-time students attended classes in the morning and then took off the rest of the day similar to semi-retirees. I remember one of my MC classmates who already had taken classes for four years. Although in his mid-twenties, he did not have a game-plan for graduation. Despite being highly intelligent and articulate, this young adult took courses as subjects interested him. Although I never asked who was paying his tuition bill, I was intrigued by his aimless strategy. He was losing money and time while he attempted to figure out his goal in life. In order to succeed, you must take your classes seriously. Community college has a great deal of importance and opportunity, which can make your college experience exceptional, if you take full advantage. Yet, students are supposed to attend community college for only two years rather than four to six years.

To prevent overstaying your welcome, you should identify a potential major and career field before you enroll in community college. Numerous community college majors offer technical/vocational training and certifications/associate's degrees for such careers as mechanic; plumber; or heating, ventilation, and air conditioning technician.[76] Earning an Associate of Applied Science degree, you will immediately start vocation-specific coursework for your career field if only an associate's degree is required.[77] Thus, you ought to know if your career of interest requires a certification or an associate's degree. Again, you have only two years to get your degree, which is not a great deal of time. You must create and follow a two-year academic plan for graduation. The academic plan should outline every course needed to graduate from college on time based on your associate's degree program. At the end of each semester, you and your academic advisor should meet to review the plan and verify that you are on track with the necessary credits for your associate's degree.

When a four-year degree is required for your career field, you must strategize your transfer plan to a four-year college.[78] If you are unsure about your major, you need to research and select it while taking general education courses at community college. You will have more time to decide on your major. This is important because you may decide to earn an Associate of Arts or Associate of Science degree.[79] For both, the coursework is more general instead of vocational or technical in nature. Your academic advisor or admissions office should help and guide you in your decision. As soon as you identify your major, if appropriate, you must immediately look for your follow-on bachelor's degree program at potential four-year colleges. You ought to contact each college's admissions office to find out if the school will accept all of your college credits. For example, you may decide to save money by taking major specific classes at your community college. Then, you truly need to make sure those credits transfer. At this juncture, I want to impress upon you that nothing exists unless there is a written record. If you want to dispute an entity's policy, decision, memory of events, or other action, you must have evidence. As a result, you should get everything in writing from the person or entity. To avoid a future denial of college credits, you should obtain a potential school's assurance in writing that all of your credits (general education and major-specific) will transfer. In addition, you need to confirm the process to facilitate the transfer.

When researching community colleges, you want to investigate their overall graduation and transfer-out rates.[80] Low graduation rates or high transfer-out rates could indicate the colleges' offered majors require transfers to four-year colleges, student academic problems, a lackadaisical administration/faculty, or a myriad of other issues. Several useful sites provide great information that you can use to research potential community colleges:

- The NCES College Navigator website[81]
  - Provides information on community colleges' overall graduation rates and transfer-out rates for students; and, offers a search engine feature to research college programs/majors, tuition and fees, and other criteria
- CNNMoney, Collegemeasures.org website[82]
  - Compiles and publishes a "success" rating for community colleges across the nation, including each community college's graduation and transfer-out rates to assign its ratings.
- StateUniversity.com[83]
  - Ranks the Top 500 community colleges
  - Compiles data on student retention, faculty salary, student to faculty ratio, each college's total cost,

financial aid information, athletics information and admissions' criteria

These sites are only tools because each community college is unique. In contrast, a college visit will help you to get the full picture of a prospective community college. You should also meet with an admissions officer during the visit. If you attend, you must stay focused on getting your degree in two years.

Section D: Private, For-profits Institutions

I want to alert you about a type of higher education institution that you should be careful about attending. For the past couple of decades, private, for-profit colleges have been booming. In television ads, these private, for-profit colleges often hype easy admission, weekend/night classes, online courses, job-specific curriculum towards a degree and greater class schedule flexibility. Private, for-profit education institutions are managed by profit-seeking owners or shareholders. Many of these schools have very low graduation rates and high tuition costs compared to public two or four-year colleges. According to a 2012 article, four-year private, for-profit institutions earned a low rate of 22% for bachelor's degree students to graduate within six years.[84] Also, private, for-profit institutions do not have a not-for-profit tax status.[85] Since they do not receive government tax dollars, private, for-profit schools usually have higher tuition costs than public community colleges and universities. Typically, the degrees that private, for-profit schools offer are limited. Also, their course credits may not transfer to other two-year and four-year colleges. Numerous private, for-profit students who may want to transfer to another school may not know the other school's transfer requirements.[86] These students waste time and money retaking courses at their new school. If you are considering a private, for-profit school, you must verify if other schools will accept your transfer credits! In addition, attendance at private, for-profit schools does not guarantee better employment or higher wages than attendance at public two-year and four-year colleges. Many private, for-profit college students have encountered high tuition and fee costs, difficulty in transferring credits, predatory student loan practices, and questionable employment returns, which raise alarming concerns. Thus, many educators and legislators have increased scrutiny about private, for-profit schools' quality, recruitment practices, and success rates for their graduates to find jobs.[87]

Private, for-profit schools are located across the nation. Normally, they target audiences through advertisements on television or radio, offering primarily online career training. Private, for-profit schools attracted 2.4 million students for the academic year 2010-2011.[88] The most popular for-profit colleges have multiple locations in several states. In actuality, a few private, for-profit schools have closed without warning. In September 2016, 136 locations of ITT Technical Institute in 38 states closed their doors in a voluntary bankruptcy filing.[89] ITT Technical Institute students lost tuition, did not obtain degrees and possibly were forced to start over at other colleges.

Attending a private, for-profit college may appear to fit many students' needs due to flexible schedules and easy admission. To be clear, I am not dismissing any past or current students who have worked hard to obtain their degrees from private, for-profit schools. Military members are especially susceptible because of deployments and access to tuition assistance to attend college. I still want to warn you of information that you should research before you select any private, for-profit college to attend. If something is too good to be true, it normally is. Compared to a 31% enrollment increase for other post-secondary institutions, enrollment grew by 225% for private, for-profit institutions from 1998 to 2008.[90] The increase in private, for-profit institution enrollment also correlated with a hike in the percentage of issued private student loans. The 2008 Project on Student Debt claimed that "almost one in four (24%) of all 2008 graduates from for-profit four-year colleges owed at least $40,000 in student loans."[91] In comparison, only 6% of graduates from public four-year colleges and 15% from private, nonprofit four-year colleges had that same amount of debt.[92] Due to their high tuition and fee costs, many of these colleges convince students to take out federal student loans to attend and then allegedly push private student loans to make up the difference. A student who has a financial crisis/setback may be left with high student debt but no degree.[93] Or, if the student has difficulty finding a job after graduation, he/she will be less likely or unable to make student loan payments. The Project on Student Debt's data also showed that federal student loan default rates were

- 9.8% for students who attended private, for-profit four-year colleges, which was more than twice as those from other four-year colleges;
- 3.6% for private, non-profit four-year college students; and,
- 4.3% for public four-year college students.[94]

These statistics highlight that some private, for-profit school students possess the highest amounts of student loan debt and default rates.

One example of a four-year, private for-profit satellite location is DeVry University in Arlington, Virginia.[95] The campus is DeVry University-Virginia. The NCES College Navigator tool provides information that a user can use to compare schools such as DeVry University-Virginia and the University of Maryland, College Park (UMCP), a public, four-year institution. Starting from academic year 2018-2019, the NCES College Navigator estimates DeVry University-Virginia's total undergraduate tuition and fees over the duration of its four-year program as $73,873.[96] This university makes no distinction between in-state versus out-of-state tuition costs. DeVry University-Virginia's estimated total undergraduate tuition and fees over the duration of its four-year program is much higher than the estimated cost of an in-state UMCP student at $45,213.[97] For the calculations, the selected tuition inflation rate for both colleges was 2%. To clarify, these undergraduate total costs over the four-year period are only estimates that do not count any financial aid funding. Still, the cost difference between the two sample schools is worth comparing this type of data for your potential schools of choice.

Next, a college's default rate is the percentage of its students who failed to repay federal student loans. In the fiscal year 2014, Devry's default rate was 12.5%[98] and UMCP's was 2.4%.[99] In addition, DeVry's total undergraduate student population in Fall 2016 was 370[100] versus UMCP's undergraduate enrollment of 28,472.[101] While DeVry's graduation rate for full-time, first-time degree-seeking students was 27%, UMCP's graduation rate was 86%. Reference transferring credits, in 2018, UMCP listed six DeVry University-Arlington courses in its transfer database.[102] Only one of those DeVry courses had a UMCP equivalent while the others required submission of a syllabus for review. The above comparisons highlight troubling information regarding costs, default rates, graduation rates an⸌ ·ferring credits that might apply to many private, for-prof⸍

The facts about private ⸍ ɑre very important to know! Private, for-profit ⸍v offer schedule flexibility and easy admissio. ɲal or working students. Despite these benefits, ·rantee better employment, higher wages, or higⱵ ⸜ for their students than public or not-for-profit cᴜ ⸍cus on graduating on time with a college degree; ⸍ ⸜ are not created equal. For that reason, youₗ ly investigate transferring credits to other schools of attending private, for-profit colleges; be especiaι

Section E: College Visits

During high school, you should exploit any college visit opportunity. College tours can help you decide if a certain college is the best fit. You will meet students/teachers, experience the environment and determine if you can think of yourself attending for two or four-years. You likely will stay and graduate if you take pleasure in attending your school. Otherwise, you will begin to drag your feet to classes or not show up at all. You want to eliminate that possible obstacle to graduating and getting your degree. So, you (and your parents) should make the trips if you have the money and time. In addition, many churches, after school/enrichment programs and organizations such as the YMCA sponsor college visits. Those schools that you visit should be your top three or four choices; especially if you have travel money constraints. You should have already done your homework to eliminate less desirable schools. Before you visit, you should contact the potential school. You can inquire if the college has guided tours that allow prospective students to talk to current students, see the campus and observe some classes. For example, you should ask if you can observe any ongoing classes, particularly for college majors of interest to you. If you do not have a specific major, you should attend a math, English, or science class. Most colleges require freshman students to take these general education classes. You should also coordinate to view one of the college dorms to gauge room space, storage size, and privacy. You might check if campus housing is available during the summer and winter breaks especially if you plan to take classes. In addition, you ought to check out the college's amenities, such as its gym(s) or student union.

In the book, "Campus Visits & College Interviews," the authors included several checklists that may help you in preparing for your college visit.[103] The book notes that exam weeks and weekends, when college is not in session, are not good times to visit a campus. In the "Chief Aspects of College Life" section, one checklist supplies questions to ask current students about their university.[104] The authors also address issues for international students and special-needs students.

Another method to check out schools is to visit local colleges/universities during their Open House or Organization Day. For instance, every April, UMCP hosts Maryland Day.[105] Each department posts instructors and students at booths to answer questions about majors and programs. With campus-wide access, parents and children can tour academic and recreational (gym, student union, etc.) buildings. You ought to investigate if your local colleges/universities have similar Open House periods. You should take the time to attend.

To recap, college visits are your time to experience these schools' environment and culture. When you visit each college, you should keep your eyes open and ask plenty of questions. You ought to use your college tours wisely in order to select the best school for you. If you love your college, you will want to stay and graduate. You also will be proud to tell others about your time at your alma mater.

Life lessons - Chapter 3: College Selection
- Research, research and research are critical for you to find the best college that you will love to attend
  - Research and making a final college selection are essential skills for you in life such as choosing a job, car, or house that is the best fit for you
- Many resources are available specifically your high school guidance counselor or the public library to help you to identify potential colleges for you to attend
- Local public two-year and four year colleges can save you money because of in-state tuition rates
  - Verify if the local college's general or core courses are transferable to other colleges
  - Check if the school is a feeder school that facilitates transfer to other colleges in the area
- Community college is a great opportunity; however, you must graduate from community college within the required two years. Stay focused!
  - When you transfer to a four-year institution, make sure you apply to your community college for your associate's degree if you earned 60 credits
- If you are considering a private, for-profit school, you must investigate its tuition costs, graduation rates, student loan default rate and ease of transferring credits
- To narrow down your top choices, avail yourself of college visits if money and time are available

CHAPTER 4:
Finances

It is late June, and it will be a long, hot summer. You graduated from high school and will be a college student in the fall. You received your desired college's acceptance and welcome letter. You also did well on your AP exams and tested out of a few courses. Congratulations! This summer before college, you should have fun: go to the beach, travel to Europe/South America, hang out with your friends, enjoy your family, and *fill in the blank*. Or, you might work. Either way, you should not completely veg out. You have some loose ends to tie up before you walk into your first college class specifically identifying money for your college dream. When you started middle school, you may have thought that paying for college was a distant problem in the future. You are not alone because many students do not have college funds or trust funds to take care of expenses, tuition, housing, books etc. Running out of money is a major factor that prevents students from graduating from college. Remember, the difference between optimistic and delusional is a plan.

Every student who decides to attend college must have his/her financial house in order. Some students are lucky to have parents who pay for their college education. Just as many parents have cried tears of anguish when they paid out exorbitant college costs only to see their child drop out before graduation. There are also numerous students who pay for college on their own without any parental help. Unfortunately, college funding requirements confuse even the savviest applicants. As early as the tenth grade, you and your parent(s) should discuss ways to pay for college namely savings, grants, loans, college funds, or merit/need-based scholarships. You ought to consider every possible scenario to fund all two or four years of college. For example, community colleges typically have very little institutional financial aid to distribute. If necessary, community college students typically must apply for financial aid from other sources including state and federal financial aid.[106] Anyway, your high school college counselor is a good resource to research options and develop a financial plan. Then, by your junior year, you need concrete numbers from your parents of exactly how much they will contribute.

To save yourself a host of pain and disappointment, you must have a tangible picture of available money for college. For instance, you may have your heart set on attending New York's Sarah Lawrence College, a private, not-for-profit college. For the academic year 2015-2016, students paid tuition and fees of $51,038.[107] By the academic year 2017-2018, the cost had increased to $54,010 according to the NCES College Navigator.[108] This example highlights that every year college costs are increasing. Unless you can foot the bill, have an inheritance from grandma, or an enormous amount of financial aid, you probably cannot afford to pay the total four-year price tag of over $223,000.[109] If you take out loans to attend, you will be saddled with enormous student loan debt. For a reality check, you also must investigate your potential earnings based on your major/degree of interest. Your potential earnings will impact your ability to quickly pay back your student loans. Thus, you must be realistic in the college that you can afford. To repeat, you and your parent(s) must have a frank discussion about college funding as early as possible. Below is a step by step plan that I will discuss in greater detail in this chapter.

- Talk to your high school counselor about financing college and possible funding sources
- Identify potential colleges and estimate the tuition and fees as well as the total cost to attend over a two or four-year period
  - Determine if you can afford your school choice
  - Research degree programs and potential earnings to pay back student loans, if applicable
  - Evaluate your desire and cost to attend an out-of-state school versus the cost of attending an in-state school
  - Consider taking general education/core courses at community college or a less expensive school, transferring those credits to a four-year school of choice (make sure credits will transfer)
- Identify if your parent(s) can contribute to your college degree and how much
- Start early in the tenth or eleventh grade to research and identify college funding sources in particular scholarships, student loans, and grants at the college, local, state and federal level
  - Use the Financial Aid Estimation Form on the FinAid.org website to get an estimate of federal financial aid that you might be eligible for[110]
  - Take advantage of the FAFSA4caster worksheet, which is another federal financial aid planning tool; it is found on the Federal Student Aid, U.S. Department of Education's website[111]
- Investigate military options to fund and attend college such as Reserved Officers Training Corps (ROTC) programs, service academies, or enlisting

- Communicate with employers, local community organizations, friends, family, and others about upcoming college attendance and solicit contributions namely gifts, scholarships, grants and/or employer tuition assistance
- Fill out the Free Application for Federal Student Aid (FAFSA) form as soon as possible
  - Accumulate financial documentation required for FAFSA form
  - Reapply and submit your FAFSA form yearly to apply for financial aid after being admitted and while attending college
- Start saving systematically for college by putting money away from working, special occasions etc. into savings vehicles like a 529 state plan
  - Calculate the total amount of money available from all sources to pay for college (two or four-year institution)
  - Identify gaps and methods to fill them such as working, work-study etc.
  - Remember the power of social media to broadcast college attendance to a wide-audience for possible funding

Now that I have set the stage, let's talk about money.

Section A: College Tuition

It is vital that you estimate how much your college dream will cost you. You and your parent(s) should know how much you can afford to pay for a college education. Tuition is the price colleges charge for a student to attend classes. A college charges tuition by credit hour, listing a course as one to five credit hours. Typically, the credit hour indicates the difficulty of the class as well as the number of times that the class will meet during the week. For a one-credit course, the instructor may teach his students one hour a week. Or, a four credit hour course can be divided into two lecture periods and a two-hour lab during the week. The instructor determines how the hours for the course are broken up, which is posted on the college's course schedule.

Students pay tuition and fee costs based on their registered courses and the associated credit hours. A student will shell out a different rate as a part-time student than a full-time student. Typically, a full-time college student takes 12 or more credit hours. A student taking six credit hours of classes will pay less than a student taking 12 or more credit hours. Usually, colleges make it easy for students to find out how much money they will need to attend their colleges. The majority of colleges and universities provide their undergraduate fee schedules and total annual cost of attendance on their official websites. In addition, you can check with a school's bursar or financial office on its current cost to attend. You should not have to search through multiple computer screens or jump through other hoops to discover the cost to attend an in-state or out-of-state college. Or else, I suggest that you run, don't walk, to the nearest exit.

I will discuss a few resources to explore colleges' tuition and other costs. These websites provide only approximations that do not take into account financial aid or a particular student's financial situation. Additionally, I did not use current academic year costs since the data is for information purposes only. For instance, the Forbes.com website provides in-state tuition and out-of-state tuition for numerous schools. For example, a Maryland resident who is a full-time student at the University of Maryland,

College Park (UMCP) would have paid approximately an in-state tuition cost of $9,996 for the 2015-2016 academic year.[112] This flat tuition rate was based on taking 12 or more credit hours per semester as a full-time student. In contrast, for the same academic year, an out-of-state resident (attending UMCP) paid an average annual tuition of $31,144.[113] Typically, schools charge in-state resident students less than out-of-state students because in-state resident students are the largest demographic to attend a local school. Also, these in-state resident students will likely obtain jobs in the state, increasing the literacy levels of the state's citizens.

In addition to Forbes.com, Collegedata.com is another good website that provides college cost estimates.[114] It supplies in-state and out-of-state tuition and fees. Under its Money Matters section, the website estimates costs for room and board, books and supplies, and payment plans. As well, the U.S. Department of Education is an excellent reference for information about college affordability and costs.[115] The above websites are not the only sources that provide college in-state and out-of-state tuition cost estimates. You can also search a school's website for the information.

When investigating colleges to attend, you should compare their *average total annual academic cost*. The total academic year cost is estimated by totaling all costs, including tuition, mandatory fees, room and board, and books and supplies. Usually, colleges will supply the average total annual academic cost on their websites. Over four years, the difference between out-of-state colleges in total average annual academic costs can be surprising. For example, UMCP and the University of Wisconsin-Milwaukee (UWM) are excellent four-year public universities. The schools are appealing to prospective students because of their abundant majors, high college rankings, and locations. For the academic year

2015-2016, UMCP's estimated average total annual academic cost was $25,742[116] for a Maryland resident and $46,285 for a non-resident student.[117] In contrast, for the academic year 2015-2016, UWM charged on average an estimated total annual cost of $23,629[118] for an in-state Wisconsin resident and $33,739 for an out-of-state resident student.[119] Although the in-state resident's average total annual academic costs were comparable, the UWM out-of-state student's cost was less expensive than a non-resident student attending UMCP. Again, these costs do not include the available financial aid that a student may have to help pay for college. At any rate, the above exercise offers an important aspect in your criteria for determining if you can afford to attend a certain out-of-state school. Although other factors may affect your decision to attend a college such as available majors, student population, and location, the cost to attend should be a weighted factor.

To pay for college, you and your parent(s) have a great deal of research and calculations to do. On a number of websites, you can find out the average cost to attend most colleges across the nation. You should apply to those colleges that you can afford to attend. If accepted, you ought to receive your college acceptance and financial aid award letters in late March or early April. Then, you should compare the cost of attendance at your top college choices. Viewing the financial aid award letter, you must verify the source, type and amounts of your college funding specifically scholarships (which are not paid back); grants (which are not paid back); work-study; student loans (federal and/or private, which must be paid back) with the associated interest rates; and your bottom line, out of pocket costs. In addition, you and your parent(s) should use a loan analyzer or calculator to compare a few lenders and their student loan terms based on monthly repayment amounts, interest rates and the length of time to repay the loans.[120]

Sensibly, the cost of your undergraduate college dream, in particular student loans or other debt, should not take more than a reasonable time such as five to ten years to pay back. Otherwise, you must really assess if you have the funds to attend a particular college. I am not trying to crush your college dreams but I also do not want you to be burdened with overwhelming student loan debt. The Consumer Financial Protection Bureau's website provides a great interactive Paying for College worksheet.[121] It allows a user to input his/her financial information and facilitates comparing college costs and financial aid offers. The worksheet considers the following items:

- All available money on hand in savings and parental contributions
- All money from scholarships and grants
- Any federal, state or college financial aid
- Any federal or private student loan amounts
- Any remaining costs that must be paid out of pocket
- Debt amount at graduation with the associated monthly payments

Researching this type of information can help you to eliminate those two or four-year institutions that you cannot afford to attend even with significant financial aid. You and your parent(s) must start early in order to make an informed decision. Then, you can accumulate the money to fund your college dream. Next, you should apply to the best four colleges that you are interested in attending and can comfortably afford. When accepted, you can attend your top contender and graduate with little or no debt.

Section B: Scholarships, College Funds, and Other Sources

No one owes you a college education. I am putting that out there for you to soak up. Of course, some parents pay for their child's education outright. Either they have more than enough money or they saved every penny to send their child to school. Many parents fully intend to fund a child's college education but unexpected issues crop up like a medical crisis or job loss that sucks up all available money. Other parents pay for private school from middle to high school in order for their child to receive exposure to the best education, network with other privileged children, or make the child more attractive to colleges. These parents may have paid over $100,000 for private high school. They have not planned to pay for college because they expect their child to receive academic or other merit-based scholarships. Unless your parents tell you that they are going to foot the bill partially or in full with hard numbers, you must assume that you have got to come up with money for college. Fortunately, you have several options to pay for college namely scholarships, college funds, and other sources. Your objective is to graduate with the least amount or no student debt.

Scholarships are a great way to pay for school because they do not have to be paid back as long as the student continues to meet the scholarship guidelines. Normally, scholarship guidelines will define the submission/performance standards, scholarship amount, and duration of the award. Scholarship submission/performance standards vary in requirements, in particular, essays, applications, community service, minimum grade point averages, or entering specific degree programs. Also, scholarships may be a one-time gift, fund a semester, pay for books only, or cover the whole period of attendance. The competition for scholarship dollars, however, can be stiff. If you do not apply, others are waiting to put in the effort and obtain the available money. Customarily, colleges offer scholarships to students as part of their offer or award letters. Luckily, colleges are not the only source for scholarships.

Governments at the local and state level offer scholarships to educate their citizens. These scholarships are investments in the community because highly skilled workers attract and create businesses. In addition, other sources for scholarships are industry associations, local community organizations, or employers. Author Leah Latimer outlines ways to pay for college in her book, "Higher Ground." Her action plans embrace churches, labor unions, professional associations, sororities and fraternities, and employers as donors.[122] For example, your parents' employer may offer scholarships for college. Otherwise, you can work for a company like Bank of America or Raytheon that offers tuition assistance or reimbursement. In addition, numerous colleges offer tuition remission in which they provide tuition benefits such as cost breaks or free undergraduate tuition to their full-time employees and their dependents. Thus, the various scholarships available are extensive. At anytime, you can search online for available scholarships based on an assortment of applicant criteria such as children of military members, residents of a certain state, or students entering specific career fields.[123] The best feature about scholarships is that you can apply for scholarships before and during college. Many are awarded, renewed, and/or offered annually. To avoid scams, though, I caution you that your searches and/or applications for any scholarships should always be free.[124]

Nevertheless, scholarships can be need-based or merit-based. Need-based scholarships refer to a student and his/her family's ability to pay for college. These scholarships are solely based on financial need. You and your parent(s) can expect to fill out paperwork, provide tax statements, and submit other documentation to display your family's financial assets. If you or your family meets the specified criteria, then you likely will receive need-based financial aid for as long as you are enrolled in school. You may be required to apply each year for certification to verify your financial status. Of course, if your family's circumstance changes notably winning a multi-million dollar lottery, you may no longer be entitled.

When a school, government agency, business, or community organization offers merit-based scholarships, it wants to recognize academic scholars, sports talent, artistically gifted students, or a more diverse demographic. There is no financial need requirement for merit-based scholarships. As I mentioned before, our society recognizes those with specialized talents, knowledge, or skills. In other words, numerous colleges and organizations offer full or partial scholarships in music, culinary arts, dance, spelling, sports, and other subjects. For instance, you can improve your chances for a music scholarship by studying and mastering an instrument like the violin, flute, saxophone, piano, etc. Or, you may excel in non-academic performance competitions, having fun while earning money for college. Specifically, the United States Bowling Congress offers monetary awards and scholarships for competitive youth league bowlers based on lane performance, leadership, and academics.

Another type of merit-based scholarship is awarded by the military. Every branch of military service has a Reserve Officers Training Corp (ROTC) program or equivalent.[125] College ROTC programs offer financial support to some students while they attend college. ROTC funding awards to students for college is very competitive. As you attend regular college classes toward your major/degree, you will also attend ROTC sponsored military science courses and training. In return for a ROTC scholarship, after graduation, you will serve in that branch of service as a military officer. ROTC programs are not offered at every college.[126] To find out more, you can research colleges that host ROTC programs or go to each military service's ROTC website. Additionally, each military branch sponsors a service academy such as the United States Military Academy. These military schools are full-scholarship institutions that commission officers for their respective military branches. Or, if you enlist in the military, you may receive a military enlistment bonus for entering a selected career specialty as well as tuition assistance to attend college. For each military option, you will sign a contract and commit to serving in the armed forces somewhere in the U.S. or overseas for a specified period time. To recap, need or merit-based scholarships are a means to fund college. In your high school junior year, you should start researching and identifying scholarships, prizes, and/or tuition benefits that you may be eligible to apply for.

Another way to pay for college is a college fund. Your parent(s) probably are not Beyonce and Jay-Z, but they can set up a college fund for you. In her book, author Leah Latimer proposes several methods to establish a college fund. These include Pre-paid Tuition Plans, certificates of deposits, mutual funds, passbook savings accounts, and other monetary vehicles.[127] Many states offer Pre-paid Tuition Plans or specialized savings plans that allow parents to contribute to a college fund. These plans are called 529 plans.[128] There are no income limits; so, parents at every income level can contribute. Each state sets its own policies for annual contribution limits, which can be as high as $380,000.[129] Since parents are not limited to their state's plan, they can shop around for the best option. Also, grandparents or others can contribute to the 529 plan to help fund it. Your parents can even solicit your help in funding the 529 plan with some of your birthday or special occasion money. In addition, you have time to accumulate and contribute some money through summer or part-time work while in high school. Your parent(s) also should begin to contribute to your college fund early. If they have not, you can prompt them to set one up as you approach your junior and senior years. Every dime helps in paying for tuition, lab fees, books, etc. Although the benefits of 529 plans are numerous, other savings options specifically mutual funds and certificates of deposit are available. Just start somewhere because a college fund is worth every penny.

Alas, many young adults fail to inform friends and family about their college attendance in August/September. To inform others, you should send out graduation announcements, specifying which college you will be attending.[130] Many times, friends and family will send $20 or $50 as a congratulatory graduation gift. In turn, you should immediately send thank you letters to the givers. People remember graduates who are grateful. Then, you should periodically follow-up with notes on making the dean's list, other significant events, and college graduation. Donors may repeat the gift gestures because they are proud of your achievements. Every little bit of money helps in paying tuition and other costs.

Another good method to broadcast the news about your college plans is social media, namely Facebook,™ Twitter,™ WhatsApp, Kickstarter, Snapchat, and Instagram.™ James Ward is a case in point.[131] In and out of homeless shelters for most of his life, Ward studied hard in high school. His hard work garnered a college acceptance from Howard University in Maryland. Ward planned to major in physics. Although he had accumulated 70 percent of the first year's tuition cost through loans, scholarships, and grants, he was short of about $14,000. Jessica Sutherland who had been homeless at one time heard of James' story. She set up a website to acquire the additional money. Through generous donations, James was able to start as a 2013 freshman class at Howard.[132] Without money, you will not attend college. You must investigate all options and select those that are feasible to fund your dream: scholarships, college funds, and other sources.

Section C: Grants and Loans

You initially might finance your education through savings, scholarships, and work; still, you may not be able to cover all of your expenses. Again, running out of money is one of the numerous reasons why most students do not graduate from college. Your goal is to graduate from college on time with a degree. Thus, you may need to apply for financial aid in the form of grants or loans to pay for school. Usually, grants and loans close the gap between the students' ability to pay, and the cost of college. In 2014-15, more than $183.8 billion was available in financial aid to undergraduates.[133] The main sources of financial aid are the federal government, state governments, colleges/universities, private organizations, and employers. The federal government's portion of financial aid comprised 67% of that $183.8 billion.[134] Federal financial aid programs include work-study, grants, and the Federal Direct Loan Program.[135] For example, work-study is a federal financial aid program that participating schools administer. While attending school, a student can earn a wage while working part-time per week on campus or off campus.[136] Work-study eligibility is based on a student's financial need while a part-time or full-time student. An added benefit is that work-study earnings do not count against the next year's financial aid.

To find out your eligibility and apply for federal financial aid, you should submit the Free Application for Federal Student Aid (FAFSA) form through your college's financial office or online at www.fafsa.gov. The federal financial aid will be allotted when you are admitted and enrolled at the school. On the form, you can elect to send the FAFSA results to colleges that you identify. If eligible, you will receive a college financial aid award letter that specifies your financial aid funding. The key to obtaining federal financial aid is to apply early because there is more money available. You need to fill out a FAFSA form as early as possible and before the deadline ends.[137] FAFSA form submission opens on Oct 1st for the following academic year. For instance, for the academic year 2017-2018, you would be eligible to file the FAFSA form between October 1st, 2016, and June 30th, 2018. Even, some colleges and state governments use the FAFSA form to offer financial aid. They may have their own deadlines for filing. Each academic year, you must also reapply and resubmit the FAFSA form to continue obtaining financial aid.

More importantly, the submitted information on the FAFSA form helps the federal government and/or colleges to determine the amount of money that a student's family can contribute towards the student's college costs. Several factors are considered, chiefly the family's size, income, and other children attending college. Typically, the family's contribution to pay a college's cost of attendance rises as the family's income increases.[138] Yet, you and your family will not know if you are eligible for financial aid unless you apply. To repeat, *at the earliest*, you and your parent(s) should submit the FAFSA form. Yet, you may not be ready to apply for college as a high school tenth grader. While researching funding sources for college, you and your parent(s) can use the FinAid.org and/or FAFSA4caster.ed.gov's free college financial planning tools. Both planning tools assess a student's eligibility for federal financial aid and calculate possible future amounts that he/she might receive.

Another form of financial aid is the grant. If a student maintains his/her GPA and remains enrolled in college, he/she normally does not have to pay back a grant. Grants are very similar to scholarships except federal financial aid does not include a scholarship category. Sources for grants are the federal government, state governments, colleges, employers, and private organizations, including nonprofit and for profit businesses. Most grant sources use a student's submitted FAFSA form to determine eligibility. Although customarily need-based, each grant requirement may have other applicant criteria in particular gender, veteran status, disabilities, high-need career fields, merit/academics, etc. In addition, submission deadlines, applications, and selection criteria vary by source. To receive state grants, students usually must live and attend college in the state. Often, a student can search for state grants through his/her college of choice or directly on his/her state's Higher Education Commission website. The Higher Education Commission, Office, or Agency administers and regulates post-secondary education programs for a state.

For eligible students, the federal government awards U.S. Department of Education grants.[139] These grants usually do not have to be repaid. Federal grants include the Pell Grant. A student is eligible for the Pell Grant based on the student's financial need, status as a full-time or part-time student, and other factors. One such factor is the undergraduate student typically cannot already have a bachelor's or higher degree. For the 2017-2018 academic years, the maximum Pell Grant award per term to a student was $5,920.[140] Every student should investigate his/her eligibility for a federal grant and apply using the FAFSA form. The College Board Advocacy & Policy Center estimates only 58% of Pell Grant eligible students who attended community college applied in 2010.[141] At four-year public institutions, the percentage of eligible students who applied for Pell Grants was 77%.[142] A College Board report listed "a lack of basic understanding, inconsistent or inaccurate information, and distrust of government agencies" as reasons that students are reluctant to apply.[143] Thus, eligible students leave a great deal of federal financial aid namely grants unused every year. That aid could have helped pay for their college education. Once more, grants are another means to pay for college. Before and during college, you should apply for grants because many are awarded, renewed, and/or offered annually. If you miss the annual deadline, you should apply the next calendar year. You have to do the research to find these opportunities.

Student loans are another means to pay for college. Unlike a scholarship or grant, the drawback of a student loan is that the student must pay back the money. All student loans are not the same. There are two categories: federal and private student loans. Below are the features of federal student loans versus private student loans: (see Figure 7).[144]

Federal Student Loans	Private Student Loans
You will not have to start repaying your federal student loans until you graduate, leave school, or change your enrollment status to less than half-time.	Many private student loans require payments while you are still in school.
The interest rate is fixed and is often lower than private loans—and much lower than some credit card interest rates. View the current interest rates on federal student loans.	Private student loans can have variable interest rates, some greater than 18%. A variable rate may substantially increase the total amount you repay.
Undergraduate students with financial need will likely qualify for a subsidized loan where the government pays the interest while you are in school on at least a half-time basis.	Private student loans are not subsidized. No one pays the interest on your loan but you.
You don't need to get a credit check for most federal student loans (except for PLUS loans). Federal student loans can help you establish a good credit record.	Private student loans may require an established credit record. The cost of a private student loan will depend on your credit score and other factors.
You won't need a cosigner to get a federal student loan in most cases.	You may need a cosigner.
Interest may be tax deductible.	Interest may not be tax deductible.
Loans can be consolidated into a Direct Consolidation Loan. Learn about your consolidation options.	Private student loans cannot be consolidated into a Direct Consolidation Loan.
If you are having trouble repaying your loan, you may be able to temporarily postpone or lower your payments.	Private student loans may not offer forbearance or deferment options.
There are several repayment plans, including an option to tie your monthly payment to your income.	You should check with your lender to find out about your repayment options.
There is no prepayment penalty fee.	You need to make sure there are no prepayment penalty fees.
You may be eligible to have some portion of your loans forgiven if you work in public service. Learn about our loan forgiveness programs.	It is unlikely that your lender will offer a loan forgiveness program.

Figure 7: Summary of Federal and Private Loan Differences
Source: Federal Student Aid, U.S. Department of Education. Public Domain.

From the chart, federal student loans usually have benefits that private student loans cannot match.[145] They are typically safer, more affordable, and more negotiable than private student loans. More importantly, the U.S. Department of Education's Federal Student Aid website offers a great repayment calculator that estimates monthly loan payments based on repayment types.[146] Viewing the information, a student can then contact his/her lender to determine eligibility and apply for a loan repayment modification or consolidation of his/her federal student loans. If a borrower qualifies, consolidation of his/her loans means combining many smaller loans into one big loan in order to make payments to one lender.[147] These actions are free services, which are especially important to know if the student would like to decrease his/her monthly loan payment amount. Even better, the Federal Student Aid office offers free help about federal student loans. It is accessible to borrowers at 1-800-4-FED-AID and on its website.

There are four federal student loan types namely Direct PLUS Loans, Direct Consolidation Loans, Direct Subsidized Loans and Direct Unsubsidized Loans.[148] Loan applicants include dependent students, independent students, parents, and graduate students. An example of a federal student loan is the Stafford Loan also known as a Federal Direct Subsidized Loan or Direct Unsubsidized Loan.[149] Subsidized Stafford Loans are based on financial need and exempt from interest payments on the loan.[150] Unsubsidized Stafford Loans are not based on need. As noted below, Stafford Loans have basic eligibility requirements (see Figure 8).[151]

Eligibility Requirements

Enrolled at least half-time at an eligible school and maintaining satisfactory academic progress

A U.S. citizen or a permanent resident of the U.S. or an eligible territory

Not currently in default. Must not owe a refund on any Title IV loan or grant

Registered with Selective Service (if borrower is a male under age 25)

Figure 8: Stafford Loan Eligibility Requirements
Source: Stafford Loans © 2013. Scholarships.com. Reproduced with permission.

Besides being a U.S. citizen, a student just has to breathe to be eligible. Stafford Loans have other great features notably

- Low interest rates that are fixed between 3% and 7%[152]
- Can be consolidated and have no prepayment penalty fees
- No requirement for a credit history or co-signer
- Offer repayment plans based on a percentage of the recipient's income
- Deferment and forbearance options - Deferment or forbearance is a temporary postponement or reduction in the payment amount. [153]

Despite these advantages, Stafford Loan applicants are small in number across the nation. The Institute for College Access & Success (TICAS) published a fact sheet that claimed 19% of private loan borrowers did not take out any Stafford loans during the academic year 2011-2012.[154] According to the TICAS fact sheet, 28% had Stafford Loans but borrowed less than the full amount available. Seriously, college students who do not take full advantage of federal financial aid should not be the norm. The federal student loan benefits and protections are immense. Thus, federal student loans are the best methods over private student loans to pursue your education, hands down.

In actuality, federal student loans and Pell Grants do have some limitations. The federal government limits the annual and lifetime amounts of federal financial aid that a student can borrow over his/her college career.[155] These amounts depend on the student's class level and dependency status. Also, any federal student loans that a student obtains at other institutions are counted in the aggregate loan amounts. In addition to loan limitations, the federal financial aid program has time restraints on a student's eligibility to receive aid. As of July 1st, 2013, first-time borrowers are only eligible to receive federal financial aid for the "maximum eligibility period" to complete their academic program.[156] The maximum length of time is 150% of the published length of a degree program. For example, a student cannot exceed six years to earn his/her bachelor's degree or three years to earn his/her associate's degree. Or, the student risks losing his/her eligibility for financial aid. Hence, the federal government is also pushing students to complete their degrees and graduate on time. In spite of these limitations, you should apply for all available federal financial aid using the FAFSA form. It is so worth the effort.

Now, let's look at private student loans. Private loan lenders consist of banks and other lending institutions similar to Sallie Mae, Wells Fargo, and Discover Financial. The borrower applies directly to the lending institution for a loan. For private student loans, the offered loans are not based on need but a borrower's good credit score and history. In 2013, private loans were approximately 14 percent of the overall loan market.[157] They totaled about $165 billion out of the $1.2 trillion in outstanding debt in July 2013.[158] Since some students may not have savings, scholarships or college funds, many of these students may be susceptible to pressure tactics that claim private student loans are their only way to pay for college. A Fox Business/Bankrate Inc. article claimed 70% of college students who had private loans were unaware of options other than private loans.[159] For borrowers, private loans are expensive over the long-term. TICAS stated private loans often have high interest rates of up to 13.74%.[160] Also, private student loans cannot be discharged in bankruptcy. Despite unemployment, health issues, withdrawing from college, or other personal circumstances, these types of loans do not provide for income-based repayment or loan forgiveness. In October 2012, the Consumer Financial Protection Bureau (CFPB) reported the largest subset of consumers with private loans "complained that they are unable to modify the repayment terms of their loan."[161] In light of private student loan issues, the CFPB's ombudsman offers guidance and help to individuals with private student loan complaints.[162]

With most private student loans, a student may not qualify because he/she does not have a credit history. As a safeguard, the lender will require the student to have a loan co-signer, such as a parent. In the event of the student's default, the loan issuer can and will come after the co-signer for payment. In addition, the student's failure to pay the college student loan can adversely affect the co-signer's credit score and future finances. The decision to co-sign a student's loans can have serious consequences. Beyond a doubt, a well-informed co-signer ought to request a co-signer release option that allows him/her to be removed from the loan after a certain period of time and consecutive, on-time payments. Not all private student loans offer or inform borrower's about release options. Based on the negative aspects of private student loans, you should be extra cautious about signing up for these loans.

Although private student loans have serious disadvantages, you may decide to rely on them if other sources do not cover your costs. Before considering a private student loan, you ought to compare several lenders. You should Google or Yelp the private student loan lenders for any customer complaints on loan servicing or lack of customer service. Also, the FinAid.org website provides an excellent loan calculator or analyzer.[163] The Bankrate.com website is another option that hosts a student loan calculator.[164] Both calculators can compute monthly loan payments and compare different student loan terms. Lastly, I want to caution you to be leery of refinancing, consolidating or transferring any federal student loans to a private student loan lender. While consolidation means combining all loans into one loan, refinancing is replacing an existing loan with a new one. By changing from a federal to private student loan, you will lose many of the benefits and protections of having a federal student loan. Yet, you may find it beneficial to refinance your private student loans.[165] Then, you have to investigate and compare private student loan terms among the prospective lenders. Even so, you ought to use private loans as a last resort. Do your research, shop around and negotiate the best student loan terms.

As a matter of fact, the terms of your student loan(s) matter. You must understand the student loan type (federal or private); interest rate; interest rate type (fixed or variable); total loan amount with interest amount added; monthly repayment amount; and any penalties in particular prepayment or late fees. For instance, you should negotiate for a low **fixed** interest rate instead of a variable rate on any loan. Your interest rate determines the additional amount that you will pay back as the price of borrowing money from the lender. Lenders often will offer teaser variable rates that are lower than fixed rates. If the variable interest rate rises on your loan, your monthly payment and interest owed to the lender will also increase. In addition, taking a longer time to pay back your student loan(s) will cost you in additional owed interest. As an example, at 8% interest over ten years for a $35,000 student loan, you will pay a projected $424.65 a month but also pay $15,957.49 in interest. Over 20 years, your minimum monthly payment will be estimated at a lower $292.75; however, you will pay $35,260.97 in interest. With the longer repayment period, you will end up paying for the original student loan twice in added interest payments. Using a Bankrate.com student loan calculator, the above calculations assume no down payment, a fixed interest rate of 8%, and only paying the minimum monthly payment.[166] Unless you accelerate your repayments on your student loan principal balance, you might be paying for your college loans in your 30's or even 40's. When possible, the best policy is to negotiate for a fixed interest rate and pay more than the minimum student loan payment on your principal balance.

Actually, the debt avalanche approach is an effective option as a loan repayment method.[167] Using the debt avalanche strategy, you would pay the minimum payment for each of your debts (to avoid fees), allocate all available cash to pay off the debt/loan with the highest interest rate, work your way down to pay off the next highest interest rate debt, and then the next. High interest loans/debt will cost you more over time if they are not paid off quickly. Once again, you want to pay more towards the principal balance. When you do so, you ought to send a check to the lender with the words "PRINCIPAL only" and the loan account number clearly written in the check's remarks section to ensure the money is applied correctly. Then, you should phone/check online with your lender and make sure that the payment was applied against the principal balance. To reiterate, you want to pay off any student loans as soon as possible.

Often, federal and even private student loans are a hedge against skyrocketing college costs; still, you must use them judiciously. In truth, student loans should only augment other methods namely scholarships, grants, and work income to cover the cost of a student's two or four-year college dream. Regrettably, numerous students take out student loans but never complete their degree. Instead of paying for school, others use the money to buy a car or other baffling reasons. That kind of behavior is foolish and irresponsible. In addition, many students do not verify their potential earnings based on their major/degree versus the repayment amount of their outstanding student debt. After graduation, countless college graduates initially earn low wages or remain unemployed for a period of time. They may have $30,000 or more in student loan debt. Financially overwhelmed, these students suffer from stress, depression, isolation, shame, denial, anxiety, and fear.

Abusing or not repaying student loans will mess up your credit and peace of mind. When your loan is in forbearance, you have postponed payments. Unfortunately, the interest continues to accrue which makes your loan amount balloon depending on your interest rate. If you are 90 days or more past due in payments, then you are delinquent on your student loan. For a default status, you have not made any payments according to the loan terms. The repercussions can be dire, including a blemish on your credit report and enormous late fees. The shock to your financial good standing becomes more disruptive because of wage garnishment; loss of tax refunds; and debt collection agencies hounding you as well as any co-signers on the loan for repayment. To prevent the above scenarios, you should not take on more federal or private student loan debt than you can afford to pay back.

When unsure how to proceed, you ought to contact your college financial office to assist you in determining the most accurate student loan amount for your needs. In spite of this, I want you to stop and read the following carefully:

- Do not sign anything until you have fully read the documents
- Take advantage of all financial advising
- Ask plenty of questions until you know what you are signing up for
- Take the time to have a trusted family member, mentor, your banker, etc. review the loan terms before you sign
- Obtain and keep a copy of all your student loan paperwork as well as all payment receipts
- Start repaying your student loans as soon as possible after graduation or while still in school
- Have a financial budget and stick with it

After you are clear on the loan terms, you (with your co-signer, as appropriate) will have to sign a binding loan agreement specifically a master promissory note, stating you will repay the loan in accordance with its terms. At that time, you should obtain a copy of your loan paperwork, get your loan servicer's complete contact information, find out where to send your monthly payments, and ask the best means to obtain payment receipts namely cancelled checks or online. As soon as you can, you must start making loan repayments. Keep a record of all your loan paperwork, receipts of your student loan payments, and cancelled checks in a marked folder. You should safeguard this folder in order to follow-up on any student loan disputes. Additionally, you must remain in communication with your lenders or loan servicers throughout the duration of the loan(s) and immediately contact them if you have any repayment issues. Periodically, you should also verify your contact information with your lender and update it, accordingly. Therefore, you must be proactive in repaying your student loans and addressing any problems.

Section D: College Accounts and Billing

You planned and have money to pay for your degree. Now, you have to monitor that your school bills such as tuition and fees are being paid. Often, colleges and universities assign a unique student identification number to each student. The student's school bills and delinquent payments are linked to his/her student identification number. For instance, UMCP permitted me to have access to my student account online to view my balances 24 hour/7 days a week. You also will likely have 24/7 access to your college student account information. Otherwise, you should find out how you can get timely account balance information.

Each semester, every college will post payment deadlines on its website and academic calendar. Then, all schools will mail, e-mail, or post online their students' balances for tuition and fees, dorm fees, health insurance, mandatory student service fees, lab/workshop fees, unpaid parking citations, late library book fees and other financial obligations. Also, schools typically will assign e-mail accounts to their students. Therefore, you need to check your student email account daily or at least once a week to keep up with your school's financial notices. More importantly, you must pay your college tuition and other unpaid balances on time. If not, the college will block you from registering for future classes, receiving student services and receiving your grades. The school may also flag your account to prevent you from obtaining your official transcript or receiving your diploma.

At the semester's start, you must check your student account balance with your school. At that time, you should pay all outstanding balances via cash, credit card, money order, payment plan, direct debit, or check. Your school will probably take payment at the financial/bursar's office in person, over-the-phone, mail, or online. When finished, all balances should be zero. For whatever reason, you may encounter problems with payment. You should immediately contact the college's bursar's office or financial aid office for recommendations. For example, you may be able to work out a payment plan with the school, apply for student loans/scholarships/grants, reduce your number of classes/credit hours, participate in work-study, or other options. Otherwise, if not paid, the school may impose late payment or collection fees, which will only increase your unpaid balance.

Students who have scholarships, grants, vouchers, or receive a stipend from a third-party entity should notify the appropriate organization if they have a change in status. For example, the Veterans Administration pays for eligible military personnel to attend a range of colleges and universities across the nation.[168] Each semester, military members or veterans must verify their eligibility for benefits with their schools. They must be attending school, registered for classes in the upcoming semester, and taking the required number of credits. In your case, an outside source or third party may pay your tuition or other fees. Your funding source may require a minimum GPA, mandate a certain number of classes/credit hours per semester, or enforce a maximum length of time to complete your degree. Specifically, you may be put on probation or suspended from federal financial aid for failing grades. Or, you might lose your eligibility for federal financial aid if you exceed 150% of the length of time to complete your bachelor's degree.[169] Since a bachelor's degree is a four-year degree, 150% would be six years. Again, you should immediately alert your funding source's administrators and the school's financial aid office if you earn any failing grades, repeat classes, or have a change of status, namely withdrawal(s) from courses/school.

Section E: Personal Finance

You must understand that money is a tool. Countless young people graduate from high school and college without the first clue about managing their finances: budgeting, saving, investing, credit cards debt, and more. Before you go to college, I want you to understand that poor financial habits will have a dire impact on your ability to buy a car, rent an apartment, pay off student debt, etc. This section is designed to increase your financial literacy; so that, you can graduate with a positive fiscal future. Primarily, you should have your own checking account when you go to college. In today's society, everyone requires access to money in order to pay for food, clothing, shelter, utilities, and other things. While attending college, you may have a job. Or, your parents might provide a stipend for you to pay for books, tuition, transportation, etc. The best place to hold that money is in a checking account. You should shop around and Google/Yelp a few options for a brick and mortar bank, an online bank, or a credit union. Each of these institutions has a different mission, branch accessibility, and fees.[170] A brick and mortar bank has an address that a customer can visit, unlike an online bank that may not have a physical presence. To simplify the discussion, I will focus on banks.

You may choose to patronize an online bank, a local bank or a national bank. Before you open an account, you (and your parents) should ask the bank representative about pertinent fees particularly monthly service fees, required minimum account balances, account inactivity fees, the minimum to open and automated teller machine (ATM) fees. You should seek out and choose a free checking account to meet your needs. Otherwise, you will be giving away your hard-earned money to the bank in fees. Also, all banks will offer online access to your bank account. You can monitor your balance with the stroke of a few computer keys. Your bank may also issue a debit card or ATM card to you. The ATM card only allows you to access money at an ATM machine. You can use a debit card to make purchases and obtain cash from ATM machines. For both cards, the money directly comes out of your checking account. The debit card is similar to a check but more portable. Most debit cards have the Visa™ or MasterCard™ logo. Some banks charge exorbitant fees if you do not use the debit/ATM card at ATM machines in their banking system. Those fees can be as high as $3. You should choose a bank that does not charge a fee or reimburses if you use an outside ATM system.

You should know how to balance your checkbook. If you do not, ask your local banker or your parent(s) for tutoring. Balancing your checkbook means accounting for every written check, debit card purchase or ATM withdrawal. You should sit down at the same time each month, open your billing statements and pay your bills on time. You can write checks or pay your bills online. If you do not balance your checkbook, you may overdraw your bank account and have insufficient funds. A bank account with insufficient funds prevents a vendor or service company from obtaining payment for products/services. Your creditors such as the electric company will be understandably upset and turn off service for nonpayment. Despite insufficient funds, you can set up overdraft coverage. With this service, the bank will happily pay the deficit and charge you a fee. Overdraft fees for insufficient funds can cost up to $35 per paid transaction. Some banks will continue to assess overdraft fees every day until you put enough money to cover the transactions into your account. Thus, in a few days, you can rack up hundreds of dollars in bank overdraft fees. On an overdrawn account, for example, payment for a cup of coffee can add up to $95 in overdraft fees within a week (the initial $35 and an additional $12 each day for five days). In contrast, you can opt-out of overdraft services, which is the best choice. The bank will just not pay for a transaction, which has no associated bank fee. The declined payment, however, will alert you that your account has insufficient funds and is overdrawn. Accordingly, you must balance your checkbook to ensure enough money is available to pay your bills.

Coupled with a checking account, I propose that you open a savings account or money market fund. Monthly, you must "pay yourself first" by direct depositing a percentage of your money such as five percent into your savings account. Your savings money should not pass through your hands: set it (up for automatic deposit) and forget it (monthly). You cannot miss what you do not see. When you earn more, remember to save a larger percentage of your income. Your target is to save three months of living expenses but the endgame is at least six month's worth. Unlike investment funds, savings is not for making money or risking. Your purpose is to have adequate accessible money for college emergencies as well as living expenses when you graduate. While in school, you could face crises ranging from buying a replacement tire on your car to paying for a hospital visit.

As you use your emergency savings, you must replenish the account as soon as possible. Thus, your savings is your cushion from financial disaster. In his book, "The Wealth Choice: Success Secrets of Black Millionaires," Dennis Kimbro explains that a savings account is important because "Saving is synonymous with peace of mind, greater options, and power: the power to leave a dead-end job or a bad relationship, or to avoid difficult circumstances altogether."[171] Thus, you should put money away systematically. If you do not start, you will have zero money today, tomorrow and into the future. By starting in college, you will become a habitual saver with money available for any circumstance. So, $25 per month over four years of college adds up to $1,200 without the compound interest. Imagine if you save even more money per month. You have the advantage of time and compound interest on your side.

This discussion may be overwhelming to you. Do not feel anxious because you have time to direct your fiscal course. I am encouraging you to take the proper steps toward financial health. While obtaining your college education, you should increase your financial literacy. If you think college is expensive, ignorance is more so. Knowledge is power. In my opinion, the practice of sensible personal finance will improve your quality of life in college, after graduation, and into retirement.

In spite of taking charge of your personal finances before and at college, you might be stressing that your savings and financial aid might not cover all of your college expenses. You are thinking that you are just scraping by. You also want to know how to handle getting money for daily needs namely toiletries, a little spending money, trips home, or laundry. College students are notorious for having "no money." These students stretch a dollar until it squeaks and cries, "Uncle!" Largely, college students repurpose, reuse and recycle. They share the burden with other broke students by borrowing clothes, hosting potluck meals, etc. College students also know that they must take advantage of all store discounts, sales, online bargains, and coupons to buy things. Your campus student identification likely provides eligibility for discounts on purchases of movie tickets, computers/software, fast food, and other things. You should Google or Yelp for student discounts or offers in order to take advantage of them. Below are a few other tips for making ends meet and generating some money:

- If you do not qualify for work-study, you can find a job on campus as a teaching assistant, library assistant, resident assistant, parking enforcement officer, campus shuttle bus driver, campus police administrative help, help desk technician in the Information Technology (IT) Department, etc. As a matter of fact, I earned income as a student IT help desk technician on campus at one time. Usually, on campus jobs accommodate the class schedules of their student employees. You can get training in new skills and knowledge while getting paid. You have to start looking early and do the legwork to find on campus employment. A good resource for your job search is your campus career center, instructors, or academic advisor.

- Join college clubs. Often, clubs host monthly club meetings, social gatherings, or guest speakers. The events are customarily in the evening. Through campus sponsored budgets or fund raising, the clubs might have pizza and soda to attract and feed club members. While meeting new people and learning something, you get a free meal. Good deal!

- Sell your textbooks at the end of the semester online, to the local booksellers around campus, or to the college book store. Buy used or rent textbooks if possible.
- Ask your parents/family to send care packages or stipends. Otherwise, make friends with other students whose parents send care packages or stipends.
- Search online for and submit scholarship and grant applications to educational foundations, industry associations, religious entities, or other entities throughout the year
- Submit the FAFSA form and apply for financial aid yearly because more money may become available
- Go to your college bursar/financial aid office, get to know the people, and apply for emergency loans or financial assistance, as appropriate - Do not wait, ask if you need help
- Lucky for you, the U.S. informal economy of making a buck is alive and thriving. Self-employed entrepreneurs within the informal economy have created legitimate businesses that may not be taxed or fall under direct government oversight through licensing. You can market and sell your skills, talent, or knowledge to buyers via online websites or mobile device apps. You can also set your own hours and standards of business.
  - o Options are babysitting, decorating, graphic designing, tutoring, or filling a specific need/service on and around campus

- o If you do a great job, your reviews will reflect high praise. Or else, you will not get repeat customers or referrals to others.
- o Become the next Mark Zuckerberg who started a billion dollar business in his dorm room
- o Numerous businesses require regulation, licensing, and oversight to prevent hurting or scamming people; so, you should be careful in researching any proposed business that you create or join
- o Please do not engage in any money making activities that are illegal, immoral, or unethical. I do not want to see your arrest on the evening news. Also, be careful of your personal safety when working with a customer for the first-time and receiving payment.
- Consider transferring to a less expensive school with a similar degree program that you can afford to attend as an in-state resident

If you are worried about money at college, you have to hustle and find ways to fund your dream. Although the above advice lists some methods to obtain money or support, let your imagination run wild to other possible avenues and follow through.

Section F: Credit Cards and Debt

I want to warn you about another stumbling block that numerous college students face: huge credit card debt. Each year, students graduate with thousands of dollars in student loan debt. Just as many have huge amounts of credit card debt. Credit card companies barrage college students with frequent applications and offers. Instead of cash, a lot of students may pay for books, food or other necessities with their credit card. Some students carry multiple credit cards in their wallets. Credit cards are not free money. Let me say it again: credits cards are not free money. Any credit card balance is <u>a loan</u> that you promise to pay back within a billing cycle, which is normally a month. Visa™, MasterCard™, and others make their money from giving short-term monetary loans to their customers. Some credit cards can have interest rates as high as 30%. A loan's interest rate determines the additional amount that a borrower will pay back plus the original amount as the price of borrowing the lender's money. The worst credit cards are department or store cards because their interest rates normally start at 18%. Regarding excessive debt, Proverb 22:7 of the King James Bible states *"The rich ruleth over the poor, and the borrower is the servant of the lender."* Therefore, you should be attentive in monitoring your credit expenses and keeping them low.

A credit card is different from a debit card. With a credit card, you are using the issuer's money instead of the money out of your checking account.[172] The possession of a credit card has many benefits. You can buy big-ticket items without having to carry around large sums of money. Often, some credit card companies offer points, airline miles for future trips, or cash back rewards to loyal customers who maintain minimum spending requirements. Also, credit cards offer theft protection. A thief can steal your cash, which you may never recover. With your debit card, a thief can steal all of the money out of your checking account. You may not notice the fraudulent activity. Then, you may have to prove that you did not make the purchases to your bank. While you wait to recover your money, you have an empty checking account.[173] Instead, a credit card affords a degree of comfort and better protection than a debit card. Typically, credit card billing statements are online. A user can track his/her spending minute by minute. In addition, your financial institution will call or text electronic fraud alerts to you if it notices suspicious activity. Your bank or credit card issuer may even shut down the credit card's future spending activity. If you lose your credit card, you will not be held liable if you notify your financial institution within its notification deadline.

Another advantage of having a credit card is your ability to build a credit history. When you use a credit card, you will acquire a Fair Isaac Credit Organization (FICO) credit score.[174] Lenders use FICO credit scores to assess a person's ability to pay his/her bills on time as well as his/her risk for delinquency. A credit score is a three-digit number that ranges from 300 to 850.[175] Creditors covet customers with high credit scores from 740 to 850, which are known as super-prime.[176] Some lenders, credit bureaus, and creditors provide clients with their credit score for free or a small fee. As your college transcript follows you, your credit score trails you in your adult working life. A high score will help you to qualify for an apartment, a low-interest car loan, or the best interest rates for a mortgage/credit card. Knowing your credit score, you have a powerful tool to make sound financial decisions and promote your credit health. Despite a low credit score, you can elevate your score over time through financial discipline. There are no quick fixes to a bad credit score. In other words, you have to systematically pay your bills on time over a sustained period of time.

In addition to knowing your credit score, I also advise you to check your credit report periodically. A credit report is a financial file that a credit bureau maintains about an individual's credit history. Equifax, TransUnion, and Experian, the three main credit bureaus, offer free annual credit reports to any individual with a credit report on file through the AnnualCreditReport.com website.[177] You should pay close attention to any erroneous entries on your credit report and correct any discrepancies immediately. You also will be able to monitor and report if someone has high-jacked your credit by opening accounts in particular credit cards or car loans in your name.

In spite of a credit card's advantages, misuse of a credit card has terrible consequences. Customers who do not pay their credit card bills in full each month or miss credit card payments incur interest, late penalties, and fees. For example, Bankrate.com provides a great credit card minimum payment-to-interest calculator that supplies the number of months to pay off a credit card balance.[178] The Bankrate.com calculations below show the impact of small minimum payments and increasing interest rates. In each scenario, the minimum monthly payment is $15. When a credit card user pays the minimum monthly payment on a $250 credit card balance at 18% interest, he/she will pay $39.85 in interest or a total amount of $289.85.[179] He/she will take 19 months to pay off this debt. If the interest rate increases to 25% on the $250 credit card balance, the credit card user will pay $60.33 in interest over 20 months. For a $500 credit card balance, the user will pay $198.34 at 18% interest over 46 months to get rid of the debt. With an interest rate increase to 25% on the $500 credit card balance, the credit card user will pay interest of $362.53 (or a total amount of $862.53) over 57 months (or 4 years and 9 months). The $362.53 interest payment is more than half the original debt. That's insane. By paying only the minimum balance each month, a cardholder will take forever to get out of debt.

If you should find yourself overwhelmed by credit card debt, I urge you to contact your credit card lenders as soon as possible. If you do not, you have the potential to ruin your credit for years to come. Thus, you ought to ask for help such as modified payment plans or reduced minimum payment amounts. Often, lenders will work with borrowers who are behind in payments. Otherwise, the creditors might not get their money back. I am cautioning you to use your credit cards responsibly -- pay more than the minimum payment and/or do not get in extreme debt in the first place. You should shop around and apply for the credit card with the lowest interest rate. To connect the dots, you ought to *negotiate for the lowest fixed interest rate* when applying for any loan specifically a student loan, credit card, car loan, or mortgage.

In this brave new world, millions of people purchase items using mobile payment apps especially Apply Pay, Google Pay, Samsung Pay, Venmo, and PayPal. Typically, the funding for the transaction is tied to a checking account or credit card. By using one of these apps, you can swipe and buy almost anything. You also can easily rack up enormous credit card debt. You will be mortgaging your future to pay back the money that you owe on your credit cards today. Thus, massive credit card debt can put you on the fast track to bankruptcy in your 20's and 30's. Do not do it!

At your age and income level, you ought to live on a budget. On the last day of the month, you should note how much money comes in (income) and how much money goes out (debts). Your debts should not be larger than your income. For simplicity, you can use an online or downloaded app budget system. Mint.com, in particular, creates a budget and tracks/pays bills.[180] In any event, I am going to give you a valuable piece of advice: "You should live within or below your means." In other words, do not buy things that you cannot afford or need. Before you make a credit card purchase, you ought to ask yourself four important questions:

- Do I need this item?
- What will be the total minimum monthly payment to pay off this item?
- How much will the new payment affect my other expenses each month?
- How long will it take to pay off this purchase?

Still, you may decide to make the credit card purchase. Once more, you should pay for the item in full at the end of the month or send in more than the minimum monthly payment. The alternatives are to save your money until you can afford the item or buy a less expensive substitute/used item – shop around. Additionally, you can get a temporary job to bring in additional income to help pay down your debt.

I want to offer a few words of caution about credit and romance. With your girlfriend or boyfriend, you may be tempted to mix finances by co-signing on loans, having joint credit card accounts, loaning large sums of money to him/her, or purchasing a car together. These actions are huge mistakes and may teach you a very hard lesson. If the relationship ends, your credit could be dragged down by huge debts or your former sweetie's poor financial habits. You probably believe that the "love of your life" would never leave you holding the bag of accumulated debt. You are putting yourself in a vulnerable financial position. It may take time to realize that your honey/boo is financially irresponsible until after the first missed payment. When any relationship starts becoming serious, you and your partner must consider divulging credit scores, credit reports and having a frank discussion on finances before you become too invested.

In summary, you must take charge of your financial future. You do not want to be another statistic of a college student who leaves school due to a lack of money. Despite your desire to attend college, you must have your financial house in order before, during and after college through improving your financial literacy. Consequently, you must know how much potential colleges will cost to attend even if you and your family have the money to completely finance your college education. Many resources are available to research colleges' tuition and other costs. Through an assortment of means, you can obtain financing to attend college. The best method to acquire funds is to start saving early as well as apply for scholarships and grants. Whenever possible, you ought to rely primarily on federal student loans instead of private student loans to supplement savings, scholarships, grants and working. Your goal is to graduate with no or little student loan debt. In addition, your use of cash, debit cards, and credit cards creates a financial picture of your spending habits. As a college student, you must maintain your credit and stay out of extreme debt. Thus, you ought to live within or below your means. You should not be a gerbil on the wheel of amassing debt. A cappuccino here, a sandwich there, weekly clothes shopping and other purchases add up quickly on a credit card. Whenever possible, keep your debts to a minimum and quickly pay them off.

Life lessons - Chapter 4: Finances
- Running out of money is a major factor that prevents students from graduating from college.
    - By your high school junior year, you need concrete numbers from your parents of exactly how much they will pay for your college degree
    - Use online resources or the college's finance office to find out potential colleges' average tuition and fees costs as well as the annual total cost to attend
    - Research potential earnings based on your degree to validate the amount of student debt that you can afford
    - If you do not pay your college student account balance, your college will block you from registering for future classes, receiving student services and obtaining your transcripts/your diploma
    - Your objective is to graduate with the least amount or no student loan debt while attending a college that you can afford
- At the earliest, you should fill out and submit the FAFSA form and apply for all applicable scholarships and grants
    - Scholarships are merit-based or need-based
    - Write essays and submit scholarship/grant applications to community organizations, employers, fraternities/sororities, on-line foundations, or any other sources that can help to fund your college dream
    - If your parents choose to save for your college education in a college fund, they have numerous vehicles to accumulate the money, including 529 state plans
- Student loans are not created equal
    - Federal loans have several advantages over private student loans, which are expensive, have high interest rates and burdensome loan terms
    - Negotiate for the lowest interest rates and the best terms on your student loans i.e., shop around
    - The FinAid.org and Bankrate.com websites provide excellent student Loan Analyzer Calculators
    - Read and keep a copy of your student loan paperwork
    - Start repaying your student loan debt as soon as possible

after graduation or while you are in college
- o Keep a copy of all student loan payments via cancelled checks or online receipts i.e., know your remaining balance
- o When paying more towards your student loan principal balance, send a check with the words "PRINCIPAL only" and the loan account number clearly written in the check's remarks section; check back and make sure the payment is applied to the principal amount and not the interest
- o Never abuse or not repay student loans because a default will mess up your credit and peace of mind
- o In the event of a student's default, a co-signer will be on the hook to repay the student's private loan(s), which can destroy his/her credit standing as well as relationship with the student
- If you are having financial problems getting by at college, then look for discounts, work, or ask for financial support/help
- Your money decisions about saving, spending and credit cards today will positively or negatively impact your future financial picture

CHAPTER 5:
Finally On Campus

At this point in your story, I hope that you have chosen your college and put your finances in order. Now, we are going to look at some other important decisions/actions that you must be proactive in making. For instance, your choice of major is critical because it impacts the classes that you take, and should be tied to your future career. A computer science major will probably write software programs and create applications for Google, Oracle, or Microsoft to solve problems. A student pursuing a major in English will probably attend graduate school for a masters or doctorate degree in order to teach at the college level. A college graduate with a criminal justice degree might work in a governmental agency like the FBI. Or, a student with a bachelor's degree in art may work at McDonald's. I am only kidding about the prospect for art majors. Although college is a great way to determine your interests, college costs money. Linda Lanis Andrews, the author of "How to Choose a College Major," articulated that "a major means taking approximately 32 class hours in a specific subject area, such as music."[181] Unless you are independently wealthy, you should have an idea about the career that you want to pursue. Otherwise, you may take six years or more to obtain a four-year degree. In this chapter, I will discuss important aspects about your first few months at college notably student orientation, determining your major, academic advisors and establishing a graduation timeline.

Section A: Student Orientation

After you receive your notification of admission, you and your parent(s) should examine your college's student orientation guide. The orientation guide (online or hard copy) outlines areas of special interest notably the deadline to accept the school's offer, placement exams, orientation activities, packing lists and other vital information. The orientation guide or webpage discusses any prerequisites prior to the first or move-in day. Thus, I am stressing that your college's student orientation guide is a must-read. Or else, your potential joyful college experience can become a trial in fixing issues that you could have addressed before you showed up.

Some schools host a student orientation day to welcome incoming students. The orientation day can be voluntary or mandatory for students and their parents. You should participate to get a snapshot picture of your school. For example, I attended the student orientation at the United States Military Academy or West Point. West Point's Orientation Day is called R-Day or Plebe Orientation. It is mandatory for all new students. That first day, I only remember a blur of getting outfitted in various uniforms, learning how to march and salute, being assigned to a room, meeting my new roommates and generally being yelled at by upper-class cadets or student cadre. The atmosphere was tense and traumatic for the 1400 newly accepted cadets. Despite this, our freshman cadet class rallied, trained and performed an amazing full-dress parade supervised by our senior cadre in less than eight hours. I am sure that we impressed the West Point school administrators, our parents and other visitors. Today, I can look back and laugh at the stress of that day. What an orientation!!!

My University of Maryland, College Park (UMCP) student orientation day was a completely different experience from West

Point. Before the first day of classes, newly admitted UMCP students must accept the admission's offer and create a university e-mail. In addition, they must register online to schedule a new student orientation session to attend. Orientation also is open to parents. At my UMCP orientation, I remember hundreds of students and parents strolling around the campus; presentations about the school from current students, faculty, and administrators; and finally major/degree specific presentations. The atmosphere was relaxed and jovial. By the end of the day, my head was spinning with a vast amount of UMCP information. Go Terps!

My community college orientation at Montgomery College (MC) was a different animal entirely from West Point or UMCP. I did not attend a new student orientation session. MC did not notify me that I had to attend one. From the first class, I learned things as I went along. In my humble opinion, every college ought to consider mandatory student orientation to communicate its services, class registration, academic standards, culture, traditions and other pertinent information. With positive orientation experiences, new students might involve themselves more fully in the total campus culture and not feel isolated. The difference in the student orientation experiences of West Point, UMCP and MC highlights that a college's student orientation is as unique as the school. Your school's student orientation should be positive and a good first impression. Hopefully, your selected school will be thorough in welcoming new, incoming students to its campus, procedures, and administration. You ought to consider going to your college's student orientation if one is available.

Section B: Selecting a Major Field of Study

As I pound my fist on the desk, I am going to let you in on a little secret. The college that you get to attend for your undergraduate degree is not as important as the major that you pursue. In "How to Choose a College Major," Linda Andrews lists some pertinent questions to ask yourself about any major, including "the required number of years to attend school for the major, the difficulty of courses, your natural ability, jobs available after graduation, salary ranges, and cost of earning the degree."[182] While you are taking your high school courses, you ought to pay close attention to the subject matters that interest you. Or, a transfer student can do this type of research before transferring from one college to another.

College is expensive and time-consuming. Some students use college as a means to pause life, which really is not the purpose of college. Although students are there to get exposure to innovative ideas and meet new people, college ought to be the means to obtain knowledge and transferable skills namely problem-solving, leadership, listening, communication, and teamwork for their future careers. Depending on the career, you may have to obtain an associate's degree, bachelor's degree, or a graduate degree. For example, in healthcare, a person can become a registered nurse with an associate's degree, a physician assistant with a bachelor's degree, or a surgeon with a graduate degree, according to the BigFuture.com website.[183] Once more, it is important that you research and know the category of college degree namely an associate's, bachelor's, master's or doctoral degree required for your chosen career. More so, you want to choose a major associated with that career field as soon as possible. The college courses that you take will accumulate credits in your major toward a specific degree. Since you want to graduate on time, you really do not want to waste time and money taking classes that will not help you in achieving that goal.

By identifying your interests early, you will be able to narrow down your choices to a potential major and future career. You may have a passion for a field of study such as veterinary science, health care, engineering, math, forestry, film production, finance, or foreign languages. You ought to follow that dream. You should seek out and talk to professionals who already are established in those careers that interest you. If possible, while in high school, you ought to research and apply for an apprenticeship/summer job in that field of interest or industry. In addition, your high school guidance counselor may be able to coordinate a meeting, phone conversation, or even a career day, featuring a mixture of professionals.[184] Or, when conducting a college visit, you might request a meeting with an upper-class student who is pursuing your major of interest or representative in that academic department. To prepare for these meetings, you ought to draft your questions ahead of time and plan for 10 to 15 minutes of conversation. Your first interview question could be, "Would you choose this career/major if you had the opportunity to do it all over again?" Depending on the answer, you will have a greater understanding of the difficulties in pursuing a specific major/career. If appropriate, you should send a thank you note to the person for his/her time. Also, you might ask this person if you can keep in touch through e-mail or phone as you investigate possible majors. You may discover a mentor who can provide future advice and guidance.

Below are additional resources that I suggest to investigate potential careers and thus solidify your choice in a major:

- The Bureau of Labor Statistics. http://www.bls.gov/ooh/

- o Lists extensive job information about wages; projected growth rate; and required knowledge, skills and education requirements by occupation
- o Has specialty categories regarding workers with vision problems, women, and veterans
- CareerOneStop. http://www.careeronestop.org/SalariesBenefits/SalariesBenefits.aspx
  - o Encourages users to explore careers, including licensed occupations, green careers, and employment trends
  - o Matches skills, interests, values, and other traits to specific jobs based on self-assessment exercises
  - o Contains a scholarship finder search engine
- Career Kids. http://www.careerkids.com/careers/
  - o Caters to high school and college students
  - o Lists several careers and hyperlinks to detailed descriptions about specific careers and the associated salaries
- MyFuture.com. http://www.myfuture.com/careers?index-field-refresh=salary&Update.x=40&Update.y=3
  - o Allows users to search for occupations by field of study, by industry, and by type of work
  - o Lists college majors that correspond to various careers
  - o Lists colleges that offer specific majors
- OkCollegeStart.org. https://secure.okcollegestart.org/Career_Center/Career_Self_Assessment/Career_Self-Assessment.aspx
  - o Has career self-assessment page

o   Evaluates the user's interests, skills, values, and personality, which can translate to possible careers

I want to caution that you must not be blinded to potential obstacles when pursuing a college major. For instance, the major may not be prized in the job market. Numerous students graduate from college but they failed to investigate the employment outlook or potential earnings for their majors/career fields. Although you might follow your passion into a particular major, you have to earn a living and be able to find a job. You do not want $90,000 in student loan debt while you compete with fifty other graduates for the same Anthropology job vacancy that pays $35,000 a year.

In addition, you must investigate the types of jobs available and actively network before graduation to find jobs associated with your major. Your best sources of information are instructors, academic advisors, college career centers, departmental career fairs, major specific internships, and mentors/professionals working in the field. When choosing a major, you need to ask what industries can I work in with my degree, what job types are available, where are the jobs concentrated and how much can I earn? Unfortunately, many students obtain degrees in such majors as Liberal Arts, Anthropology, Fine Arts, Communications, Social Work, Philosophy, or anything ending in "Studies." Often, these graduates need more advanced degrees in the field, which requires additional time in college and money. Or, the major is too general and does not readily correlate to a specific occupation, i.e., this means unemployment. While in college, numerous students fail to identify the specific industries and careers that they could translate their majors into filling. They have degrees but do not know how or where to apply them. Due to these obstacles to employment, the graduates never work in their major or field of study.

Another issue may be that you may not have the prerequisite academic preparation to pursue a particular major. In high school, you probably have a good idea of your academic weaknesses and strengths. You may be a high school senior who has only taken math up to Algebra II. Then, you should carefully reconsider selecting a math intensive major for a career like mechanical engineer, statistician, or accountant. These majors require calculus I, calculus II and higher level math. In effect, you will be spending extra time and money to take remedial college math courses to acquire the necessary knowledge. Thus, you ought to research the required academic prerequisites for a potential major. Then, if possible, you can structure your high school academic program to mirror the curriculum required to succeed in the specific major. Lastly, many students choose a major but they do not have any natural ability. A student may want to be a surgeon because their parents and siblings were physicians but he/she could not cut a straight line in a pie crust with a sharp knife.

If you are unsure and panicking about your major, RELAX. Now that I have given you the hard sell, I want to reassure you. You probably will not walk into your first freshman class knowing your major. You have time. Many college students do not select their majors until their first, second, or even third year in college. You may also flip flop semester-to-semester in your decision about a major. To be clear, you do not want to follow the example of the ones who are figuring out their majors in their third year of college. Obviously, the more research about majors that you can do, and the more experience in the career field that you can get will help in your major selection. Otherwise, to avoid high student loan debt, you ought to consider applying for a school deferment or gap year before college.[185] Then, you can join the work force and increase your experiences until you are ready to figure out what you want to do in your career life.

At a four-year institution, you will take your general education courses in your first and second years of college. During that time, you can seek out information on available majors and careers. For example, every campus career center is available to transition students into the job-market. Many career centers offer job-related guidance on obtaining major specific internships or researching potential career fields. Also, most college websites offer comprehensive descriptions of their major programs to facilitate students' selection of majors. For instance, the University of Maryland, College Park (UMCP)'s undergraduate departments/colleges correlate to 90+ undergraduate majors.[186] The UMCP admission's web page lists 12 colleges, including the College of Arts and Humanities and the A. James Clark School of Engineering.[187] By clicking on the hyperlink for a specific college, a prospective student can examine the majors unique to that department. As an example, nine undergraduate engineering majors fall under the A. James Clark School of Engineering. As the prospective student clicks on each major, he/she will be hyperlinked to a separate website for that major.

In particular, the Aerospace Engineering website has a wealth of information for undergraduate students in particular a comprehensive description of each engineering course.[188] The site also provides a recommended course sequence by semester, including required math and science courses from freshman to senior year. As the student takes these sequenced courses, he/she accumulates expertise in the major, which should translate to proficiency in the career field. UMCP is not unique in listing its course requirements for each major. If interested in a major, you might call the department in your potential/current college or visit to find out more. You also might talk to current students who are pursuing the major.

A college's Registrar's Office is another source of information about specific majors. For example, the UMCP Office of the Registrar (TESTUDO)'s website supplies the calendar year's Schedule of Classes online.[189] The TESTUDO website lists general education courses, all courses with links to the associated major, course descriptions, course availability, instructors' names, course prerequisites, the days and times that the course occurs, and book requirements. Armed with this information, a current student can register for classes, depending on course availability. All colleges have similar registration information, whether online or in a paper course catalog. In your case, you should navigate to your prospective/current department or Office the Registrar's website to view major-specific courses and their requirements. With a little research, you can decide if a specific major is appealing to you.

College exposes students to new ideas, people, organizations, and activities. In addition, it can be an opportunity to pursue fields of study that interest you for a future career. It helps if you have already researched some subject areas or majors as a high school or transfer student. While completing your general education courses, you have time to make an informed decision about a specific major. In your future career, the key to success is to match up the interests that you genuinely enjoy with the set of skills that you can do really well while earning a top-notch living for them. When you have a career that you love, you will be asking yourself, "I get paid for this when I would do it for free?"

Section C: Academic Advisors

You may not have signed up for classes at the student orientation. Your next step is to identify the classes that you are taking for your first semester. More importantly, you must have a progression plan for the classes that you need to obtain your degree and graduate on time. Your academic advisor should be your guide in this process. A college academic advisor is a student's side-kick, who is concerned about the student's best interest. The academic advisor is Robin to the student's Batman. During your initial meeting, you ought to discuss in detail your plans to enter a specific major/degree program. At this point, your academic advisor and you should have a frank discussion about your previous academic preparation, your advance placement exam results, your goals in attending college and your specific major/degree's course requirements. You ought to arrive with a notepad, pen, and questions because this exchange will chart your academic course toward obtaining *your* degree. With the input of your college academic advisor, you will register for your classes. Your interaction with your academic advisor should be continuous throughout your college years. He/she is your first contact for basically everything college-related especially declaring a major, changing majors, changing schools, failing grades, participating in a study abroad program, or any other issue impacting your future graduation. Academic advisors know the ins and outs of their particular school or degree program. If you have not met your advisor or do not even know his/her name, you have another task to add onto your to-do list. Academic advisors keep students on track toward graduation.

At UMCP, I ascertained that academic advisors are vital to a productive and effective college experience. I entered UMCP as a computer science major. The Computer Science Department required all of its students to schedule a 30 minute face-to-face meeting with an undergraduate computer science advisor at the end of each semester.[190] Until I met with my advisor, I had a registration block that prevented registering for the next semester's classes. At the meeting, the topic of conversation was registering for classes in the upcoming semester and filling out my four-year academic plan worksheet.[191] Although the format varies, a two or four-year academic plan records a student's required general education courses, degree/major specific courses, elective courses by semester, earned credits, and class year. Using the four-year plan format, I registered for my courses based on their availability for the semester. My academic advisor and I also verified that I had the required prerequisite courses for more advanced courses. A prerequisite course saves a student from walking into a classroom without the basic knowledge to pass a course.

Thus, the academic plan is a great flexible chart that tracks changes and helps each student stay within his/her graduation timeline. A two or four-year academic plan is particularly useful for an academic advisor in calculating credits if a student changes his/her major or transfers from another school. To use the plan, the student and academic advisor should meet each semester as the student progresses. On the academic plan, they will list the student's earned credits from completed courses, semester GPAs and the total number of remaining required credits. A student's expected graduation date can be earlier or later depending on remedial courses, failed classes, changing majors, etc. For instance, to reach 120 credit hours for a bachelor's degree, a student should take 15 credit hours per semester in order to graduate within four years. The credit hours needed per semester will change if the student takes summer and/or winter classes. In addition, the student and advisor will calculate the number of credit hours differently if the school schedules classes by quarters.[192] Unlike a semester system, an academic year based on quarters has four terms that last 10-12 weeks per term. To obtain a bachelor's degree and graduate, a student requires at least 180 to 192 quarter hours depending on the major. With the variable nature of earning credits, a student's use of a two or four-year academic plan is vital to the his/her graduating from college on time.

When you declare a specific major, your general academic advisor may change to a major specific advisor. For example, many science, technology, engineering, and math programs assign instructors who have Ph.D.'s in the subject matter as advisors for undergraduate juniors and seniors. The major specific faculty advisors are quite familiar with appropriate course scheduling, course content and the amount of work required for each course. In addition, a major specific advisor may be a student's future instructor. It is important that you get to know your academic or faculty advisor. Additionally, you can use your two or four-year plan to open dialogue with your new advisor.

Many students do not ever meet with their academic advisors. Even worse, many colleges do not require students to meet with an advisor or have a plan for graduation. These colleges have an economic conflict of interest because they make money from students who never graduate but continue to take irrelevant courses. In your situation, you should keep rotating through the academic advisor department until you find an advisor who cares about your best interest and academic goals. When you find a knowledgeable and effective academic advisor, you should meet with him/her at the end of each semester. At that time, you must verify your progress toward graduating on time and register for future courses in accordance with your two or four-year plan.

In summary, your academic advisor is your best bet for meeting your graduation timeline. Your academic advisor has the expertise and knowledge to help you make practical academic and career decisions. Incidentally, your school may not require a two or four-year academic plan. You and your academic advisor ought to draft informal ones. The effort will save you money and time which will help you to graduate on time. You still have to pass your classes but you at least will have a consultant and a definite progression plan.

Section D: Honors Programs, Internships, and Study Abroad

This section deals with supplementary college activities namely honors programs, study abroad programs, internships and fully exploiting college breaks that may or may not help you graduate on time. I encourage you to read it anyway. These activities make you more attractive to graduate schools and employers similarly to taking AP/IB courses makes your high school transcript more appealing to college administrators. So, let's begin. Regarding Honors Programs, full-time students earning a 3.5 or higher GPA are typically eligible to become members of their colleges or departments' honors programs. Across the nation, two-year and four-year institutions sponsor Honors Programs. For instance, the National Collegiate Honors Council (NCHC) website publicizes its two-year institution or community college members by state.[193] Honors Programs have numerous perks specifically access to merit-scholarships, special honors courses taken with non-honors courses, small class size, superior instructors, honors advisors, field trips, seminars, conferences, tutorials, internships, independent study and some study abroad opportunities.[194] The

Honors Program courses are more challenging and the instruction is top-notch. Honors scholars come from different majors, backgrounds, nationalities, and interests such as student government or athletics. Additionally, Honors Program students typically have a higher graduation or transfer rate . . . due to the exposure to accomplished professors and the best courses.[195] To investigate, you can visit a specific school's website for more on its honors program in particular its application procedure.

Besides honors programs, other opportunities exist for academic recognition at two and four-year institutions. You may receive an invitation to join a national honors society, like Phi Theta Kappa for two-year colleges.[196] With my Phi Theta Kappa membership, I received a special honors emblem on my diploma, an honors cord at graduation, and a notation on my MC transcript. For inclusion in an honors society, a student must meet a GPA minimum and have completed 15 hours of coursework towards an associate's degree. Another academic honor is the Dean's List. At the end of each semester, each college or department recognizes full-time students who have 3.5 or higher GPAs on the aptly named Dean's List. The college also publicizes the student's Dean's List status on his/her transcript for that term. Many students list their Dean's List standing on their resumes or transfer college admission applications. Your participation in honors programs, honor societies and/or dean's lists shows a desire to strive for the highest standards of academic excellence. Your professors will notice your focus and maturity when you earn stellar grades. If necessary, he/she may endorse you for an internship or write letters of recommendation for you. I maintained a cumulative 4.0 GPA at Montgomery College (MC). When I applied to UMCP, three of my MC teachers wrote letters of recommendation for me. I can credit their help in my eventual admittance. Hence, you should aspire to achieve academic recognition especially through those programs available in college.

While in college, you ought to consider applying and participating in a college internship. It will give you a chance for work experience. Preferably, the internship should be in your major. Internships look great on college graduates' resumes. Also, the internship might lead to a full-time position within the same organization. Internships can be paid or unpaid; so, you have to decide if an unpaid internship is economically feasible. To research possible internship positions, you can start by looking at the websites of companies that hire based on your specific degree/major. Additionally, you can check with your college career center, your academic advisor, or even your instructors for internship information. Your school's career center also should provide assistance in drafting your resume and preparing you for the internship interview process.

The best plan for acquiring an internship is to apply early. An internship application typically consists of a resume, transcript, essay, and letters of recommendation. Numerous internship applications are due between February and March for the following summer. Each has specified minimum GPA requirements and class levels (junior, senior, etc.). Before you apply for an internship, you should sanitize your social media profiles of any inappropriate material. Numerous potential employers and human resources recruiters search social media websites for information on interns and candidates before hiring. When you start applying for internships, you also ought to compile a list of references. These references will be those college instructors and employers who may write letters of recommendation for you. Do not write down a reference's contact information on an application until you ask the person for permission. For letters of recommendation, you should ask and notify the potential writers not less than four weeks prior to the deadline. As a courtesy, you might provide a short resume of your college accomplishments to help the writer in drafting the recommendation. When you find out the final decision, you ought to provide feedback about your selection or non-selection for the internship. Then, you should send thank you e-mails because you might need to use these references again.

As an intern, you typically will gain exposure to a 9 to 5 work environment, experience on-the-job training and understand employer expectations. Usually, you will be supervised by a supervisor/mentor who will guide and counsel you about the organization's culture. You also can use your internship to network and meet others who potentially can offer future employment opportunities. In fact, a few months prior to your college graduation, you want to secure interviews with several companies in order to obtain a job. Employers have the upper hand in choosing and hiring potential employees. Typically, they like to hire college graduates with "real-world" knowledge and work experience. Your parents think you are special, but in the business world, you will have to prove yourself. Your internship may help in that pursuit. The internship may be the resume highlight that tips a potential job in your favor. Otherwise, you will be like every other college graduate applicant without work experience. If you do not participate in an internship, you will in due course find employment. Then, you can show your employer that you have worth by being a problem-solver, developing new ideas, having confidence, being a leader, and showing your college education has prepared you with the appropriate knowledge to thrive in any work environment (Ok, I am done with the pep talk but do not let anyone underestimate you or your degree's importance).

During college, you might participate in a study abroad program. Study abroad or student exchange program are broad terms which encompass attending another school overseas or in the United States.[197] By travelling outside your comfort zone, you will experience diverse populations, languages, cultures, and perspectives. You will gain a better awareness of yourself and others. In an increasingly globalized community, U.S. businesses and organizations desire college graduates who are confident and skilled in interacting with people from different countries. For example, the duration of the study abroad program can be a few weeks, a couple of months, half a semester, or an entire academic year. The locations are just as diverse, including Costa Rica, Belize, Mexico, Canada, Spain, Croatia, Peru, or Botswana. Study abroad programs can occur throughout the year or during school breaks. Due to time conflicts, you may not be able to enroll in a formal study abroad or exchange program. You ought to consider travelling outside the country on your own. The purpose is just to see and experience how other people live. Thus, you will widen your horizons and understand that you "are not in Kansas anymore." The experience is priceless.

For any study abroad program, you must do your research. Each college or department website will publish study abroad program descriptions and eligibility requirements. You will be required to meet face-to-face with a study abroad coordinator. You should also speak with former study abroad participants. Some colleges award college credits based on the study abroad programs' duration and coursework. You must verify if your chosen degree/major program requires a study abroad experience for graduation. Thus, you should meet with your academic advisor to expose any issues regarding your major, study abroad participation and graduating on time. You should also check with the college's financial aid office to determine how study abroad program participation will impact your school costs. To be clear, a study abroad experience should be more fun than an obligation. While travelling, eat some Birds Nest Soup, Hakarl, or Kopi Luwak for me! Or, not. If you take part in a study abroad, you and your resume will stand out.

Finally, you should fully take advantage of your college breaks. School breaks are prime opportunities to take a class and graduate early, earn money, gain experience from an internship, or participate in a study abroad/exchange program. Each academic year, school breaks equal about four and a half months of unencumbered time. I know that you want to use all of your time off and hang out with friends and family. You ought to have a balance. When you graduate, you will receive about two to three weeks of annual vacation from your employer. You ought to use college as a means to get into that mindset. I have said time and time again that your goal when you attend college is to graduate on time. You might graduate early if you take summer and winter term courses. During these two terms, the available courses are limited but typically shorter in duration than fall/spring terms. You will still have free time to hang out with friends. Those extra earned credits will add up over the two or four years in college. Otherwise, you might work during your breaks. The extra money offers a means to pay for college books, tuition, gas, or other incidentals. You can also put aside money for your post-graduation life. You may feel that I am pressuring you to abandon your college experience too soon. When you graduate early, you might use that extra time and money before starting your job to surf the Australian coast, bike across Norway, or swim with the fish in Thailand. Yet again, your college breaks are prime time.

Life lessons - Chapter 5: Finally On Campus
- Read your student orientation guide and take part in student orientation to observe how your school welcomes new students to its culture, services, etc.
- College is an opportunity to choose a major and obtain a degree in a specific career field
    - Discover your interests while in high school to identify potential college majors
    - Investigate potential careers and thus solidify your choice in a major through websites such as the Bureau of Labor Statistics and OKCollegeStart.org
    - Your choice of a college major is critical to taking classes toward your degree
    - Speaking with professionals and current students in your desired career field can help you to narrow down your choice of majors
    - Review your college's or department's website to view course requirements for majors that you are interested in
- Your advisor is Robin to your Batman, keeping you on track toward graduation
    - Meet with him/her at least once a semester throughout your college years
    - Fill out a two or four-year academic plan and use it
- Your participation in an honors program, study abroad/exchange program and/or internship helps you stand out to graduate programs and employers
    - Apply early when eligible
    - Balance fun with taking advantage of your college breaks to participate in a study abroad/exchange program, take academic courses, work and/or take part in an internship program

CHAPTER 6:
Class Registration

After consulting with your advisor, you must register for classes each semester at the earliest to graduate on time. You are probably wondering "what's the big deal?" By waiting too long, you may be denied the ability to take the classes that you need. Students register for classes based on vacancies, credit hours, class time of day, major/degree, eligibility or department approval. Most registrars' offices allow students to register online for each semester.[198] Some colleges restrict registration periods based on students' class levels; so, seniors may get priority. You will be competing with everybody else who needs those classes too. If you wait, other reasons may prevent you from enrolling in classes. For example, the class is full because the instructor is very popular. Another issue is some required courses are offered every other semester or term. In addition, some schools' online registrations automatically sync classes to ensure a student has adequate travel time between classes. You may not be able to register for classes that have a time conflict. You need to know this immediately and work with your advisor to determine alternative classes. When your registration period opens, you must register quickly instead of scrambling for classes in a hit or miss fashion. As a freshman, you should understand the registration process to make it quick and stress-free. Additionally, your two or four-year academic plan will guide you in making deliberate decisions about the classes to take. Ask your advisor if you have any questions about your school's registration process. Let's go into greater detail.

Section A: Course Descriptions

Most colleges list their course catalog and schedule of classes on their Office of the Registrar's website. These are critical to find and read because they list all programs and requirements. In them, you also will find course descriptions. Usually, a course description contains its title, course number, number of credit hours, instructors, sections, total seats available, waitlist numbers, any prerequisites, and the days and time for the course. When selecting classes for the semester, you have to know their number of credit hours and the times/locations of the classes. For example, you may end up short if you do not take the 12 credit hours necessary for full-time status. A part-time status may affect your scholarship, tuition assistance or any other financing. When you take a course, the course description will list any prerequisite courses and the minimum completion grade. Additionally, the course description displays any required textbooks. Thus, you will have ample time to order them before the class begins.

To earn your degree, some of your courses will be electives. You might register for an elective because you read the course description and discover an interest in the subject matter. Normally, elective are not associated with your required courses for your major. The subject matter is optional but you must complete a certain number of electives to complete your degree. Your chosen electives ought to be based on an interest or curiosity about a particular subject. Electives are like toppings namely whip cream, crushed peanuts, chocolate sauce, or sprinkles on your ice cream sundae. They make your college experience richer because you choose them. Electives are supposed to spur new perspectives, introduce you to a different social circle of classmates outside your major, and be less demanding. Typically, you will take electives after you have completed your general education courses. In consultation with your academic advisor and a review of your academic plan, you will balance taking electives with required courses for your degree/major each semester. You might also use your electives to create a secondary concentration of courses (also known as a minor).

Anyway, you need to have access to your college's course catalogue, schedule of classes and course descriptions to enroll in the right classes toward your degree and graduation from college on time. Course descriptions are also important if you wish to transfer to another school. A college may use another school's course descriptions to determine the academic content/merit of specific courses. When the college determines a course is comparable to its college course, the school may award course credit and exempt you from taking that course.

Section B: Waitlists

Seniors normally have priority to register for classes. Students in the lower classes have fierce competition to enroll in the remaining seats left for some courses. When a required course is full, you should register on its waitlist. The waitlist is a standing list of students who will be allowed to take the course if seats become available. Having your name on a course's waitlist is like winning the lottery or flying standby. Sometimes, the department or instructor for the course will open up more seats for the class. More likely, an enrolled student will decide to "drop" the course, which frees up a seat. When either scenario occurs, the registrar's office notifies the first waitlist student about the opening. You might be that lucky person. You will have a specified time frame to register. Otherwise, the next student on the list gets the opportunity to fill the slot. Sometimes, waitlist students attend the first few days of the particular class. If they get into the course, then they have not missed any classroom instruction. No one may drop from the course or the instructor may not open up more seats. In that case, the waitlist expires. Then, waitlist students will have to take the course in a later semester. Your college should have instructions on waitlist procedures. It is imperative that you are aware of the offering periods for your required classes and register early.

Section C: Add/Drop/Withdrawal

During the first few weeks of the semester, colleges allow students to modify their class schedules. Unlike high school, students are not stuck taking classes arbitrarily assigned by administrators. Most colleges typically permit students to perform add or drop classes online. On the Registrar's Office website, the online Academic Calendar lists dates for everything specifically registration deadlines, adding a class, dropping a class, withdrawal deadlines and the first/last day of classes. You must know these vital dates. If more seats open for a class or waitlist slots become available, then you can register and "add" the course to your schedules. You must do so by the add course deadline. Also, a student may be unable to take a course for some reason. Then, he/she must formally remove the registered course from his/her schedule. Normally, the student "drops" the course(s) online or at the registrar's office. The drop status informs the school that the student is no longer taking a course. Then, a course seat opens up for another student to add the course. In order to receive a refund or forgo a fee, a student has to drop the course by the college's course drop deadline. The course drop does not count against the student. The drop status will not show up on his/her permanent record. You need to be aware of the drop date; or else, leaving the class later will cost you money.

After the drop deadline, you can leave the class but the request becomes a withdrawal. You do not need a reason to withdraw. You might use a withdrawal if you have been receiving poor grades up to this point and fear failing the class. Or, you may have a conflict or heavy course load that you just cannot take the class now. Thus, a course withdrawal is not a failure but an informed, adult decision. Before you withdraw, you need to meet and discuss your withdrawal decision with your academic advisor. For instance, your full-time status may be affected by the loss of the class's credits. <u>Nevertheless, you must withdraw by the withdrawal deadline.</u> Regrettably, the college will charge you a withdrawal fee, which can be steep. Withdrawals also will show up on your transcript as a "W" but will not affect your GPA.

You should use course withdrawals sparingly. Some colleges limit the number of student withdrawals per semester. If you reach that limit, your college will not allow you to withdraw from the course(s). Actually, employers and graduate schools also may wonder about excessive withdrawals on your transcript which can call into question your academic readiness. Or, you might be put on probation or suspended from federal financial aid. After July 1st, 2013, the federal government mandated a "maximum eligibility period" for new borrowers to complete their academic programs. These students must not exceed the maximum length of time to earn a degree in order to remain eligible for federal financial aid specifically Federal Direct Subsidized Loans and Pell Grants.[199] Thus, you must complete your degree program within

150% of the allowable time frame. To remain eligible for federal financial aid, this means you have three years (or 90 attempted credit hours) to complete an associate's degree and six years (or 180 attempted credit hours) to earn a bachelor's degree. All unsuccessfully completed credit hours namely withdrawals, incompletes, and failed credits are counted in those attempted credit hours.

Despite the reasons, take it seriously that you must formally drop or withdraw from a class through the registrar's office before you stop attending any class. By correctly using drops or withdrawals, you can keep your GPA intact. Please, do not just walk away. The consequences are bad. You will earn an "F" grade because of your failure to complete the coursework. Also, the school will charge you the full tuition and fees for that class. Worse still, you took a seat from another student. At the earliest opportunity, you want to drop or if necessary withdraw from a course within the deadline.

Life lessons - Chapter 6: Class Registration
- Register for class each semester at the earliest to graduate on time
  - Everyone is competing for the same vacant class seats
  - Course offerings may close because the class is full, only offered every other term, or other reason
  - Understand the registration process and register for classes using your two or four-year academic plan
- A course description tells you everything about a class; so, use it to discover any course prerequisites, course times, the location and the required textbook
- If you do not get in a full class, sign-up on the waitlist
  - Another student may drop the course
  - Class seats may open up
  - Attend the course to keep up with the class work until you know if the waitlist has expired
- College Academic Calendars list all important dates
  - Know critical deadlines namely add course, drop course and withdrawal cut-off dates
  - "Dropped" courses do not count against a student
  - Course withdrawals show up on a student's transcript as a "W" but do not affect his/her GPA
  - Use withdrawals sparingly because you must complete your degree program within 150% of the allowable time frame to remain eligible for federal financial aid
- Formally drop or withdraw from a course through the Registrar's Office or receive a grade of "F"

CHAPTER 7:
The Classroom

As I have said before, colleges and universities are not extensions of high school. The college classroom is where 35% or more of your time will be spent per course. It should be fun, engaging and challenging. Ok, maybe, 20% of that 35% will be those things. The other percentage will be working outside the classroom in the form of researching, studying, preparing for class and completing assignments. You must use your time effectively, especially when you take your major specific classes. Your goal is to graduate on time. Your other college goals should be to learn, grow and exercise your independence as an adult. When you put in the effort, your ability to gain knowledge and apply it is unlimited. Instead, many students give up when faced with an academic challenge because the material is new or requires more work than they anticipated. Or, they are just not motivated by the subject matter to do the hard work of studying and preparing for class.

In college, many instructors attempt to foster students' curiosity and teach them new perspectives. While your college advisor is your sidekick Robin, your college instructor is Alfred. He/she is there to mentor you but also kick you in the butt when you need it. Since you are paying your money to obtain your degree, you should value your class time and give each professor/instructor a chance. My point is that you should get to know your teachers. When possible, talk to them after class and try to appreciate the class subject matter. If you knew every subject, you would be teaching the course. On the contrary, your teachers already have their degree and extensively know their course material. From your class, you might obtain a nugget of information that may change your life. So, suck it up and do your best to pay attention in your classes. Otherwise, you should give up your classroom seat to someone who wants to be there. Now, I will go through the process to prepare and succeed in your classes.

Section A: Instructors and Teaching Assistants

Every teacher deserves respect, especially in person, e-mail or written correspondence. Teachers have a hard job, trying to influence and cultivate young minds. Some college professors teach their students in an interesting, thought-provoking manner. These instructors have a great deal of experience in their fields, knowledge, and enthusiasm. They get a rush from working with students day to day. In a history of the play course, my college professor taught a new perspective about Shakespeare's *Othello*. For years, I thought that the play was boring. I really did not understand the fuss and fascination. The teacher, though, brought to life the complexity of the language, the imagery, and the characters *Othello*, *Iago*, and *Desdemona*. I thoroughly enjoyed the teacher's discussions about *Othello*, and the other plays in the course. I was sad for the class to end. That is teaching.

In contrast, other instructors make their classes an excruciating experience. On Youtube.com, students frequently rant about their boring teachers. Although I do not condone the rants, I understand these students' frustration. Frequently, these "boring" college teachers talk at their students rather than connecting with them. For example, one of my undergraduate instructors presented 60 or more PowerPoint slides during each 50 minute class period. Instead of a dialogue with students, the instructor looked at the projector screen and read to us. The class was agonizing death by PowerPoint. Some teachers take up space and make their classes mind-numbing.

Your comprehension of the course material is crucial to passing your courses. You have to connect with your teacher and the subject matter. Usually, freshmen or transfer students do not have the social networks to investigate each professor's teaching ability. The old days of finding out about teachers by word of mouth are passé. The RateMyProfessor.com website is a tool that you might find useful when registering for courses.[200] Moreover, the RateMyProfessor.com website encourages college students from across the country to rate their professors on their teaching ability. With the click of a mouse, you can find out about rated instructors. You will be forewarned about coursework, teaching styles, and possibly exam difficulty. The site does not have comments about every instructor. Fortunately, more schools have their own variations of RateMyProfessor.com.

Despite the RateMyProfessor.com website's usefulness, I caution you to read all comments about a professor to look for patterns. Some students' RateMyProfessor.com comments are biased. The students may be at fault for their bad experience due to their poor attendance or academic performance. These students blame their teachers. You should form your own opinion and also speak to former students of the class. Other factors render instructor rating websites useless. For instance, a college might not list a particular course instructor until the first day of class. Or, a poorly rated instructor is the only one that teaches that particular course.

When you have an ineffective course instructor, you will have a very painful semester. You need to pass the course and understand the material; so, here are two tips. When the course is not a requirement, you might consider dropping the course and enrolling later. You have to judiciously plan and investigate if the course is available in the future. Or, many freshman and sophomore required courses have multiple sections that different instructors teach. You can "drop" the original course and then "add" the same course number with a different section by the appropriate deadlines. Poof, you have a new teacher. Just make sure the other instructor's class has space.

At this point, I have a few comments about teaching assistants (TAs). Some courses have as many as 200 students in a class. Realistically, a teacher cannot adequately grade, help, and answer questions for 200 or more students. To assist him/her, the instructor may have one or more TAs. Each TA is responsible for 30 to 40 students. The TAs are normally graduate students. Although they may be a few years older, they have a great deal of knowledge and authority to impact your grade. TAs grade papers, answer questions, host office hours or lead separate lecture sessions. The TA's activities are supposed to reinforce the instructor's lectures. Some TAs are better at explaining concepts than the teacher. They are a great resource if you are having academic problems in class. When you interact with TAs, you should treat them with respect.

Section B: The Syllabus

The syllabus is the most important document in the course. The instructor will review the syllabus on the first day of class. The syllabus lists

- The instructor's name, e-mail address and telephone number
- Office hours
- Class days and times
- Course learning objectives
- The grading policy, including the percentage range for each letter grade, A through F
- Every deadline, homework assignment and textbook requirement.

At the earliest opportunity, you should read the syllabus again and highlight important dates in particular exams and assignment submissions. Then, you ought to record these special events on your calendar. Other tracking options include recording the assignment submission dates on the calendar of a smartphone, tablet or any other preferred electronic device. With this action, you can set reminder notifications for one week prior to the due dates. Usually, the syllabus will also cover communication between the instructor and his/her students outside of the classroom. At this point, I urge you to confirm the method that your instructor will use to broadcast information. If it will be via email, for example, you should make sure that you check your student email account daily or link your student email account to the email account that you use regularly. Many unwise students throw their syllabuses in their backpacks and never look at them again. They rely on their instructors to announce everything in class. These students are due for a painful wake-up call.

When you annotate requirement deadlines on your calendar, you should also anticipate the additional prep time necessary to turn your assignments in early. Most students wait until the last minute to turn in assignments. The additional stress is unnecessary.

Instead, you ought to plan on submitting your work at least a day ahead of time. Otherwise, your computer will pick the deadline time to crash. Maybe, the submission website will be down for maintenance. Or, you will win two tickets to attend a Taylor Swift or Little Big Town concert scheduled on the same day as your assignment due date. By completing assignments early, you will be able to go out with your friends; join college academic/sports/social clubs; and enjoy your free time without worrying about an upcoming paper, project, exam, etc. When you miss an assignment submission, you should contact your instructor as soon as possible (but not later than the next class period). By being informed, the instructor might award partial credit for the late assignment instead of an "F" or zero grade. In his/her course syllabus, the instructor will say if he/she gives partial credit for late assignments. Once more, try to turn in your assignments early.

One last note: I want to advise you to keep/scan your course syllabi. A course syllabus describes the required books, the assignments, the scope, and basic content for the course. In the future, you may have a large time gap in schooling or want to transfer course credit to another school. Your copies of syllabi might save you from retaking general education or other courses at your new school. After a review of the syllabus, your new college may determine the course is comparable to its college course. As a result, the school may award transfer credit and exempt you from taking its course.

Section C: Class Attendance

Say it with me: You won't know what is going on in class unless you attend. For example, your instructor may put up the diagram that makes a particular formula work. Or, the teacher may give out every answer to the next quiz. You will not get those answers if you are not there. When you attend your classes, you have your best chance to ask questions and clarify points that you do not understand. For your classes, you ought to be on time. Teachers are very conscious of late or missing students. Today, college instructors have attendance rosters with students' pictures on them. When you are consistently late or absent, that instructor will make a point of identifying you. Late students typically disrupt class as they move toward open seats despite attempts to be quiet. Also, you do not want to have to ask for a hand out because you were late. Another consequence is missing announcements, notably the instructor will only accept a hard copy paper assignment in class rather than an e-mailed version. You cannot take notes if you are not there. If you perform poorly on exams or other assignments, your instructor will unapologetically handout "D" or "F" grades to you. When you cry to him/her, your professor will have very little sympathy and point out your terrible attendance record. Your attendance makes a difference.

When you attend classes on time, your course grades also will likely benefit from your participation in class discussions. Participation can be speaking up in class, showing up on time, or how the instructor defines it in the course syllabus. Typically, teachers often give points to students for contributing to the class discussion as part of their overall grades. Frequently, you will have to answer a professor's question or make a classroom presentation. You are probably asking the question, "*Why?*" When their students look at them with blank stares, teachers get bored and frustrated too. From their students' participation, teachers also can assess if students understand the classroom material. To repeat, you might improve your grade if you attend class, open your mouth and say something relevant to the discussion.

Sadly, you may freeze up when speaking in public. You are not alone. Some people would prefer a root canal instead of public speaking. In addition, many students unconsciously use mental pauses namely "Um," "You know?" and "Like" to the point of incoherency. To reduce your anxiety, you might join the debate team or enroll in a college oral communications course as an elective.[201] As an alternative, you can reduce most verbal fillers by practicing in front of someone, recording and listening to yourself, or rehearsing in front of the mirror. With public speaking practice as well as preparing for class, you will sound natural, confident and interested in your topic. Trust me. Your participation allows your teacher to get to know you and establish a relationship. He/she may be a future reference or a letter of recommendation writer. Hence, you must get ready for public speaking in your college classes.

By the way, I also advise you to stay informed of current events and financial matters in order to know/understand the issues affecting your world. Then, you will be able to form opinions and intelligently converse on a wide range of topics. In addition, you will hone your critical thinking, listening skills, comprehension, problem-solving, vocabulary, and language. All of these improved abilities will help you in your college classes mainly in class discussions and participation. My recommendations to keep up to date are four Public Broadcasting Service (PBS) shows that are available on television and online for viewing namely the PBS NewsHour, Frontline, Washington Week and Nightly Business Report. You ought to consider periodically watching one or more of these shows. Furthermore, you will impress your instructors, classmates, future employers, and others in social gatherings with your sophisticated view of the world.

Reference your classroom attendance, if you are going to be absent from class due to an illness, a sports activity, or other legitimate reason, you should notify your instructor ahead of time or as soon as possible. The syllabus should spell-out the make-up policy for exams, quizzes, etc. Otherwise, your grade may be adversely affected due to earning zero points on those missed assignments. Also, you should ask a reliable person such as a study group partner to provide a copy of his/her notes for the missed class to you. Thus, you will have intentionally identified someone who you trust to discuss his/her notes in detail with you and clarify your questions.

Some readers will rage that attendance is common sense advice to students. Common sense is not common. For instance, one of our UMCP classmates e-mailed everyone that he had not attended class since the previous exam. He audaciously begged for lecture notes for the upcoming exam. Some unwise student probably took pity on this poor soul instead of deleting the e-mail. Unlike the requesting student, I would not put my faith in passing the next exam based on understanding a random person's notes. Thus, you should think about the consequences of repeatedly being late/missing classes and refrain from doing it.

Section D: Taking Notes

In college, successfully taking notes is essential to passing your classes and graduating. Let's face it. High school teachers tell you the important items to study at a slow, modulated pace. In contrast, the information comes fast and furious in college courses. The college environment is geared toward teaching masses of young adults at different knowledge levels in a short amount of time. Many college students have very poor note-taking and studying skills. The instructors may not care if students do not keep up. Literally, you are supposed to filter through the vast amounts of information and successfully regurgitate the main points on exams, projects, and papers.

On day one, the college professor will give his/her first lecture. Unlike in high school, college classes will probably not dismiss early. You should have a pen and paper or your computer handy for notes. You ought to be prepared to capture the pearls of wisdom that drop from the lips of your erudite professor. Yeah, right. If you have ever watched any of the "Peanuts" cartoons, the teacher in the classroom is never seen. The audience only hears his/her voice, which is a series of sounds similar to "waa, waa, waa, waa." For the first two or three class periods, your college professor will sound just like that. In freshmen courses, many professors talk non-stop without input from their students. These teachers will ask for one or two responses from the class but basically, they often talk, talk, and talk. They realize that their students cannot contribute to the classroom discussion because the students lack a baseline of knowledge, mostly in math, science, and technical courses. The key to success in this type of class is to take notes, write down diagrams (or take a smartphone picture of the blackboard), review the notes, and go to office hours if you do not understand elements of the lecture.

At the start of class, you should write the date and class name on the top of your note page(s). Unless you are using an individual binder for each class, your notes will become mixed together over time. Recording the date and class name, you should be able to link notes to the syllabus outline, organize for studying and prepare for exams. An alternative is to take notes on your laptop or tablet. While taking notes, you will be unable to capture every word during a lecture. You should concentrate on listening, outlining, and summarizing—recording key definitions, instructor blackboard scribbles, any diagrams, and unfamiliar concepts. Some students bring mini-recorders and record lectures, which may supplement the written notes. When your teacher emphasizes a particular item, you should put an asterisk next to that reference or underline that note. The item may be an exam question. Many teachers use PowerPoint slides. You can print them out or type your comments directly on them with your laptop. Later, you can read through the teacher's slides and identify any points that you missed or do not understand. In addition, you can typically tie the material in class with your assigned reading or homework.

During the week, you must carve out time to review your notes from that week's classes. To emphasize again, this is not high school; therefore, you must devote time to studying or your grades will reflect that shortcoming. When possible, you should find a quiet place to study. You also ought to determine the best time of the day that you concentrate, which may be morning, afternoon, or evening. Then, you should study as if you have a quiz for the next class period. This includes completing homework assignments, which is especially critical in technical classes. As the course progresses, you can quickly review the older notes and focus on the newest notes. Although the review can get tedious, you will be able to refresh your memory about older concepts and identify gaps in your knowledge. If necessary, you can go to office hours with your TA or professor to clarify issues. By studying your notes, you will better understand the information presented in the class. Over time, you will become comfortable with the material. At exam time, you will not have to relearn every concept in a cram session. Most students give up in frustration when cramming for an exam due to the volume of information. Then, the students are tired because they did not get a good night sleep. Cram sessions do not work. Instead, students should study and review their notes throughout the course to prepare for exams.

Due to your schedule, you may feel that you just do not have the time to devote each week to review your notes. Then, I recommend that you start studying at least a week before an upcoming exam. You should not make this option a habit. Depending on the class, most exam information is memorization. Thus, a week will provide a period long enough to reread textbook passages, go through your huge volume of notes, work some homework problems (as appropriate), ask clarifying questions in class, or visit office hours. One of my worst college experiences was the conflict of a major exam and paper that were due on the same day. Yes, I waited until the last minute on that paper. However, I started studying a week before the exam date. When my paper took more effort than anticipated, I was not too worried about my early morning exam. I was prepared for it. I submitted the paper that morning online, dragged myself to class and took the exam. I was dead tired. That was one of the longest days of my life because I had other classes immediately following the exam. So, you need to read through your notes weekly. If you do not have the time, you ought to begin studying in earnest a week ahead of the exam date.

When you cannot seem to find time to study, you might have a time management problem. College offers many distractions. You may be juggling too many things namely work, clubs, a significant other, volunteer activities, sports, etc. If cannot seem to say "No" to even minor diversions, you ought to seek out help from your college counseling center. Many campus counseling centers offer training and assistance in learning time management techniques. Otherwise, you ought to visit your old friend, your academic advisor, to find out where you can obtain time management coaching. As a full-time student, you will take 12 or more credit hours per semester. You must successfully complete your assignments in order to graduate on time. Thus, you need to prioritize and manage your time to study. By the way, when your schedule permits it, you ought to consider scheduling your daily classes in blocks of two or three back to back courses. Yes, you will have to register for that 8 am class! This strategy allows you to have larger intervals of time to study, complete homework, or work because your day is not broken up.

To enhance your note-taking, you also might form a study group with other students in your class. The group of two or four people can discuss notes from the class, clarify confusing ideas and identify important points from the class. If you miss a class, you can ask a reliable study group partner for notes. Group study sessions are especially effective before exams. The study group might create a study guide that outlines key definitions and explains concepts. A study group, though, should not take up more than an hour per week. Instead of studying your notes alone, you might not feel so isolated or frustrated with a study group.

Section E: Reading

While in high school, you should practice reading for speed and retention of several types of material (i.e., magazines, books, and newspapers). A 2013 U.S. Department of Education, National Institute of Literacy study estimated 14% or 32 million U.S. adults cannot read.[202] In addition, 19% of high school graduates cannot read.[203] Every college course will require some type of reading. You cannot get around it. Your objective is to hone your reading skills before you get to college. In your neighborhood, you must have seen that big building with all the computers, DVDs, *free* books and other reading material namely newspapers, journals and magazines. With a library card, you can find something interesting to read and check-out several *free* books, magazines, etc. The added benefit of your recreational reading will translate to better reading comprehension in your high school and college classes.

To bring everyone to the same level of knowledge, college instructors assign pre-class readings or hands-on homework. In fact, your course instructor may list a textbook on his/her syllabus. Textbooks are essential to many instructors' curriculum, including the subjects of math, chemistry, physics, geography, or English. The textbook provides supplemental reading to reinforce the ideas/concepts of the class. On the first day, your professor will let you know if the textbook is required. If so, the teacher will probably pull quiz and exam questions straight from the book. Therefore, teachers expect you to read the assignments, do the assigned homework, and discuss the material in class. They will not spoon feed every detail about the reading. You may be bored in a class when the teacher talks non-stop to you. Well, the teacher is probably just as aggravated. Often, students stare mutely back because they have not read the assignment or completed the homework for the class. Unfortunately, many college textbooks are boring. Some may even be confusing. But, if you have chosen the college path, keeping up with the reading and assigned homework is part of the deal.

In high school, the school district normally provides the books to its students. In college, you will be buying the textbooks. Unfortunately, textbook costs are outrageous and seem to steadily increase. The National Association of College Stores estimates that college students paid on average $313 on required course material during the fall 2014 term.[204] Instead of the college bookstore, you might purchase your textbooks cheaper from alternative vendors such as Amazon.com. To save money, you also should investigate renting your books, purchasing e-Books, checking out library-owned textbooks (maybe an older edition), buying them from a departing college student, or getting textbooks from department book swaps in which graduating students donate their books to raise money. Thus, you ought to obtain any required textbooks for class but you have options on the price that you pay.

Nonetheless, some teachers assign crazy amounts of reading. In one of my college courses, our class read seven tedious books during the course. The teacher assigned between 130 and 240 pages of reading per week. I was swamped. In a similar fashion, you may find it hard to keep up, especially when you are a full-time student with several classes. Yet, you can overcome the reading challenge with the following tips:

- Scan each chapter, as appropriate
- Read the chapter introduction and summary
- Outline the author's main points per section
- Take note of key definitions
- Write down any questions about information that you do not understand to ask in class

When you browse through the reading materials ahead of time, your classroom lectures will have more meaning. In the classroom, the teacher will discuss major points and concepts. You should pay attention, take notes and determine if you can tie the discussion back to your reading. From the class discussion, you can also take the time to reread sections that you might have originally glossed over. You may even understand what your teacher is talking about over time and be able to participate in the discussion. When you engage, you will have more fun. Ok, maybe not. Anyway, I suggest you try and keep up with your course reading. Basically, you will improve your comprehension of the course material and the chances of passing the course.

Section F: Exams

In college, you will take exams every couple of weeks in your various classes. You cannot avoid them; so, you ought to prepare yourself. If you do not pass the course's exams, you will definitely not pass the course or graduate. Every course syllabus lists its exam schedule. The worst mistake for a student is to miss an exam; so, please annotate exam dates on your calendar. From the syllabus, you also can find out the percentage of your grade that each exam represents. You ought to know this information to determine your exam's grade impact on your overall course grade. At any rate, through exams, college instructors will assess their students' retention and ability to apply the information from labs, lectures, readings, and homework. Most instructors build on and test the subject matter for a course from the first day of class. These types of tests are called cumulative exams. Some instructors administer cumulative mid-term and final exams. Or else, many instructors administer one cumulative final exam without a mid-term. Others may give three or four non-cumulative exams throughout the semester. In other words, the instructor will only test the block of material from the previous exam up to the current exam. Exams can be in class or online. In addition, some exams are open book. This means that you can use your notes to complete the test. A closed book exam means that the student only uses the knowledge in his/her head. Depending on the instructor, either exam can be hard.

In advance, the teacher will review the format for the exam, which may consist of fill-in the blank phrase/word, true or false, multiple choice, and/or essays. The hardest exam types are multiple choice and true/false questions because the instructor will make every answer appear factual. When taking a multiple choice or true/false exam, you must read each question carefully. Then, you should underline key phrases in the question specifically "all" or "not" that may immediately knock out wrong answers. During the exam, you may not know the correct answer. You should not panic. Since exam time is limited, you ought to mark the debatable question with an asterisk, and temporarily move on. Do not forget to return to the unanswered question(s). With a few minutes left, you ought to just mark your best guess.

If your exam has essay questions, your teacher may provide the topics ahead of time. Otherwise, the contents of the essay will remain a mystery until test time. Hopefully, the teacher has covered the main points throughout the course. In addition, your syllabus and notes should form the basis for your answers. While reviewing your notes, you should concentrate on major themes. When possible, you ought to associate specific examples to your answer from the readings and class discussions. During the essay portion of the exam, you should jot down a quick outline for each question to organize your thoughts. Or else, you may start writing on a tangent that does not answer the essay question. For a second time, it is crucial to provide specific examples rather than writing in generalities. In addition, you should leave some extra time to re-read your completed essay and make on-the-spot corrections. At this point, you ought to check off each concept to make sure you have answered the entire question. When satisfied, you should cross out your outline to separate it from the final product. For any exam, you must have a system to progress through the exam in an orderly manner. The above tips should help you to not panic when the exam is put in front of you.

For some exams specifically in math, computer science, and engineering, students work math problems, write a computer program, or solve a technical problem on the exam. These types of technical exams may be difficult for some students who are not familiar with them. To help, college departments may post previous exams and solutions online in a TESTBANK.[205] The resource is fantastic for students. In class review sessions, instructors/TAs may use TESTBANK exams to prepare their students for upcoming exams. Or, students can review the TESTBANK exams on their own. For an upcoming exam, you should print TESTBANK exams and attempt each question that mirrors those in your course. The TESTBANK's practice questions may look like gobbledygook. You have time to go to your instructor or TA's office hours for help. You ought to ask your instructor or the specific department if previous exams are available in a TESTBANK. Also, some clubs (i.e. the Math Club, Engineering Society) may have previous exams on hand for club members. Despite TESTBANK resources, I urge you to remember that nothing takes the place of sitting in class.

To prepare mentally and physically, you ought to get a minimum of six hours of sleep before your exam. In addition, you should grab a quick snack, depending on the exam's start time. You ought to arrive at least 15 minutes early to get comfortable and seated. Some college professors will not let a student take an exam if the student is late. Occasionally, a late student will find the exam room's door locked. In addition, the instructor will alert the class to any other special materials to bring. Many instructors use Scantron, mark-sense bubble forms to quickly grade exams. Each student will need to bring one or two number 2 pencil(s)/mechanical pencils with erasers. For math or science classes, students may need to bring a calculator as well as pencil. In addition, students should bring pens and their student identifications, as appropriate. Lastly, teachers require students to turn off or silence all devices such as phones and tablets.

After an exam, you should ask to see your hard copy exam to find out what you missed. Although it is rare, sometimes an instructor grades an exam incorrectly. Furthermore, if the class is a prerequisite for a future course, you can identify concepts or processes that you did not understand. Your follow-up is particularly important if a final exam is cumulative. Typically, final exams are graded after the class concludes. You should meet with the teacher if you have a failing final exam or course grade.

Life lessons - Chapter 7: The Classroom
- Try to connect with your teacher and appreciate the class subject
  - Your classroom comprehension is vital to passing your courses
  - RateMyProfessor.com is a valuable tool to identify good and poor teachers
  - If you have an ineffective teacher, you can try switching sections before the drop course and add course deadlines
- Your syllabus is the most important document in your course
  - Record all major events especially exams and assignment submissions on your calendar with reminder notifications
  - Submit your assignments/homework in early, if possible
- Attend all of your classes or you will miss important information, concepts and principles
  - Be on time to class
  - Participate in class discussions
- Note-taking is important
  - It is the only way to filter the vast amounts of information in class and prepare for exams, projects and papers
  - Review your notes every week instead of cramming weeks of notes just before an exam; devote time to studying
  - Identify any gaps in your knowledge and set up a time to meet with the instructor/TA during office hours
  - Form a study group to help you to clarify confusing ideas and identify important points from class
- Practice reading for speed and retention before you get to college
- Have a systematic plan to organize and answer exam questions before you sit down
  - Read the questions carefully
  - Do not panic
  - Write an short outline of your points before you tackle an essay question
  - Ask if previous exams are available for practice in technical subjects like math, computer science, etc.
  - After an exam, you should ask your instructor to review it in order to identify concepts that you did not understand

CHAPTER 8:
Papers and Projects

The importance of this paragraph is to make sure that you account for your use of other's work. College instructors typically assign due dates for papers, projects, and exams on the same day or within days of each other. Many college teachers will not remind their class of upcoming assignments. You will run yourself ragged trying to catch up. Truthfully, procrastination will make your life miserable in college. Writing assignments are uniquely challenging. At three in the morning, every first draft looks great. Those assignments usually contain grammatical errors, misspellings, incomplete thoughts, or irrelevant themes. As the clock ticks, you may be less inclined to correctly cite your sources. The cost can be devastating: dismissal from school or receiving an "F" grade. When you turn in your work, you must account for any outside source/help that you use in papers, computer programs, projects and other class assignments.

Section A: Honor Codes and Plagiarism

Every college has an honor code.[206] All colleges punish students who are caught cheating, stealing, and/or lying. A student's ethical misbehavior has devastating consequences, including ruining his/her reputation, suspension, expulsion and/or a grade of "F" in the class. Also, the college will annotate the offense on the student's transcript. Such an unethical individual breaches a trust that he/she is obtaining academic success and knowledge based on his/her own merits and work. For instance, a student's cheating is unacceptable because it is dishonest and unfair to others who do the "right thing." Cheating is also wrong since it undermines the purpose of going to school, which is to study and apply that knowledge in a profession. No college will grant a degree to a student who is found guilty of cheating. The potential graduate's actions cast doubt on his/her knowledge, character and integrity. In another example, a student may be found guilty of plagiarism, which is stealing someone else's work. The student may have been under pressure to write a paper but he/she did not start until the night before its due date. To compensate, he/she may steal ideas or passages from an obscure paper on the internet or in a book. The student thinks he/she will not get caught. The student will be tragically wrong. In today's digital world, teachers can check for plagiarism on various online websites in particular Doc Cop, Purdue OWL, Paper Rater, and the Plagiarism Checker.[207] Therefore, you should avoid cheating, stealing and/or lying to cover up misconduct in school. Or else, you are putting your graduation in jeopardy because there is no justification for these offenses.

To prevent plagiarism, you can take steps that include keeping careful notes when you use charts, quotes, word for word passages, or any idea that is not yours. If you are not sure, you might consider using Paper Rater.[208] This free online proofreading website assists students in checking their papers for plagiarism. In addition, several free online websites as well as Microsoft (MS) Word helps students to format citations.[209] The user inputs the appropriate source information into the citation program. The program will display the source's bibliography and footnote format.[210] These citation tools have formats for books, websites, journal articles, films, etc. You do not have to rack your brain to get the citation in the right format. Some tools will even create a bibliography list from the compiled citations.[211] With these resources, you should cite sources for papers, assignments or projects, accordingly. In summary, I caution you that honesty is the best policy in your academics as well as in your professional life. You should never compromise your integrity and ethics. In addition, you must not tolerate those who are dishonest or unethical either.

Section B: Writing

You will have to write numerous papers in college. You must know how to write essays, research papers and reviews of literature in order to get good grades in your college courses. Some writing projects will be enjoyable and fun while others will be serious and thought-provoking. In college, writing exercises display your understanding of the material and ability to communicate your position. Twitter, texting abbreviations, and non-sentences in instant messaging do not translate well to college essays. Also, numerous students, majoring in math, science, and other technical majors may think that they do not have to use their writing skills in college. They are wrong. Writing assignments will be diverse and cross many different college majors including engineering, business, health sciences, and education. Your writing ability will affect every aspect of your college life as well as into your career/profession.

Normally, a college instructor will supply the general subject for term papers, research papers, or essays for his/her course students. In addition, he/she will provide a rubric, which is a detailed description of the written requirement and grading scale. The rubric lists the discussion topic, minimum page length, due date and other information. The rubric may also address if and how graphics, pictures, or diagrams should be attached to the paper. It is important that you closely review this document and ask questions if necessary. Failure to follow the instructions will adversely affect your grade. You should not turn in 10 pages if your teacher wants a maximum of five pages. When your teacher requires a minimum of seven pages, you should not turn in three pages.

In college, you might receive a paper topic such as, "Is Lady Macbeth a strong or weak character in Shakespeare's play, *Macbeth*?"[212] For your class, you may have already read the play. You should not write your paper in a vacuum. In other words, your teacher probably has discussed the play, characters, key terms, and concepts in detail during the class period. You ought to review your classroom notes, any lecture slides/presentations, and other classroom sources. You will want to incorporate any appropriate themes, specific examples and terms into your paper. Many students are guilty of missing several class periods. They have no idea what the teacher talked about in class. These absentee students often use vague fillers to answer questions in writing assignments. The teacher will not be impressed. Unless they are teaching a creative writing class, professors want students to use class discussion information to create thought-provoking arguments in papers.

After reviewing classroom notes, articles, and slides, you are ready for your second reading of *Macbeth*. On the second review, you will look for specific examples to form an idea about Lady Macbeth's character. As you read, you should take notes about Lady Macbeth's actions and words, which show her strength or weakness. Your notes ought to be the basis for a rough outline of your paper. The key to taking notes is to organize, organize, and organize some more. Your research notes should not be a jumbled mess. Or else, you will not remember where you obtained a quote or passage. That is a recipe for plagiarism. To organize, you might record each source's ideas, passages, or quotes on a separate page or note card. You should place the date that you accessed any online source on the top of your notes. You will use it later for your bibliography.

After reading the play, you still may not understand Lady Macbeth's motivation or character. Then, you will have to research the topic. Many assigned college papers force students to research specific topics.[213] Research involves more than finding random articles online or reading Wikipedia, which contains varying degrees of factual information. The authors are usually not scrutinized for accuracy. In the rubric, your instructor will address any off-limits research sources. When possible, you should use at least three scholarly sources, including books, magazines and journal articles. Scholarly books, magazines, or journals typically have extensive citations and bibliographies documenting their sources. You can find these on the school's library web catalog or other online resources. If you are unsure of a scholarly source's reputation, you can ask your teacher or a librarian at the college. To research *Macbeth*, for example, you might use Sparknotes, which offers plot reviews and character analysis.[214] You would credit any Sparknotes ideas as a source.

From your notes and research, you should draw a conclusion about Lady Macbeth. Your conclusion will be the basis of your thesis statement or main point of your paper.[215] Every paper or essay should have a compelling thesis statement. Now, you are ready to organize your notes into a refined outline of your intended discussion points. At this juncture, you may want to speak with your instructor about your paper. In actuality, you ought to present your thesis statement and outline for his/her review. The meeting will ensure you are answering the assigned question in accordance with your teacher's instructions.

Your thesis statement will focus your paper. For example, "In Shakespeare's play *Macbeth,* Lady Macbeth is a weak character because Lady Macbeth changes from an ambitious and determined woman into a guilt-ridden and mentally fragile soul." The rest of the paper will analyze and discuss specific language or actions that you gathered to support the conclusion of Lady Macbeth's weakness. Unlike high school, your college instructor will want you to show evidence of a particular position with concrete examples. This is where your research and note taking will help you immensely. The paper should flow and use transitions to tie your examples into a coherent argument. You ought to discard note cards that are not relevant to your argument from your pile. Finally, the concluding paragraph of the paper typically does not introduce new information that you have not previously discussed. This guideline varies by instructor. Instead, the concluding paragraph will summarize selected points that support your thesis. Your conclusion should be strong and persuasive.

Your first draft of the paper is complete. Now, you should run the Spelling and Grammar check function in MS Word or use an online checker like Grammarly. These programs will identify spelling errors and grammatical issues. Many teachers take off points by as much as a letter grade for typographical errors, poor spelling and incorrect grammar in papers. The next step is to print out the paper. Instead of reading the draft immediately, I want you to set it aside. If you can afford the time, you should reserve one or two hours to watch TV, get a drink, eat some dinner, and relax. After the break, you ought to review the paper's rubric once again.

While reading through the draft, you can fill in any gaps. Simultaneously, you are reading your paper for errors that the spelling/grammar checker did not catch.

You may be pleased with your paper. You ought to consider having a second person review it. Most colleges have writing centers to review students' papers.[216] Or, a professor sometimes permits his/her students to submit papers early for a review. Before the deadline, the instructor will return the students' papers with comments for revisions. When the opportunity arises, you would be smart to turn in your best final draft for early submission. At this point, you should make any final corrections and submit that paper in before the deadline. Hopefully, that paper will come back with an "A" grade.

The above techniques can be used for any type of paper. They also prevent plagiarism since sources are noted and cited correctly. The key to successful paper writing is

- Starting early
- Reviewing the rubric
- Outlining your paper and crafting a strong thesis statement
- Taking good notes and using specific examples
- Citing sources
- Having someone else review your best final draft

As you gain more experience, you will get quicker and better at producing well-written products for your classes. Your good grades will move you towards graduating on time.

Section C: Group Projects

In upper-level courses, you may be required to work on a group project. Your instructor may assign the project among teams of four to five students. A group's project should follow steps similar to an individual paper namely start early, develop the thesis statement/research question, cite sources, get the instructor's feedback, proofread the final draft and turn in the assignment on time. From the onset, the group ought to assign tasks that each member will perform according to specific deadlines. Depending on the project, the group's grade and morale can be adversely affected by a non-contributing team member. As a group, the members should meet with the member who is not meeting expectations in either effort or input. In particular, the member may constantly miss meetings and/or deadlines. Although the conversation might be awkward or difficult, they must ask for a change of behavior/performance and give a specific deadline. Also, the group should politely document the member's unacceptable performance, preferably by e-mail. If the "unsatisfactory" member does not step-up and improve his/her behavior, the group members ought to get the instructor involved. Thus, group members should inform the instructor before the first major graded assignment or progress report. Otherwise, the instructor has little time or evidence to take action. As a precursor to future college classes, internships, and work environments, your group assignments will test your ability to work with all types of people. You ought to use the group project experience to develop and improve your teamwork, accountability, problem-solving, communication, public speaking and writing.

Life lessons - Chapter 8: Papers and Projects
- Cite sources when using others' work
    o Procrastination is a student's worst habit
    o Every college has an honor code that prohibits cheating, stealing (in particular, plagiarism) and lying
    o You risk suspension, expulsion and other consequences for ethical misconduct notably plagiarism or cheating
    o Several online websites and MS Word can help you to format your bibliography citations
- You will have to write numerous papers in college
    o Start early
    o Take good notes
    o Use specific examples
    o Cite sources
    o Have someone else review your best final draft for typographical, spelling and grammar errors
- Group projects improve teamwork, accountability, problem solving, communication, public speaking and writing

CHAPTER 9:
Academic Resources

The most important part of the academic process is to keep track of your grades in your classes. Your grades are an essential element of graduating on time. After the first major graded course assignment or exam, you must get help if you perform poorly. The course material will only get harder because most classes build on earlier principles. If you do not "drop" the course or improve your future assignment grades, you will fail and repeat the class. Your instructor may or may not seek you out if you are failing his/her course. In class, a teacher who looks out at the sea of faces may fail to reach the struggling student. He/she does not have the time or responsibility to corral students into seeking help. To keep students on track, many university registrar offices host secure online databases that provide students with immediate access to their course grades. In turn, a college instructor enters his/her students' grades into the online database in which the students have access to graded assignments, quizzes, and exams.[217] In addition, all colleges/universities send out failing course grade notices via e-mail or regular mail to affected students by the fourth week of the semester. These students are fully aware of failing course grades. The warning is supposed to give the students a chance to turn around poor/failing grades. In your case, your instructor and/or university will alert you about any failing course grades. You will have ample notification; so, please do not live in Egypt also known as the land of denial. Yet again, do not delay getting help due to embarrassment or an unrealistic idea that you can "catch up." You must be proactive to make changes and obtain help.

To take the initiative, you have a first line of defense against repeating a class. At any point, you can manually calculate your tentative course grade in a class. Somewhere, on the course syllabus, the instructor will list the grading criteria for his/her class. During the course, you may be doing worse or better than you think, depending on the instructor's grading system. Thus, you will need to understand the grading scheme for your calculations to work. Using the syllabus, you can calculate the necessary points after each graded assignment that you will need to earn in order to pass the class. For instance, an instructor may calculate assignment grades based on a 100 point scale. The grades may be adjusted since some assignments may be more important than others. For example, the numerical grade 90 to 100 may correlate to a letter grade of "A" while 80 to 89 is a "B". The mid-term exam might be worth 15% of the grade using a 100 point scale. If you received 95 points on the mid-term exam, then you earned an A. Since it is 15% of your total grade, you would multiply 95 points times 15% for 14.25. The 14.25 is a portion of the cumulative 100 points. As you receive results, you would apply the same process for each of your assignments and exams. For your final course grade, you would add all of your adjusted assignment and exam grades together based against the 100 point scale. For example, for the class, a total overall number of 90 means you would have a cumulative course letter grade of "A" (remember 90 to 100 is an "A"). This was one example but it depends on your instructor. If you do not understand the grading system, you need to ask your instructor to explain it. Therefore, you will know if you are doing poorly in your class. Additionally, you should not suffer in silence if you are having problems. The best strategy for academic success is to obtain assistance early. You can seek help through office hours, tutoring, or online resources such as Youtube.com. These resources provide a wealth of academic support that you should not ignore.

Section A: Office Hours

Often, students do not go to the instructor or teaching assistant (TA) office hours when they have difficulty understanding the material in class. Crazy, huh? To restate it, many students do not avail themselves of face-to-face time with the person responsible for their grades. They try to tough it out and fix the issues on their own. Instead, every student should meet with his instructor or TA as early as possible when faced with a problem in a course. During class, instructors are divided between hitting the lecture's course objective and answering questions. Immediately after class, an instructor or TA does not have much time to answer questions in great detail because another class may be flowing in or for other reasons. Hence, colleges have mandated that instructors must hold office hours to aid students.

On the first day, every instructor communicates his/her office hours: location, specific days and times. The syllabus also will list office hours. Those days or times may not be convenient. Fortunately, most instructors will schedule alternative appointment times convenient to the student. You may be afraid or intimidated by your instructor, but he/she is there to help you. You cannot pass the course if you do not understand the material. You have no excuse not to reach out. For office hours, you should come prepared with specific questions about the class, homework, assignment, reading, exams, or whatever. The instructor will be there to address those questions. For technical courses in particular math or science, you should calculate enough hands-on problems in the textbook to understand the process. You may be unsure about particular problems but you can show that you made an attempt when you are able to visit your instructor during his/her office hours. Thus, office hours can be very important to your success in a course.

Supplementing instructors' office hours, TAs host separate office hour days and times for students. In a course with a large student enrollment, the TA provides the course's primary interface with students. Some students underestimate the help that TAs can offer. As a TA, I often worked on my own homework because no one showed up for my office hours. You should not make that mistake of dismissing TA office hours' attendance. In my undergraduate Calculus II course, for instance, I tanked on the first exam and received a distressingly low grade. Thereafter, I went to my TA's office hours every week until the final exam. The Calculus II TA was a math major, earning his graduate degree. Each session, he patiently went over the assigned weekly homework and my graded class exams with me until I could solve each problem and understood the concepts. Since no other students showed up during those sessions, he was my personal tutor during office hours. I credit that TA with helping me to pass that course.

Office hours are in place to help you. You should arrive prepared to work. Bring your notes, questions and attempted assignments/homework that you did not understand. If consulted early, an instructor or TA will work with you to develop actions or provide the one-on-one teaching necessary to pass the course. A note of caution: your instructor and TA are similar to your bosses at a job. Thus, they should be given the same level of deference. Some instructors and TA's are relaxed in their interactions with their students. They are not your peers. In all communications especially e-mail, you ought to ensure that you use words of respect in particular "Please," "Would you...?," "I respectfully request" and "Thank you." You must ensure your communications are cordial and fact-based. In the event those communications are viewed by an outside source, your interaction will not be viewed as inappropriate or disrespectful. Since some instructors and TA's have seen and heard it all from students, your civil communications will be viewed as a breath of fresh air.

Additionally, office hours afford an opportunity for you to discuss issues about an assignment or course grade. If you think that you received a grade due to error or other reason, you have the ability to dispute or appeal your grade with your instructor. You must inform the instructor as soon as possible instead of waiting months after you receive the grade. Only the instructor can re-grade a paper/exam/project or change an overall grade. Time is of the essence because the grade appeal process has a finite period to occur. First, you ought to look over the syllabus to understand the grading policy. Second, you must gather your evidence to dispute the grade, which means pulling out the specific assignment or all of your graded work namely exams, papers, and projects. Third, you should review your assignment(s) for any instructor comments/notes explaining why you earned your grade. For your next step, you should contact your instructor and make an appointment to meet during his/her office hours.

When you meet with your teacher, you ought to bring your evidence and syllabus. You should respectfully explain your concerns relevant to your grade(s) in a clear and concise manner. If you are not satisfied with the instructor's explanations, you should document your understanding of the meeting's outcome in a short, respectful email to your instructor. Then, you have the option of contacting your instructor's department chair to start the grade dispute or appeal process. Before you appeal, you should review your college's website or contact the Registrar's Office about the college's formal grade appeal process. Another source of information is your academic advisor. After you have researched the policy, the appeal process is not to be taken lightly. Unless he/she has shown a persistent pattern of behavior, the instructor will have all of his/her documentation to show his/her grading policy, your graded work, and any attempts on your part to come to office hours. If you feel that you are right and have the evidence, though, you should follow through with a formal grade dispute or appeal. In spite of this, you have a responsibility to talk to your instructor before filing a formal grade appeal. During the meeting, he/she then has an opportunity to explain or correct any grading issue(s), as appropriate.

Section B: Academic Departments and Other College Resources

If office hours are not meeting your needs, your major's academic department or other campus organizations may offer supplemental tutoring. On weekday evenings, for instance, the UMCP Math Department offers free tutoring in a program called Math Success.[218] Any math students who are having trouble can attend the free math tutoring sessions at the designated location. The tutors help solve and explain any homework problems in Calculus I, Calculus II, Differential Equations, Linear Algebra and other math subjects. All tutors are juniors or seniors, pursuing majors in mathematics. In another example, the UMCP computer science department also provides free tutoring in programming for students every afternoon. In addition, the UMCP English Department runs the Writing Center, which is available to all campus students. By appointment, a Writing Center representative will proofread any UMCP undergraduate student's paper prior to its submission. At your school, you should check if a specific department offers similar subject matter tutoring/help for academic problems.

Academic departments are not alone in providing assistance to students. Depending on your school, a mixture of other organizations also may provide campus-wide tutoring support. For example, the UMCP Office of Multi-Ethnic Student Education (OMSE) provides tutoring in Math, English, Chemistry, and a myriad of other subjects.[219] During the week, any UMCP student can go to the OMSE offices and receive free tutoring assistance. Another campus resource is the counseling center. It offers academic counseling to students, specifically, techniques to improve studying, note-taking, and exam preparation.[220] Therefore, good colleges offer an abundance of student academic support/assistance to their students. When having academic issues, you must seek help early. If you are unsure where to start, you should ask your instructor or academic advisor.

Section C: Online Resources

Besides college's resources, several websites provide in-depth college-level instruction. You must be proactive in turning poor grades around. You may have to devote additional time to studying and understanding that class' concepts. You may be wondering where you will get the time. The alternative is to retake a class and graduate late. So, you may find the following helpful and supplement attending office hours.

- Khanacademy.com.[221]
  - o Covers numerous academic subjects, including computer science, math, science and economics, and humanities
  - o Free, online and self-paced
  - o Explains complex concepts
- Wolfram Alpha website.[222]
  - o Computes solutions to mathematical problems
  - o Covers many areas such as integration, derivatives, limits, and vector analysis
  - o Offers step-by-step solutions, alternate forms, and accompanying graphs
  - o Good for double-checking answers or obtaining a hint (You still need to understand the basic, underlying concepts of solving the problem; so, try to solve the problem yourself first.)
- Youtube.com.[223]
  - o One-stop shop for finding nuggets of information about a wide range of subjects
  - o Platform that several college-level institutions offer free courses in math, English, computer science, biology, chemistry, or astronomy
  - o Offers tutorials on almost any topic by typing the subject in its search engine
  - o Quality of the instruction may be questionable
- Massive Open Online Courses (MOOCs).[224]
  - o Usually free, self-paced online courses but some charge a fee
  - o Sponsored by several entities, notably, Udemy, ITundesU, Stanford, UC Berkeley, Duke, Harvard, UCLA, Yale, and Carnegie Mellon

- o Open to all and promote participation
- o Do not award diplomas
- OpenCourseWare.[225]
  - o Free, self-paced online courses hosted on universities and colleges' websites
  - o Sponsored by several college/university entities, like Stanford University, Massachusetts Institute of Technology and Yale
  - o No registration for classes
  - o Video-recording of scholars and teachers' lectures in their course classrooms
  - o Posts the course name, syllabus, lectures and course materials online with the course book available for online purchase at the school's bookstore
  - o Does not grant credits, degrees, or certificates
- Coursera.[226]
  - o Partners with different universities to provide free self-paced online courses
  - o Rotating courses in diverse subjects
  - o Register and sign-up on the website for a specific course from an upcoming list of scheduled courses
  - o Available in six languages, including English, Chinese, French, and Spanish
  - o Colleges can host their own Coursera courses
  - o Mirrors web-based courses sponsored by MOOCs or OpenCourseWare

To help you pass your class or classes, you can use these resources to supplement your college lectures, office hours, or even for college prep. You want to graduate from college on time; so, the delay of a failed course will definitely put a crimp in that plan.

Section D: Paid Tutors

You might benefit from a one-on-one paid tutoring if you are failing a course or failed the first major exam in a course. Otherwise, you may fall further and further behind. Since students learn at different levels, some need more help than others. Sometimes, a student cannot grasp a subject despite countless office hours and online resources. He/she is on his/her own to seek help as soon as possible. A paid tutor is a major time commitment and expense. The tutor can devote time to explain the subject matter, help prepare for an exam or teach throughout the semester to pass a course. A paid tutor is a last resort when you have exhausted the free alternatives. Unlike the free help, the tutor's fees may put a dent in your budget.

Paid tutors are especially good for technical courses like science, math, engineering, and computer science. Some college academic departments provide tutors' names and contact information. Tutors may also advertise on college billboards, dorm walls, or other means. The potential tutee ought to interview two or three different tutors. Frequently, tutors are graduate students, college juniors, or college seniors. You should also compare costs among tutors. When selecting a tutor, you must investigate the credentials of the tutor, i.e., the tutor's grade in the specific class, when the tutor took the course, the tutor's course instructor and any previous experience as a tutor. The tutor's grade is important because his/her comprehension of the material is essential to his/her ability to explain it. Lastly, you and the tutor must verify if your schedules are compatible.

Your paid tutor ought to tailor instruction sessions to your needs. The first meeting should be free. He/she ought to use the first session to evaluate your level of knowledge and specific gaps in understanding. The tutor should also examine your past assignments and previous test scores. If hired, your tutor ought to submit a draft lesson plan for review to you within one to two weeks. It should parallel the course's syllabus. The lesson plan must include the number of weekly tutoring hours and tentative dates/times, the topics per session, hourly cost per session and the payment structure (per week/month). Each tutoring session ought to reinforce the classroom instruction for you. In many cases, a paid tutor may provide the singular break-through that you need to understand the course material. Again, you must get help at the earliest from available resources to benefit from needed academic intervention.

Life lessons - Chapter 9: Academic Resources
- Obtain help if you perform poorly after the first major course exam or assignment
    o Know how to calculate your course grade by using the syllabus grading criteria or asking your instructor
    o Pre-empt course(s) failing grades immediately by asking for help from your instructor or TA
    o Your instructor and the college will officially notify you if you are failing the course; however, do not wait until then to get help
    o If you have a concern about an assignment grade or final course grade, you must discuss it with your instructor as soon as possible
- Several free resources are available to help you improve your grade in order to pass a course
    o Office hours permit you to meet face-to-face with your instructor or TA about academic issues
    o Check if specific academic departments or other college organizations offer free tutoring in subjects such as math, English, computer science, etc.
    o Several websites like Khanacademy.com and Youtube.com provide in-depth instruction in numerous subjects
- A paid tutor is a last resort to free tutoring/help but may provide the singular break-through that you need to understand the course material

CHAPTER 10:
Failing Courses

Retaking any class will cost time and additional money. This may also impact a student's graduation timeline and financial aid eligibility. Nonetheless, many colleges sanction a second chance for a student to pass a failed class. When a student fails a required course with a "D" or "F" grade, he/she may immediately sign up to take it again. The student then "repeats" the course but must pass the class this time with a grade of "C" or better. Throughout the semester, the student should remain in communication with his/her advisor as he/she improves his/her grade. If the student passes the course, he/she may apply to the school for grade forgiveness. Each college has a different grade forgiveness policy. Grade forgiveness permits the student to use the most recent and highest course grade to count in his/her cumulative GPA calculation. The student's failing grade for the course remains on his/her transcript but the grade does not count in the overall GPA calculation. Most schools are very strict in the processing and approval of a student's "grade forgiveness." Some colleges only permit freshmen to apply for grade forgiveness. Although grade forgiveness allows a student to improve his/her GPA, he/she should not abuse the process. A student's best bet is to work hard, study and pass his/her classes the first time. Frankly, "D" or "F" grades in a course indicate a lack of prerequisite knowledge/skills; an inability to understand and apply the coursework; or personal issues. If a student does not pass a required course a second time, the academic department for the major may discharge the student from the program. Failing a course twice, that student should genuinely reassess his/her major and career goals.

In your situation, you may have failed a course. If applicable, you ought to check with your school Registrar's Office whether it has a grade forgiveness policy and how it is applied. Either way, you will need to repeat the course to complete your degree. If you fail a required course a second time, you should consider whether a change of major is an option. After you have chosen your major, though, you may have huge reservations about changing it. The cost and time may be deterrents because you will have to take additional classes for the new major in order to graduate. Do not despair because the change in major may be for the best. For every obstacle or failure in life, you have to have a backup plan and go on with your life. The mark of a person's character is not how he/she deals with success upon success but rather how he/she overcomes and succeeds despite obstacles or failure. In college, your focus should be learning about yourself beyond your comfort zone. Despite the touchy-feely sentiment of the last few sentences, nevertheless, your main purpose is to graduate on time (Gotcha!). The most important thing is to graduate and get your degree. This chapter goes through the process to determine if you should change your major.

Section A: Failing Grade(s)

A student might earn numerous poor grades specifically "Ds" and "Fs" in required courses while pursuing his/her major. The school will issue ample warnings to the student, especially, when his/her GPA falls below the required minimum level. As a result, the school will formally place the student on academic probation if he/she continues to fail to meet academic standards or does not show required improvement. If that is the case, he/she ought to assess if a change in major is warranted. For instance, UMCP has a highly ranked computer science program. Former students include tech industry titans, in particular, Sergey Brin, co-founder of Google.[227] Only the most accomplished students (who typically have previous programming experience) survive. At instructor and TA office hours, computer science students often are lined up for help similar to customers waiting for the newest iPhone at the Apple Store. The UMCP freshman computer science courses often do not cater to students' different levels of knowledge and skill. A computer science major should be able to program or his/her grade point average (GPA) plunges fast and brutally. UMCP's weeding out process still has produced over 600 Ph.D.s since the computer science program began in 1973.[228]

At UMCP, I noted that the successful computer science students programmed all the time. These students would practice, practice, and practice. These students actually enjoyed the challenge of getting a program to work. They also excelled in the required advanced math courses, which eliminated many computer science "wannabes." In contrast, the less than stellar computer science students were in the major for the wrong reasons. Or, they performed poorly in their computer science courses or required advanced math courses. Instead of wasting time and money, these students should have taken a hard look at their interests and prior academic preparation.

At the earliest, if you have poor or failing grades, you have to take the initiative. Otherwise, you may be ejected from your major. You may be paralyzed by anxiety. Your frustration level may be so high, and your GPA so low that you may make a rash decision to switch majors, switch colleges, or drop out. That is a mistake. You have to look at the big picture. Questions to ask yourself include: "Do you still want this degree in this field of study?" and "Are you hungry to do the work?" You also may be asking yourself, "What do I do now?" Breath, stop for a minute and think. You should reflect on all of your grades for that semester. You may be confusing a challenging course or semester with a perceived lack of aptitude. When doing well in other classes, you may be struggling in one particular class. That one class does not define you. If you can just pass that one class, you can pursue your degree. You will have to work hard, study hard, and get help to bring up your grade. Or, if you are in a technical major, you may often get low grades. Job recruiters understand the difference between getting "C" grades in technical courses versus getting "Cs" in liberal arts courses. These "C" students with technical degrees are marketable and valuable because employers need their skills. Before you cut your losses in your specific major, you must verify your options. For that reason, you should talk to someone of authority in the school.

Initially, you ought to meet with the instructor(s) in the course(s) that you are failing. You should discuss your failing coursework, including additional coaching/tutoring and the potential for a turnaround. Alas, the meeting with your instructor and additional office hours may not produce improvement. Before the deadline, you should consider "dropping" or "withdrawing" from those classes until a later date. During the interval, you will have an opportunity to get additional academic help, take other classes namely electives, and make some decisions. Immediately, though, you should discuss the problems with your academic advisor. Since you have been in touch periodically, your situation should not be a surprise. Remember, there may also be financial consequences namely probation or suspension of federal financial aid. When you have failing grades and/or course withdrawals, you should discuss them with a representative from your college bursar's office. When you have exhausted all tutoring assistance and delays, you may still get failing grades in your required courses. You need to make a decision as soon as possible on whether you need to change majors. Time is not on your side.

Section B: Changing Majors

As illustrated above, students are only successful in their chosen major when they are dedicated and have the required proficiency. After much thought, you may finally decide to change your major, particularly, if you have poor/failing grades in your courses. As soon as possible, you need to make an appointment and speak to your academic advisor. Before your face-to-face meeting with your advisor, you ought to investigate your school or department's academic probation policy. Every college posts this information online, including academic suspension, dismissal from the school for academic deficiencies, and readmission. You should read through the policy. Then, your academic advisor only will be confirming or denying what you already suspect. At your meeting, the advisor should address issues namely your GPA, tutoring, academic probation, and dismissal. After the conversation, you might discover that your situation may not be as dire as you believe. In that case, you and your advisor can also discuss the best course of action including potential new majors. To prepare ahead of time, you ought to research new majors. The process is similar to your search for your first major. This time, you have a better understanding of your likes, dislikes, and aptitudes for specific majors. For instance, you may substitute your major with a minor or secondary concentration of courses that you have been pursuing. Anyway, every student's situation is different. A student may be failing all of his/her classes, including general education classes. If that is the case, then the strategies and outcomes will be completely different. Again, you need to talk to your advisor. Accordingly, you and your academic advisor should tailor a plan of action designed specifically for you. Then, you can make an informed decision rather than a knee-jerk reaction about leaving the major or even the school.

Despite the previous focus on failing grades, you might have other motives for changing your major. In spite of passing all of your courses, you might have lost the appetite for pursuing your chosen major/degree or discovered a passion for another career field. For my bachelor's degree at the University of Maryland, College Park (UMCP), I thought that I had the determination to thrive in computer science. Nope, I was wrong. For a year, I was a UMCP computer science major student who hated programming. I also realized that a college major should encompass subjects that I would be willing to do every day in a career. After a discussion with my academic advisor and some research, I switched majors. It happens. My experience should alert you to similar issues that you might encounter. You might have made a mistake in pursuing your major. Do not despair or beat yourself up. After exposure to their major's requirements, many students change their major because the major was not what they expected. Sometimes, a person's path is winding rather than a straight line. To start the process of changing your major, you should follow the same procedure outlined above i.e., investigating new majors and meeting with your current academic advisor to discuss alternatives.

After you have decided to switch majors, you should make an appointment at the earliest opportunity with the new department/major's academic advisor. You must accept the reality of the situation and be proactive. Each department/major has its own policies and procedures for accepting new students. The new academic advisor will counsel you about that major's required classes for degree completion. In any event, you and the new advisor should draft a revised two or four-year academic plan for your graduation timeline. Then, you may have to submit an application for acceptance to the new academic department. If accepted, you will now have a new major. Your new advisor will help you coordinate any additional documentation with the Office of the Registrar. For example, the college's registrar might mask your failed grades (Ds or Fs) earned in courses that do not count toward your new major. The masked credits and grades will appear on your transcript except they will not be calculated in your GPA. Customarily, grade masking applies to first-year transfer students or those with only a semester of major specific classes. You should contact your Registrar's Office to investigate.

The new academic advisor may also direct you to the school's financial/bursar's office. At that time, you can determine if switching majors will affect your school financing. You will need to take appropriate steps, accordingly. To close the loop, you should inform your old academic advisor when the change of major will occur. By keeping everyone informed, you will facilitate a smooth transition. If you are having academic problems, be realistic and get help as soon as possible. Again, you are controlling your own destiny rather than succumbing to paralyzing fear.

Section C: Telling Your Parents

You should tell your parents as soon as you realize that you are retaking a course, failing several courses, changing majors (voluntarily or not), or switching schools. Any of these circumstances may change your expected graduation timeline. Every year, parents are in the dark about whether their child is graduating, failing, changing majors, etc. Your parent(s) may be paying for your college degree. Changing your major may extend your graduation timeline which will cost additional money for new classes. Your parent(s) may only be willing to pay for two or four years of college; so, you will have to work and pay for the extra tuition. You have to take responsibility and keep them informed of any changes in your academic status. You may be afraid to tell your parent(s). Your family may give you some grief initially; still, you and they must discuss the financial burden and solutions as calm, mature adults. Or else, the situation will be much worse when your family and friends show up for your non-existent graduation. Do not let the news fester. During this stressful time in your life, you will need your family's support. They will care more about your emotional and mental well-being than any disappointment with a postponed graduation. If you have done all you can to pass your classes, you are not a failure by any means. With swift action, you should be able to overcome the disappointment of switching majors or other change in status. In the long run, your initial major may not have been for you.

Life lessons - Chapter 10: Failing Courses
- Failing grades in required courses for your major do not define you
  - Approach your instructor(s) for assistance
  - Assess if you should change to another major
  - Discuss the options with your academic advisor in particular possibly "dropping" or "withdrawing" from a course until a later date to get help
  - Inform the bursar's office to verify if there are any financial aid implications
  - Be proactive and get help as soon as possible
- Choosing a new major
  - Meet with an academic advisor of the department for a new major(s) that you are interested in
  - Submit an acceptance application to the department, as appropriate
  - Develop a new two or four-year academic plan for graduation with your new advisor
  - Notify the Registrar's Office, financial office and your old academic advisor of the change in major
- Tell your parent(s) if a failing course grade or change of major will effect financing college, especially scholarships/loans, and your graduation timeline

CHAPTER 11:
Outside the Classroom

In college, you are going to meet new, exciting people. You will venture to places that you have never been before. You are away from home, experiencing an adventure in independence. Have fun! On the other hand, you must be aware of threats to your safety and well-being. There is danger for those in the wrong place and time. You must protect yourself and take precautions: be conscious of your environment and the people around you. For example, you may run or walk alone for exercise. You might also run with earbuds or walk with your eyes fixed on your phone. These activities should not be issues. The problem comes from other people. On the prowl, others may see you as an oblivious prey. The outcomes can be your phone ripped from your hands, an attack from behind, or other physical harm. Or, you might walk across campus at night. Robbers/muggers try to blend in with students on campus and look for potential victims to ambush in isolated places. Your safety is paramount. You do not want to end up in the hospital and miss several weeks of class due to an unwarranted attack. Below are discussions to raise your awareness about campus safety, personal safety, responsible sex and other issues.

Section A: Campus Safety

Safety and security are paramount to your happiness at school. When researching colleges, you ought to investigate the schools' crime statistics and their surrounding areas. Every school's website should furnish crime statistics and have a clear comprehensive sexual assault policy.[229] You and your parent(s) also ought to Google search news articles about the schools' reported crimes and its handling of the incidents. In addition, the U.S. Department of Education maintains the "Campus Safety and Security" website.[230] You can search for a school by name or schools by several criteria. For a specific school, you can find out its security officer, Title IX coordinator and information on criminal offenses, hate crimes, arrests, etc. Additionally, the website http://www.city-data.com provides a vast amount of information about cities within the U.S. It provides crime data, registered sex offenders in local areas and other data. These websites are worth checking out.

Frequently, some good schools are in questionable neighbors in major cities. In Washington D.C., Georgetown University, George Washington, and Howard University were prime examples of such schools. During the 1980's and 1990's, crime and violence were rampant in the city. In the last few years, Washington D.C. went through gentrification as baby boomers and young professionals returned to the city. Now, these universities are tucked among retail shopping, business-occupied office spaces, high-end condos, and transportation conduits such as buses and metro stops. Some pockets within D.C., however, are not the best. According to city-data.com for D.C., 67% of the reported crimes are thefts.[231] City-data.com also claims that Washington D.C. has higher crime than 95.7% of other U.S. cities.[232]

In addition to the surrounding area, you must look at the statistics for crime on campus. Although you may feel safe in your dorm, you should take precautions specifically locking your dorm room at night or when you are gone. A scary scenario would be waking up to find a stranger in your room who wants to assault or rob you. Such a situation would be traumatic. You must be alert that criminals are constantly looking for targets of opportunity. I also suggest that you enroll in a self-defense class to be able to protect yourself. Additionally, you should discuss campus safety with your roommates. Hopefully, they, in turn, will safeguard against "supposed" friends or strangers gaining unauthorized entry to your shared unsecured dorm room. Thus, you must check out a college's crime and safety statistics as both will impact your college life. No place is completely safe: urban, suburban, or rural. If you fear for your life when you live on or near the campus, your preferred college may not be the best choice.

Section B: Personal Safety

In your free time, you may push the limits, go out on a limb and trust your gut with a new person or situation. My mother always warned me that "Nothing good ever happens at 2 o'clock in the morning." So, be judicious with your personal safety. You want to be around to attend classes and graduate from college. You should listen to trusted friends (and family) who are trying to protect you from a stupid act or risky behavior. Outside of your family's safety net and trusted friends, few people have your best interest at heart. With good friends, you should be able to hang out without worry. Unfortunately, I have seen newspaper articles again and again about men and women disappearing after a night out with "friends." Associates who desert you at a party are not your friends. You should not be stranded somewhere, having to hitch a ride with a stranger because these people left you for someone or something. In addition, friends don't let friends do stupid things. To ensure this, your group should have a rotating designated driver, purse watcher, table holder, coat checker, etc. In other words, one person in the group must stay on guard and sober. For each excursion, you and your group should make a pact to listen when confronted by the "rational" friend's safety concerns in order to reel in the craziness.

When you leave your dorm or apartment for a night on the town, you must let someone know where you are going. When possible, you should use a buddy system in which you and a friend go out together. If you don't have anyone to call or it is late at night, then you might consider texting a friend or leaving a voicemail on your own phone. You should give as much detail specifically a departure time, the destination, an expected time of return, any friends going with you and the mode of transportation. I have left a voicemail on my answering machine like this a time or two. I have been relieved when I was the one to hear and erase the message. The action meant that I made it home fine.

As another measure, you (man or woman) can download an assortment of smartphone safety apps to provide a level of security. For instance, the free Circle of 6 app for smartphones sends pre-written text messages to six pre-identified contacts.[233] The first message sends your GPS location with a pick-up request. The second message sends a request for your friends to call you as soon as possible. When you identify reliable friends for the Circle of 6 app, you should consider picking friends with operational cars. Another appropriate app for personal safety is Friend Radar, which is a fast and easy way to locate a "lost" friend within a hundred feet.[234] Reference your phone, you should create a contact in it called "in case of emergency." This contact should correspond to a local friend's name and telephone number. If someone finds (not steals) your phone, he/she can immediately call the emergency contact person. When your phone requires a password to unlock it, you should set your locked screen to show the emergency telephone number as "emergency: xxx-xxx-xxxx." On your locked phone, I also suggest you display the first initial of your first name, your full last name, two-digit state code, and zip code, providing a starting point to identify you.

When alone at an event or party, you need to be on your guard and constantly aware of your surroundings. Try to resist leaving an event or place with someone you do not know. Joran Van Der Sloot did not seem like the proverbial boogeyman.[235] He was handsome and a lawyer's son. He allegedly was the last person to see Natalee Holloway. She was a high school graduate who disappeared on a graduation trip to Aruba in 2005. Van Der Sloot allegedly was also the last person to see Stephany Flores, a Peruvian business student. In 2010, Van Der Sloot was convicted of killing Flores in a Lima hotel room.[236] Evil comes in many guises, including attractive packaging. For instance, you may decide to spend time with someone who is not well-known to you. In that case, you ought to be conscious of your safety. When possible, you ought to snap a picture of your companion with your smartphone. Then, you should send that person's photo, name and telephone number to your computer or a close friend's smartphone. If uncomfortable in a situation, you must leave quickly. Right now, you are probably rolling your eyes. You are thinking that the excitement and spontaneity will go out the window when meeting someone new at a party or nightclub. As of December 2016, the FBI's National Crime Information Center reported 88,040 active missing person records for the operational year.[237] Of these numbers, 42,807 (48.6%) were classified as juveniles and defined as under 21 years of age. The family and friends of these missing young people are desperate to find their whereabouts. Do not play Russian roulette with your personal safety.

When attending a party on or off-campus, you must drink only out of closed beer, water, soda, or drink containers. Sometimes, there may be a communal punch bowl. Stay away from it. You do not know if someone has spiked it with liquor or other substances. At a party or bar with a new person or group of people, you should not leave your drink or food unattended; lose sight of your drink or food; or, accept a drink or food from anyone other than the bar's official bartender/hostess. For your safety, you should get a new drink or plate yourself because sexual predators and bad people put roofies in drinks or food.[238] Roofies are typically sedatives, depressants, or psychoactive drugs similar to Rohypnol, or Liquid Ecstasy. Roofies come in liquid or pill (crushed) forms. Roofies cause memory loss, unconsciousness or loss of self-control, making the drugged person vulnerable to sexual assault, robbery, kidnapping, murder, etc.

Although there is no absolute way to prevent a roofie attack or exposure to an unknown drugging substance, you must be wary. When possible, you ought to go out with a trusted friend; so that, you can watch out for each other. According to descriptions of the effects, the roofie experience is traumatic and scary.[239] If you feel sick or disoriented, you should not leave alone or with a stranger. Instead, you must immediately alert your friend(s) or the manager that you need help. You also ought to go to a hospital or emergency room because a roofie overdose can be deadly. Additionally, you should consider filing a police report about the incident. It is probably not the first time the perpetrator has spiked someone's drink or food. If you are the survivor of such an appalling attack, you should seek counseling. The roofie concern is real because the consequences can be dire – sexual assault, a sexually transmitted infection (STI), robbery, kidnapping or death. If it happens to you, you are not at fault because there are just evil people who use roofies against the unsuspecting. These situations occur at parties, social gatherings or on dates. At college, you must look out for your personal welfare. You do not want to be the subject of an "Amber Alert" or episode of "True Crime".

Section C: Online Interactions

Sexting is the new calling card or sexual foreplay. Sexting is when intimates send sexually provocative photos/messages back and forth between media devices. The pics can be partially or fully nude. Sexting has an impact on your personal safety and possible your future goals. You should not engage in such behavior. When you send an explicit photo/post, you trust that the other person will not do something despicable with it. In other words, you are giving your control to someone else. It opens you up to blackmail, bullying and internet exploitation. Yes, you may be Sexting with your boyfriend/girlfriend. People break up all the time. Many young women and men are crying tears of grief because of an ex's betrayal. The unscrupulous ex sold/posted intimate personal sex tapes or pics for money, in anger, to embarrass, or to hurt his/her former significant other. Or, a third-party stole or purchased the tapes/photos. Then, the third party sold them to media outlets or posted them on porn websites. Think about famous individuals who for fun, experimentation, or other unwise reasons created or posed for provocative photos/videos that someone leaked to the public. They did not realize that a racy photo/videotape could have devastating consequences after the act. Anyway, do not engage in Sexting or creating videos/photos that you would be embarrassed to share with friends and family. When images or videos are put online, they are there forever. You can spend the rest of your life trying to restore your reputation and reclaim your dignity.

If you are going to voluntarily post images or personal information, you should lock down the security on your social media profiles. Facebook, Instagram, Twitter, Tinder, and texts can be hacked. Also, do not "friend" people that you do not know. Some internet thieves steal online pictures and use them to fake personal profiles. The thief is known as a catfish. Also, many employers look at potential candidate's social media websites to weed out those with questionable judgment, poor behavior, etc. You ought to consider giving access only to trusted friends and family on your social media sites. Celebrities who post indelicate information or pictures online are terrible role models for young people. These celebrities do it because they seek fame at any cost to privacy or personal safety. These types of people are called media whores. If you would not show your parents, employer, or your best buddy an image or post, you ought to reconsider putting it on your social media website. You should keep some mystery about yourself.

Lastly, you might experiment with the internet to meet new people. Tinder, Yellow, Match.com, Plentyoffish.com, and e-Harmony are just a few of the many online dating sites out there. Basically, you are on your own because many sites do not conduct background checks. Once more, you must take necessary precautions to protect yourself. Internet dating breeds intimacy and instant friendship where none really exists. Sociopaths and psychopaths are expert manipulators who lure their intended victims into lowering their guards. They will try to obtain personal information in particular addresses and telephone numbers of intended victims. You might think that you are chatting with another high school or college student. Actually, he/she could actually be a creepy, sexual predator or a potential killer, sitting at home in his/her droopy underwear and trolling for victims.

If you hook-up with one of your internet "dates," you should meet initially in a public place. You also ought to send a picture of the person to a friend. At the end of the date, you should arrange to phone or FaceTime that friend. Your friend ought to call you if you do not call (not text). The expiration for no contact is two days, which should result in a report to the police. Here are a few other safety tips: look at your date's wedding finger for a tan line (and ask if he/she is married); ask to see a picture identification at some point; conduct Google and Facebook searches of his/her name; do not invite him/her to your home or meet in a secluded place until you have dated for a few weeks; meet his/her friends after a few dates, as appropriate; and give your "date's" contact information to someone whom you trust.

Section D: Responsible Sex and Birth Control

Despite the title of this section, I am not advocating pre-marital sex for anyone. Abstinence has always been in vogue. You can choose abstinence, which is as important as choosing to have sex. You want your college experience to be happy and satisfying. Sex is included in this book because poor choices can ravage your mind, health, and soul. Sometimes, the intensity of a relationship that goes wrong has caused many college students to drop out of school or have mental breakdowns. So, you must go into any sexual encounter with eyes wide open and your mind aware of the consequences. I want to emphasize that you and your partner have no timetable for sex. Your relationship can thrive without sex.

Either way, you should practice responsible sexual intimacy. Sex is not a one-sided proposition.

Sex has many facets especially cuddling, oral sex, mutual masturbation, and other pleasurable activities. You and your mate should feel safe, fun, passion and empowered; otherwise, trust and satisfaction wanes. For example, your partner may constantly pressure you for sex. You must take it as a warning sign. This person does not respect your choices. You have the right to say, "No." There is a difference between remorse and force. A person's remorse is questioning his/her voluntary decision or action while force is the lack of a choice. In other words, your partner and you must be sensitive to any reluctance, uncertainty, fear, mental impairment (in particular being drunk/high), or resistance. If there is, I advise each of you to just walk away from the encounter. Thus, both of you must be clear that sex is consensual to diminish remorse and prevent force. With an agreement to engage in sex, you and your mate specifically man-woman, woman-woman, and man-man pairings must speak up about your desires. Please do not permit your voice to be silenced. Sex must never be judgmental, pressured, soul-crushing, dishonest, distressing, or unsatisfying. Otherwise, you should move on to someone who cherishes and respects you.

When having sex, you must consider the health and emotional risks. Or else, you and your partner risk leaving school because of an unplanned pregnancy or other health issues. You should take precautions to use birth control every time. For example, Bedsider.org provides a comparison of all forms of birth control.[240] The website offers interactive discussions about each method, including effectiveness and side effects. If sexually active, you also can discuss birth control options with your doctor or Student Health Center. Most college health clinics provide condoms and how to apply them properly for *FREE*. Sleeping with a new partner, you should use condoms as well as a secondary birth control method. This safe sex practice prevents pregnancy and the spread of sexually transmitted infections (STIs) especially HIV/AIDS, genital warts, pubic lice, Chlamydia, gonorrhea, herpes or syphilis. Since many people do not have symptoms, your partner could be affected by an STI and not know it. Many STIs can cause infertility, cancer, nervous system damage, recurring symptoms (herpes) for life, and even lead to death if untreated. Being infected by one of these diseases will adversely affect your psyche and health. For instance, a person can get pubic lice from sexual contact or contact with fiber materials namely clothing, bed linens, or towels that the infested person used. To protect yourself, you should have a frank discussion with your partner. Both of you must get tested for STIs if you both have been sexually active with other partners. Depending on the type of sexual activity, STI exposure can be anywhere: throat, genital areas, or rectum. Accordingly, get tested! You can find out more from your doctor or at the campus health clinic.

A casual sex hook-up without protection is not mature or wise. Typically, the sexual partners really do not know each other. Thus, you need to protect yourself and your future. You should consider carrying one or two condoms in your purse or wallet. In the heat of the moment, your partner may say he/she does not have one. Then, you can whip out your own. Also, you must change out the condoms occasionally based on their expiration dates. Yes, condoms have expiration dates. If your partner refuses to use a condom, he/she does not have your best interest at heart. With that pattern of behavior, he/she may have an STI or be an unplanned pregnancy waiting to happen. Also, you should not engage in risky sexual behavior while under the influence of drugs or alcohol.

Both impair judgment. For example, beer goggles cause people to dim-wittedly place the other person's sexual history on the back burner.

While in college, you or your partner do not want an unplanned pregnancy. When one partner does not want to be a parent, he/she may abandon the other partner to deal with the situation. Thus, he/she will not take responsibility emotionally or financially for this new child. With an unplanned pregnancy, you might be the only parent who provides love and financial support. If you want to observe the fear and uncertainty of an unplanned pregnancy, MTV hosts the television show, "16 and Pregnant." The show is a candid look at the trials and tribulations of young unprepared mothers and fathers. These shows are heart-wrenching and not pretty to watch. With an unplanned pregnancy, your options are raising the child without finishing college; having/raising your child while you work and go to school; asking your parent(s) to raise your child until you finish college and graduate; adoption; or an abortion. Each decision has consequences and disrupts your plans for the future – graduation and obtaining a college degree.

You may decide to leave school to raise your baby. Children of a single parent or two parents, lacking skills or a higher education degree, are likely to live in poverty. Of the more than 800,000 children and youth experiencing homelessness in the U.S., two-thirds of their parents lacked a high school diploma, and 75 percent of these parents were unemployed in 2013 according to the book, "Cities and Urban Life."[241] Raising children is not cheap. In 2015, the estimated price tag to raise a child until 18 years old was $233,610.[242] Unbelievably, this amount does not even include the child's future college. Instead, the approximate cost only covers a child's housing, food, education, childcare, clothing, medical expenses and dental expenses. In spite of the price tag, you and hopefully your partner will be able to earn a living in order to handle these costs.

In an optimal situation, a woman might have a committed partner to share the burden of the adoption or abortion decision. When faced with such a situation, you (and your partner, if appropriate) ought to investigate the facts and obtain medical input. As solutions for an unplanned pregnancy, adoption and abortion are viable choices. Each also has problems and consequences. The parent(s) may not be allowed to have future interaction with the baby after the adoption is complete. For an alternative, abortion is legal but one of the hardest decisions. Despite the anti-abortion movement's outcry, the decision is never done on a whim or for convenience. Abortion is a personal decision that no one else has the right to judge. In addition, adoption and abortion also can create problematic legal situations for the unmarried birth father.[243] Unplanned pregnancies can take an emotional and financial toll on both parties involved. In summary, you must think about your goal of graduating from college on time and how to attain it. Remain focused on your goal. Children are expensive but can also be rays of sunshine in your life. When you eventually have children, you should feel joy in the occasions. You want to love and take care of them without mental misgivings and financial fears. Therefore, you should be responsible in your sexual encounters and behavior. When you practice responsible safe sex, you are preventing an unplanned pregnancy or the spread of an STI to you.

Section E: Self-Respect

I am going to take a few minutes to discuss relationships. You should be open to new relationships and consider dating often. Then, you will know what you like and dislike about a partner. You ought to take your time. College is a prime dating pool for young, enthusiastic and optimistic mates. You are all there for the same graduation goal and hopefully, have similar ambitions. When people first meet you, they will present their best face to you. You must observe a person's behavior over time instead of what they say or how they look. If you date or sleep with someone, your best option is to select your partner wisely. No one is perfect; so, a relationship depends on compatibility, tolerance, attraction, and compromise. When you find the right person, you should be rewarded with a helpmate, companion, and friend. He/she must respect and treat you well. With one-night stands and casual sex, you are not in a position to really know your partner. For example, the other person could be mentally unstable. By the time you realize it, your safety and well-being could be in jeopardy.

My mother always said, "Do not sleep with a stupid or a mean person." When an individual is naive or inexperienced, he/she is susceptible to falling into a relationship with these types of people. Stupid and mean people hold you back. They do not support you or rejoice in your advancement. Instead, they are jealous of your achievements and attempt to trap you into their expectations. The best ways to identify these people are to observe their interactions with other people, have a few long conversations with them, and meet their friends and family.

Regarding stupid people, most reasonable people will make changes to their behavior or views if they discover a new idea that makes sense. Despite this, stupid people know something is wrong in their thinking. They choose not to change their behavior despite every bit of evidence. In an interaction, you might point out flaws in their logic. Although they acknowledge the inconsistencies, stupid people quickly become defensive. They think that you are putting them down or think that you are better than them. They do not respect education, knowledge and respectful disagreement. Stupid people are a drag on your finances, your peace of mind, your values and your time. If an unplanned pregnancy happens, you might get stuck with this dim person while you (alone probably) or both of you (probably not) raise your child for the next 18 years. Dense people usually cause chaos/confusion in their wake. Keep your distance to maintain your sanity.

In contrast, a mean person uses physical violence or intimidation to get his/her way. In a relationship, any hitting, choking, shaking, screaming, habitual lying, stalking, or e-mail/text harassment is a sign that the offending boyfriend/girlfriend needs anger management and/or psychiatric help. Also, sexual harassment, sexual assault, or rape may happen in a toxic relationship. Strangely, you probably think your partner's possessive behavior is an expression of love. Snap out of it! When observing demeaning or manipulative behavior in a partner, you should run to the nearest exit. Take heed of the initial warning signs. This type of irrational, possessive boyfriend/girlfriend will attempt to isolate you from friends and family. Your "mean" partner will not support your dreams to discover and explore new things. Typically, he/she will seek to keep his unacceptable behavior hidden from others outside of the relationship. First Lady Eleanor Roosevelt was speaking the truth when she said, "No one can make you feel inferior without your consent." Do not suffer in silence. Speak up and report the incident

193

as soon as possible. No one has the right to touch you or your property without your permission.

For the abuser, the relationship is about power and control. Poisonous relationships have a pattern of violence that escalates with a break-up. After a brief period, the toxic person may beg for another chance. You may feel vulnerable. Do not give a "mean" partner another chance to bring the crazy. You must withdraw from the insanity and drama. This abuse dynamics applies to heterosexual, same-sex, low-income, or wealthy couples. You cannot change this type of person or make him/her happy. Although you might feel embarrassed, guilt, or responsibility, you are not at fault. For this reason, you should consult with your campus counseling center to sever ties with your boyfriend/girlfriend, report the event(s), and break the cycle. Stop all contact with the other person. If the other person approaches you, sprint the other way. Then, you must contact the police or school administrators immediately! You might have personal items within a shared space such as an apartment. In that scenario, you must take someone with you or request police personnel on site to retrieve them. Otherwise, you should give up that *stuff* for lost.

A former or current boyfriend/girlfriend may threaten you verbally with death or bodily harm. You must take such threats seriously, ask for help, and immediately report the incident. Yeardley Love was a 22 year-old, University of Virginia lacrosse player. George Huguely V, her former college boyfriend, viciously beat and killed her.[244] Huguely was an allegedly violent man, who drank alcohol to excess. After their break-up, he purportedly sent threatening e-mails to Yeardley. Although her family prompted her to file a restraining order, Yeardley chose not to do it. If faced with a similar circumstance, you must report the threats especially when the abuser is another college student. This is not the time for you to exercise your independence as a young adult. You and your parents should file a complaint with the school. Colleges are obligated to protect their students and respond to sexual misconduct/abuse in accordance with Title IX.[245] Your college should intervene by allowing you to switch classes, prohibiting the threatening person's contact with you, suspending or expelling him/her from the school and offering counseling to you.

Your school may not be responsive, the behavior may continue, or the person is not a college student. You (and your parents, if needed) should immediately go to the local police (not the campus police) and apply for a restraining/protective order. The order should stipulate that the abuser cannot have any contact with you at any location, in person, or by phone.[246] Protective orders are in a nationwide law enforcement database. Numerous law enforcement agencies also are requiring offenders to wear a GPS tracking ankle bracelet.[247] Make sure that you document all incidents, contact, violations and any witnesses. Thus, the police can take immediate action if there is a violation. The police or law enforcement representative ought to notify your college's campus police and administrators of the order. You and your parents, however, should also inform school administrators and campus police. Finally, through the court system, you must follow-up to ensure a temporary restraining order becomes a permanent protective order. So, it is extremely important to record all violations and contact, in particular, any visits, text messages, or emails.

You are in college to get your education. You should not have to learn or leave school under the threat of violence. With any luck, the initial restraining/protective order will make the abuser pause and calm down to a rational level. If threats, stalking, harassment or other aggressive behavior continue, you will have to file formal charges and take the person to court. The court may impose fines, counseling and/or jail time. Remember, all abusive people are mentally unbalanced. I advise you to make your safety and well-being a priority. Again, keep away from "stupid" or "mean" people in a relationship. You should not trivialize the situation; be vigilant.

Section F: Rape and Sexual Assault

You should feel safe from sexual assault and rape on campus. Sexual assault is unwanted sexual contact/touching while rape is unwanted physical penetration. Rape also occurs when a person cannot give permission for sex. When either partner is incapacitated, drunk or unconscious, the sex is not consensual. Although your college or university may actively raise awareness about these crimes, you may not give these offenses much thought. Yet, you must stay alert to your surroundings and the people who populate them. According to 2015 Rape, Abuse, and Incest National Network statistics, 11.2% of all college students (among graduate and undergraduate students) experience rape or sexual assault.[248] Of that percentage, 23.1% are female undergraduates and 5.4% are male undergraduates. In theory, no one has the right to sexually touch you unless you give your permission. When you say "no" to sex, he/she should stop. Unfortunately, many sexual offenders willingly violate others' sexual boundaries. In a 2014 Special Report, the Bureau of Justice Statistics (BJS) estimated that approximately 80% of sexual assaults/rapes against college students and nonstudents were committed by someone known to the victim.[249] Not all sexual assault attackers and rapists are the frightening assailant lurking in the alley. The BJS Report also stated that rape and sexual assault crimes against students (80%) were also more than likely to go unreported to the police than with nonstudent victimizations (67%).[250] A survivor may be afraid to report the offense, does not want to get the offender in trouble, or sometimes blames himself/herself rather than the culprit. For the perpetrator, sexual assault and rape are about control, force and violence. Thus, the survivor is not at fault for someone else's behavior or actions.

Sexual assault or rape can occur off campus or on campus. With the attack, you may be in shock and hurt. I encourage you to call a friend or family member to go through the reporting process with you. If you are off-campus, you should immediately report the assault or rape directly to the local police instead of the campus police. When the incident occurs on campus, campus law enforcement normally is first on the scene.[251] Campus police know the campus layout and locations of buildings. Depending on the emergency, the campus police typically also contact the local police department.[252] Unfortunately, some college police forces have botched investigations or do not have the resources to handle sex crimes. According to a BJS report for academic year 2011-2012, only 68% of U.S. four-year colleges and universities use sworn police officers with certified training and full arrest powers granted by a state or local authority.[253] If campus security officers instead of campus certified police officers show up, you may want to respectfully request the additional presence of local police officers. The local police will know the proper steps to collect forensic evidence and coordinate a free medical exam.[254] The medical exam also known as a rape kit can last between two and four hours. After the incident, you should not bathe/shower, comb/brush your hair, change clothes/shoes, or douche (for women). After you file your report, you must follow-up to obtain a

197

copy of the police report and a status of the investigation. In extreme cases, you might be unwilling to go to the police. At that point, you can go directly to a hospital or medical center for treatment, emergency contraception, and a medical exam.[255] You still should call a friend or family member to go through the reporting process with you.

Although you feel vulnerable and scared, you can anticipate support from the police, your parents, hospital personnel, and college administrators. For instance, your parents may be miles away but you should get them involved right away. They care about your welfare and emotional health. You do not have to face this traumatic situation alone. Under Title IX, school administrators must investigate and take your report seriously.[256] They can allow you to change classes to prevent interaction with the perpetrator or expel/suspend a perpetrator from school. The school's response to protect you should be swift while the investigation is occurring. In addition, you should seek free mental health counseling on campus or at a local off-campus rape-crisis center. Often, sexual assault and rape survivors can become paralyzed with fear and anxiety. The BJS reported that "fewer than 1 in 5 female students (16%) and non-students (18%) who are victims of rape and sexual assault received assistance from a victim services agency."[257] In seeking counseling, your mental recovery is addressed and you can take back control. Sexual assault and rape are horrible crimes that impact the victim and his/her family. It is imperative that you *immediately* notify your parent(s) and the proper authorities (law enforcement and/or school administrators) if you are a sexual assault or rape survivor. The culprit must be exposed and brought to justice to prevent future sexual misconduct/crimes.

Life lessons – Chapter 11: Outside the Classroom
- You must be aware of threats to your safety and well-being
  - When researching colleges, you ought to investigate the schools' crime statistics and their surrounding areas
  - If you can, you should use a buddy system in which you and a friend go out together
  - If you go out alone, let someone know where, when and what time you will return
  - Do not drink food or drink that has been out of your sight
- Social media/the internet are tools
  - Avoid Sexting, which can make you vulnerable to bullying, blackmail or sexual exploitation
  - Lock down the security on your social media accounts to permit only friends and family access
- Safe responsible sex is important to your well-being at college
  - Abstinence is a viable choice too
  - Casual or risky sex can expose you to adverse consequences
  - Condoms prevent unplanned pregnancy and the spread of sexually transmitted infections (STIs) while other birth control methods prevent unplanned pregnancy
  - Get tested if you are sexually active
  - Choose your partners wisely for relationships and sexual partners
- Rape and sexual assault are crimes
  - Report the offender immediately to police and school administrators
  - Take someone (a friend or family member) with you to make the report because you may be hurt or in shock
  - Inform and get your parents involved for their support
  - A school must respond swiftly to a reported incident and conduct an investigation (under the Department of Education's Title IX)
  - Get mental health counseling on or off-campus if a survivor

CHAPTER 12:
College Life

You can attend college but you will be miserable if you only focus on academics 24/7. Every day, you will want to be somewhere else. College is stressful. You have papers, exams, quizzes, projects, and other deadlines. You run from class to class, event to event, sports practice to dinner, and other places. Your family, friends and significant others also want some of your time. Sometimes, you won't know if you are coming or going. With the paper chase, you have to find a practical way to deal with stress. Unproductive methods of dealing with stress include over-eating, drugs, alcohol, and smoking. Each of these things will get you in trouble. You must release tension in a productive way. In college and during your work career, you should prioritize your time. You need to plan and participate in activities other than studying or working. Your recreational time can be used to be alone and reflect but some of that time also should include other people. Periodically, lift your head from your college books and look at the world around you. Thus, don't isolate yourself with only academic pursuits but have a balance.

To fill some of your free time, you can participate in sports teams, recreational clubs, academic clubs, social clubs and fraternities/sororities. You also might attend a campus/local church, synagogue, mosque, temple, gurdwara, or other places of reflection to quench your spiritual thirst. As another alternative, you can volunteer at a charitable organization such as a food pantry or animal shelter within your college community. By engaging in any of these diverse activities, you can make friends instead of sitting in your dorm room and stressing over your grades. Friends are a wonderful support system. They offer conversation, traveling companions and exposure to new things, for instance, different foods, cultures, religions, etc. Some of your college friends will become as close to you as your family. When you have true, good friends, you do not feel isolated or trapped. Other methods to relieve stress are engaging in physical activity for example running, walking, bicycling, bowling, horseback riding, and racquetball. Erase the frown from your face for a few hours—with canoeing, dancing, a movie, a trip into town, playing cards, attending a party, calling home, pizza with some friends, reading a book, listening to tunes, becoming skilled at the guitar, or even watching "Keeping Up With the Kardashians"—the horror, the horror. Therefore, this chapter deals with strategies to increase your acceptance of your new environment. While in school, you cannot live on "facts" alone. You have to feed your soul and have fun!

Section A: College Connection

While attending college, many students do not cultivate a connection with their fellow students. These isolated students go to work, go to school, do homework, go to sleep, go to work, go to school, do homework, go to sleep, and yada, yada, yada. To combat this situation, you should think about joining a few social or academic clubs while you attend college. Many academic departments have student chapters that are degree specific such as the Society of Automotive Engineers. These types of clubs can offer networking and internship opportunities. Or, you might join a club based on an interest. For instance, if you are a business major, you might become an active member of the finance or math club. Typically, every college website lists its student organizations, which allows searches by name, keyword, or categories. At the very least, you can meet other students for coffee, get to know others on social network apps, or create a study group.

When investigating a specific two or four-year institution, you ought to check if it participates in a national or state athletic conference. Participating in or attending college sports, you can cultivate a connection to your college or university. For instance, numerous community colleges are members of the National Junior College Athletic Association (NJCAA) and compete in intramural baseball, basketball, cheerleading, soccer, softball, tennis, track & field, and volleyball.[258] The NJCAA is the national governing body for two-year college athletics. You ought to feel pride in attending your college or university. Thus, you should go to a few sports games each semester. School spirit is not just for cheerleaders. Additionally, you can bond with other students through your college's sports teams. To enrich your college experience, you have to create friendship with other people at college.

Lastly, you should not forget the people back home. To lessen homesickness, you ought to call, text, or video chat with your supportive family and old good friends. They can fill you in on hometown gossip and happenings. I am sure that your parent(s) will be happy to take a few minutes to hear your voice and listen to your stories about that hard exam, night out with friends, or "A+" grade on your 15-page research paper. Thus, you should develop relationships with new friends on campus as well as maintain those encouraging connections back home. Otherwise, you will experience two or four long, lonely years in college.

Section B: Roommates

Be a good roommate. If you are living with other people in dorms, your college experience will be miserable if tension and strife permeate the living space. Typically, students live in dorm rooms in which the school may assign one or two roommates. In college, you are going to have roommate(s) who may become your best friends for life. Then, you'll meet others who you would not spit on if they were on fire. In reality, you will not become best buds with every roommate. Either way, you and your roommate(s) have to co-exist. Not everyone has been trained at home to be respectful, courteous and friendly. To show respect to your roommate(s), you should speak in the morning and the evening by saying with a smile "Good morning", "What's up", "Hello", "Hola", or whatever. Otherwise, you will seem rude and discourteous. If the other person does not respond, then greet him/her anyway. It is hard to stay mad at or indifferent to someone when he/she smiles and wishes you a good day.

Roommates have a shared space, which necessitates cooperation, respect, tolerance, and courtesy. In other words, you should try to live by the golden rule of "Do unto others as you would have them do unto you." It is very difficult for occupants to live, study, or sleep when chaos and confusion reign daily in a room or apartment. However, murder is not permitted when roommates cannot get along. During your college search, you should visit each college's dorm rooms or view a schematic to verify the dorm room size for comfort and privacy. Also, you ought to find out if suites are available which typically have individual rooms connected to a common living space. Lastly, you should investigate how dorm rooms are assigned i.e., first come, first serve; by questionnaire; or randomly. With a little additional research, you may be able to reduce the potential for roommate conflicts. At the beginning of the semester, you and your roommate(s) should sit down and negotiate daily interaction in your shared space. Roommates have to **communicate**, **communicate**, and **communicate**. This is the most critical component of cooperative living. The other big issues of contention are likely to center around guests of the opposite sex, borrowing, cleaning and noise/light levels. I will go through each of these in detail.

In college, you or your roommate(s) may experiment with dating and sex. Generally, you should not have sleepovers in the room with sexual partners, significant others, friends with benefits or occasional lays, unless you and your roommate(s) mutually agree. In addition, some people consider pre-marital sex to be wrong. Thus, sleepovers are disrespectful to your roommate(s). The apartment or room is yours too, but the atmosphere will be better if each roommate respects the other's right to say, "No." Your roommate(s) may want to study, chill or just dress after a shower without the embarrassment of inadvertent exposure. Also, your roommate may not want to witness your sexual escapades. If sleepovers are discussed and permitted, you should notify your roommate(s) at least one to two days ahead of time that your boyfriend/girlfriend will be spending the night. Then, they can take action by locking their doors and wearing headphones, as necessary. Your lover must not stay over at your place for more than two nights each week. Otherwise, he/she has become another roommate without paying the appropriate rent/dorm fees. You must again respect your roommate(s)' desire to limit your lover's sleepover times. Instead, you and your partner can go to his or her apartment/dorm room until you overstay your welcome there too. This is where saving your money comes in handy to get a hotel or motel room. When your roommate is the offending party partaking in excessive or unwanted sleepovers in the dorm room, you should talk to him/her about your concerns and displeasure as soon as possible. Your roommate should be responsive and act accordingly. No one should lose the use of his/her room because his/her roommate is not concerned about privacy.

Ask before borrowing. If you are from a big family, remember how frustrated you became when your little sister or brother borrowed your clothes or equipment without asking. It is the same premise. Also, you should not eat or drink your roommates' food and beverages without replacing them or paying for the items. You and your roommate(s) should set ground rules about eating or drinking the last of something. You may be eyeing that last donut, but make sure your roommate will not go ballistic if he/she has been waiting to eat that chocolate covered delight all day. Ask and replace, as needed.

Keep a tidy room and clean up your shared spaces. Clutter, filth, clothes/shoes everywhere and dirty dishes with the accompanying foul smells are unacceptable. These breed vermin and unsanitary health conditions. In addition, a lot of people cannot study, organize or function in such a chaotic environment. I know that you are away from home for the first time, but try to remember that no one is your maid. As roommates, you should come up with a cleaning plan that everyone agrees to follow. These are shared duties namely washing dishes, sweeping, mopping, and bathroom duty that you can divide weekly among roommates. Everyone has to do his/her share.

The next bone of contention is noise and light levels. People differ in their noise and light tolerance. For example, I cannot sleep if the TV, radio, or any lights are on. I have an aunt who cannot sleep unless lights are on, the TV is at full blast, and the radio is on at a low murmur. We could not be roommates unless we brainstormed a compromise. If not, we would have to go our separate ways. In the room, everyone ought to be considerate, especially at night. To show respect, in general, each roommate should only host a party or invite numerous friends over when he/she notifies the other roommate(s) well in advance. With this in mind, you or your roommates may have exams, which require a good night's sleep. Whenever possible, use headphones and a desk lamp if you are studying while your roommate(s) sleep. If possible, hang a calendar, indicating major academic events including papers, exams, and presentations. The calendar will keep everyone in the room aware of important dates which necessitate restricted noise and light levels. When you and your roommate(s) follow the actions above, the outcome ought to prevent anger, frustration, and hate.

When you and your roommate(s) have a disagreement, you should be factual in your comments, reiterate policies/agreements, and do not engage in personal attacks. To ensure harmony, personal issues between roommates must be resolved fairly and as soon as possible. Once more, roommates have to directly **communicate**, **communicate**, and **communicate**. If you and your roommate(s) have declared open warfare, though, then you may have to coordinate an intervention. For example, you may have a roommate who steals, uses illegal drugs, has emotional/personality issues, or is just incompatible. On campus, you need to ask the dorm Resident Assistant (RA) for help. Living in the dorm or residence hall, the RA is responsible for ensuring the dorm's quality of life, safety, and security for residents. He/she receives training in conflict resolution between residents. When necessary, he/she can instigate a room change.

Although the majority of college freshmen and sophomores live on-campus in dorms, some juniors and seniors typically have a choice. While you live off-campus, your ability for conflict resolution is harder because of your lease or rental agreement obligation. During roommate(s) selection process, you do not want to make a spur of the moment decision. Whenever possible, you might check-out your roommate candidate on Google or other social media platforms. You are not creepy or stalking the person but investigating someone who may live with you. Then, you ought to interview your potential roommate(s) in person before you share a residence. Thus, his/her answers to your questions may identify beforehand incompatibility and possible conflict. This interview is especially important because rent will be due each month even if a roommate does not pay or moves out early. Having a college roommate, you must understand each other's expectation to have a pleasant experience. Select some or all of the questions from the list below to start the conversation (see Figure 9).

Questions for a Potential Roommate
Getting to know you

1. What's your major? When do you graduate?

2. What are your study habits?

3. Do you have a few or a lot of exams, projects and papers for the semester?

4. What types of things really bug you when sharing a space with someone else?

5. Have you had a roommate(s) before?

6. Tell me about a time you had to resolve a problem with a roommate?

7. When do you need or plan to move in?

8. Tell me what you consider to be quiet hours for studying, relaxing or sleeping?

9. What kind of music do you like? How loud?

10. Are you typically an "early bird "or "late owl"?

Getting down to business

1. What is your source of income to pay the rent, utilities, etc.? Are you currently employed? If yes, how long have you worked there?

2. What would a person who knows you (other than a family member) say about you?

3. How often should we do chores to keep the place clean in particular washing dishes, washing clothes, sweeping, mopping etc.? What cleaning activities do you like and dislike?

4. How do you feel about overnight guests? Should we set a limit or time when guests should stay?

5. How do you feel about TV, radio or noise levels in general while relaxing in the room, sleeping or studying?

6. How do you spend a regular weekend?

7. What are your thoughts regarding smoking, drinking, or drug use?

8. Do you have any dietary restrictions or allergies such as to pet hair, smoke, etc.?

9. Are you open to sharing personal items like shoes, clothes, computer or printer? How do you want to resupply or pay for shared items for instance garbage bags, milk, bread, paper towels, etc.? Should we mark our food or just replace what we drink/eat?

10. Are you bringing any furniture, appliances, or other items to set up in the room? Will you want to paint the walls or decorate with your own style?

11. Do you have a pet or plan on getting one while living here?

Let's Talk...build rapport

Would you mind going out for a coffee or drinks to talk a little more in a few days? (This opportunity allows you to verify compatibility).

Figure 9: Getting to Know a Potential Roommate Questions

Based on the responses, you may have a new roommate or politely reject the individual if major issues, lifestyle, or incompatibility exist. In the end, you and your roommate(s) will be sharing space for at least a semester. The best plan of action is to communicate and respect one another to avoid chaos and confusion.

Section C: Tolerance

At college, you have to be tolerant of other people's race, religion, gender, sexuality, etc. In recent years, college students have been suspended, expelled and arrested for discriminatory and horrific misbehavior, in particular, posting online racial slurs, engaging in sexual harassment/misconduct/disparagement, creating hate-filled homophobic or anti-Semitic videos/websites/tweets, or just bullying others. Additionally, bullying, which includes harassment, threats, or physical violence, is a major problem in high schools and colleges. Bullying can be in person or via social media. Picking on someone because he/she is different or vulnerable is immature, ignorant and hateful. In this day and age, any college student who engages in the aforementioned behaviors must be degenerate or stupid. Campus authorities frequently punish them immediately to send a clear message that intolerance will not be condoned. If you engage in intolerant behavior or actions, then you can and should expect adverse consequences.

Often, intelligence, empathy, civility, curiosity, and open-mindedness are underrated in discourse between individuals. Most people have prejudices because they really do not know about another culture, religion, or race. Your campus may have diverse populations because students come from across the nation as well as many other countries. For instance, on numerous campuses, college students exhibit every type of hairstyle, clothing fashion statement, and cultural/religious/ethnic symbol. It is fascinating and sometimes amusing to "people watch." Your college experience will be enhanced with exposure to others who may not share your values, background or future goals. You also have an excellent opportunity to socialize and discover how to deal with different people. You can create a study abroad experience on your college campus. You may not "love" your neighbor, but you can learn to understand him/her. In other words, you should not be so quick to judge the differences of other people but interact and be open to learning from them. Every person deserves respect and courtesy.

As a child, you exist in a small circle that is your world. Your friends and family probably are similar to you. When you venture out into the world as a young adult to attend college, you have to remember that not everyone is like you. The world is a big place. As of June 2017, there are over 7.6 billion people in the world.[259] Their religions consist of Hinduism, Buddhism, Christianity (includes Catholicism and Protestantism), Judaism, Islam, Daoism and assorted others. Homosexuals, heterosexuals, transgender people, and others share the same planet. Many individuals function and thrive with disabilities such as Down syndrome or navigate through life in a wheelchair. The different U.S. political parties include Republican, Democrat, Libertarian, etc. The college experience offers a hodgepodge of diversity that widens your circle of friends and acquaintances.

You may have prejudices but the problem comes when you turn them into discriminatory or mean actions. Thus, you will not be allowed to violate the morals and values of common decency and acceptance. If you cannot act accordingly, you need to go someplace else. The college community will not tolerate you. In the same vein, you should speak up against bigotry, racism, cruelty, bullying, or intolerance by others. You must not excuse these blatant behaviors/actions against you or someone else because they are wrong. Typically, intolerant behavior festers because individuals do not step in to help. They may feel powerless or fear retaliation from others. Despite these possible fears or uncertainties, you have a moral obligation to immediately report discriminatory actions or bullying to your parents, school administrators, someone in authority, or any reliable adult. Continue to speak up until they intervene. In truth, intolerance thrives in the shadows but withers under public scrutiny.

In their formative years, children are open to new people, ideas, and concepts. They are taught intolerance from their parents or other adults. It is so sad to see a child spout hatred that has no basis in fact. In an experiment, young kids watched a video of wedding proposals and marriages between gay couples in 2013.[260] Some of the kids were surprised by the same-sex couples' marriages but many were caught up in the joy of the occasion. At the time, most of the children were shocked to hear that numerous states banned same-sex marriage. Again, intolerance and hate are taught. To co-exist with others, tolerance and compromise ought to be a part of your character. We share an existence in this world. You should listen, observe and make your own decisions about people. In college, you ought to consider suppressing judgment and practicing openness.

Section D: Physical Fitness

When worrying about your next exam or paper, you are obliged to take care of your physical well-being. Staying fit is a great stress reliever, especially in the high-pressure environment of college. Additionally, daily exercise can help you to burn off excess energy, increase immunity to illness and improve stamina. These benefits, in turn, help you to focus and remain alert in class. As you work out, you are actually increasing your ability to concentrate, earn better grades and graduate on time. Unless you are in ROTC or attending a military service academy, you will have no one to push you to stay in shape while in college. You will be tempted to let your weight take care of itself. That may work for the first few months but you will quickly find that your pants do not fit anymore. Many college students eat too much junk food, drink too much beer, and stay up too many nights into the wee hours. Those students will find a spare tire around their middle by the time they hit their senior year. Typically, it is very common for a student to get the freshman 15 (pounds) due to stress and poor eating habits. Yet, the freshman 15 is nothing to get worried about if the student takes control with physical activity and proper nutrition.

To combat unnecessary extra pounds, you should plan to exercise daily or every other day at least 30 minutes to an hour. The exercise should encompass strength, flexibility and cardiovascular training. Your college's gym probably has aerobics, yoga and exercise equipment available. Since you are paying tuition and fees, you might as well capitalize on using the gym. In addition, you will find almost infinite individual exercise plans on the internet. Another way to exercise is to briskly walk or bike from class to class across campus. Or, you can grab some friends and work out together. The key to a sustainable exercise routine is to find a regimen that you enjoy and can easily do.

While getting in shape, you should consider getting between six and eight hours of sleep nightly if possible. Sleep regenerates your mind, helping you to think clearly. Otherwise, inadequate sleep will make it harder for you to concentrate in class or read (those sometimes boring course assignments) because you are falling asleep. When tired, you also will not want to get up and exercise. In the end, your mind and body will thank you for the exercise and ample sleep.

Section E: Diet

Diet is also important to your physical and mental well-being at college. College can be exhausting; so, you need to function at peak levels in class. Hunger causes weakness in your body and mind. You really cannot live on pizza alone. I know because I tried. Pizza reigns supreme on college campuses. It is quick and easy to order. Although pizza has the four food groups (vegetables, dairy, grains, and meat), it is packed with salt, fat, sugar, and other preservatives. In class, you probably will find it hard to concentrate on an empty stomach. You ought to buy easy snack items that you can pop in your book bag. When you shop, you should try stocking up on fruits and vegetables in particular apples, oranges, bananas, celery, and carrots. Other items might include whole wheat pita bread with hummus, raisins, beef jerky, almonds or other healthy snacks. The more color and variety of your food will ensure you eat a diversified selection of nutrients, minerals, and vitamins. I am not talking about Skittles. Also, you ought to steer toward the healthier selections in your campus's dining facility. If you are unsure about the right things to eat, most schools offer counseling about nutrition and diet.[261] Or, you can create your own menus, using internet resources. You do not have to give up pizza, hot dogs, and chips entirely. You can make these items a treat to intersperse with the good stuff.

Unfortunately, many students suffer from eating disorders, which may include binge eating, anorexia nervosa, and bulimia. Signs of these disorders are excessive exercising, preoccupation with food, distorted body image, fear of gaining weight and a refusal to eat. These disorders affect women and men. The images in the media including television and magazines depict young people who supposedly have easy lives and perfect bodies. Social media especially bombards teens and young adults with these false ideals. In actuality, real-life young women and men will never live up to those expectations or subjective judgments. I want you to understand that the media's "perfect" reality is a myth. No one is perfect. Everyone has trivial physical quirks such as smelly feet, cellulite, wiggly bellies, acne, sweaty hands, hairy knuckles, or bad hair days that turn into years. Instead of surface issues, the most important traits that people should "work on" are their character and how they treat others. As a result, the best way to live your life is to accept and love yourself, which are the truest signs of mental and physical well-being. College life can be stressful and competitive. Your eating disorder may escalate because of daily college requirements, damaging your health more. If suffering from such a malady, you will eventually lose your ability to tackle academics. You must seek professional help immediately. Eating disorders are treatable with long-term counseling. You do not have to hide your disorder or be ashamed. All colleges have student health clinics, which can offer treatment or referrals. With awareness and help, you can meet the challenges of college with a new attitude of mental and physical health.

Another issue with diet is the prevalence of food insecurity on college campuses. Since college is expensive, students may be strapped for money to buy enough food to live. In response, many colleges have created on-campus "food pantries."[262] A food pantry supplies canned goods, bread, peanut butter and other staples to help its hungry clients. The cost is usually free. If you do not have food for the next meal or several days, you should investigate if your college has a food pantry or would consider opening up one.

In addition to diet, you should drink plenty of water each day. Your body is made up of a little over 70% water. You have to replenish it. To add flavor or variety to your water, you can use tea bags, flavor packets, or real fruit juices specifically a wedge of lemon, lime, or orange. These alternatives are inexpensive. Tea bags, flavor packets, and real fruit juices also allow the drinker to control the added sugar. You are saving money and your waistline. In contrast, soda, sports drinks, specialty coffees and juices have massive amounts of sugar.[263] When you drink four or five sodas a day with your meals, specifically, you are consuming unnecessary calories and adding weight to your waistline. For instance, one teaspoon of sugar equals about four grams of sugar. One 12-ounce can of regular Coke contains about nine teaspoons (or 36 grams) of sugar. You might be opening your fifth daily soda today. Imagine you have already swallowed 36 teaspoons (or 144 grams) of sugar. The recommended daily allowance for sugar is about six teaspoons for women and nine teaspoons for men.[264] Any unused sugar above the daily allowance just turns to fat. Over time, substantial sugar consumption particularly found in processed foods and drinks is one of the leading causes of diabetes, obesity and heart disease. So, you ought to read nutrition labels on your food/drinks and verify their sugar content. In moderation, pizza, chips, beer, soda and sleepless nights are O.K. but do not make them mainstays of your college life.

Section F: Mental Health

Mental health is a big problem on college campuses. Most mentally ill people, including those with long-term depression and bi-polar conditions, are not violent or suicidal. Some control their symptoms with medication. Few treatment facilities and beds are available to deal with the huge population of mentally ill people across the nation. Often, hospital emergency rooms only deal in crisis and are inadequate for long-term care. If you suffer from mental illness, you cannot run away from your mental problems by going to college. You will be busy with class assignments, jobs, friends and other distractions. The stressful college atmosphere may exacerbate your mental illness. Unless you are vigilant, you might forget your medication or deliberately stop taking your medication in order to concentrate. At your college, effective mental health treatment requires communication between you, school administrators, the mental health clinic professionals and the police to help and act, as appropriate.

If you suffer from mental illness, you ought to choose and apply to potential schools with appropriate mental health resources. You should research each potential school by contacting the campus mental health center or reviewing the college's website. Questions to ask should include the number and credentials of counseling providers; the cost of individual sessions; the availability of peer-to-peer counseling; and the ability to schedule appointments online.[265] When accepted for enrollment, you can then inform school administrators of your specific needs. Then, you, college administrators, your academic advisor, and campus mental health center can coordinate a viable plan of action to integrate your academic needs with mental health supervision.[266] As a resource, the Leader21 Committee is a comprehensive guide on student mental health rights.[267] It notes that savvy college administrators have established academic protocols to accommodate course withdrawals, authorize class absences for treatment, or communicate with teachers to facilitate working with the student. Otherwise, with the hectic pace of college, your mental health issue can easily escalate into an explosive situation.

While at college, you might be only having trouble coping with your new environment, notably loneliness, academics, relationships, dorm life, stress, anxiety, and homesickness. You do not have to suffer alone. Before reaching an unmanageable state of mental distress, you should seek help immediately. Although you might talk to family or friends, you also ought to contact the campus counseling center. Typically, the campus counseling center is a resource for students in distress. You just may be having troubles with the new environment of campus living. Still, these types of adjustment issues might impact your academic performance. In addition, most college counseling centers typically offer confidential group counseling for diverse student populations such as veterans, students of Color, or lesbian, gay, bisexual, and transgender students. Group counseling sessions can provide support, an avenue to discuss adjustment issues and coping skills regarding your new college environment. Finally, as needed, the college's counseling center can often provide referrals to other campus resources namely academic tutoring.

Your next source of help is your school's mental health services when your emotional distress persists. Mental illness requires comprehensive, long-term treatment. Please understand that mental illness including depression, bipolar disorder, post-traumatic stress disorder, or anxiety disorder is not a character flaw but a legitimate, treatable ailment. Without treatment, psychological issues may adversely affect your ability to function in your classes, lead to poor academic performance, paranoia and isolation. If you are struggling and hurting, there is hope. In the wake of college shootings, colleges are aggressively promoting mental health services, incorporating suicide prevention programs and outside referrals. Many colleges offer access to crisis counseling hotlines on a 24/7 basis, including holidays. To seek additional help, the National Suicide Prevention Lifeline provides emotional support to those in suicidal crisis and emotional distress 24 hours a day, 7 days a week.[268] The help is free and confidential online or via telephone at 1-800-273-8255 (1-800-273-TALK).

In addition, you may request a referral to an outside mental health provider because you may realize that your campus mental health center is not meeting your needs. Outside mental health care providers can run the gamut, including a private mental health professional, the state's social and health services, or national mental health support groups.[269] For an outside referral, you ought to confirm your school mental health clinic's policies and any insurance premium requirements. Since passage of the Affordable Care Act, your parents also should verify if you are covered for off-campus mental health treatment under their health care plan. Before or during a mental health crisis, you should seek aid because a burden is best shared with friends, family, professional counseling and those who want to help you. You are not alone.

A student on the edge might not seek care because of different reasons, for example, the perceived stigma, embarrassment, anxiety about confidentiality, lack of insurance, or fear of dismissal from school.[270] The risk to others as well as the student outweighs these concerns. Fortunately, numerous colleges and universities now emphasize early recognition of students' mental issues and intervention to staff, faculty and other students. While in school, you may observe a friend, roommate, or other person having serious personal issues. Depending on the situation, you may be the first observer of early warning signs. These may include substance abuse, suicidal comments, depression, isolation, menacing threats, violence against others, erratic behavior, or excessive changes in appearance/cleanliness. You must not ignore the problem, hoping that it will fix itself over time. You should speak to the person if you know him/her well. Also, you ought to encourage them to get help through proper mental health channels. Otherwise, you should report the affected person's suspected mental health issues before the problem reaches critical stages. Campus administrators and the police typically have protocols in place to assist in these types of situations. You must immediately notify them as well as your dorm RA.

In 2012, James Holmes killed 12 people and injured 70 at the Aurora Colorado movie theater.[271] He was a neuroscience graduate student at the University of Colorado. According to a CNN report, Holmes told a friend that he wanted to kill people before the shooting. In hindsight, his behavior should have raised warning flags if campus administers, law enforcement or an alert classmate had connected the dots. A myriad of red-tape and privacy issues make many college administrators slow to react. If you do not see results in a timely manner, you should inform your parents. In turn, they need to escalate the issue to the president of the college, the local police chief, and/or the state's attorney general. Do not wait to act. You may save a life or lives.

Life lessons – Chapter 12: College Life
- Do not isolate yourself at college
  - Form a connection with your classmates and college community
  - Join social or academic clubs
  - Participate in or attend your college's sport activities
- Be a good roommate (enough said)
- Intolerant, bullying and discriminatory acts against people for their religion, race, gender, sexual orientation, or nationality will get you suspended, expelled, or arrested faster than you can pack your bags
  - Do not do it!
  - Be civil, curious and open-minded
- Take care of your physical well-being through frequent physical activity like running, walking, biking, yoga, etc.
- You cannot think if you have a poor diet
  - Try to add more color and variety to your food namely vegetables and whole grains
  - Get help if you are suffering from an eating disorder
  - Ask your academic advisor or college administrators if your college has a food pantry that offers free food staples to students
  - Stay away from consuming sugary drinks and drink more water (flavored if needed)
- Many colleges have mental illness protocols in place to help students
  - You must communicate your mental health needs to your school administrator, academic advisor and campus mental health center
  - Ask for help from your college counseling center with issues regarding your new college environment
  - Ask for help from your college mental health clinic if your emotional distress persists
  - If the college mental health clinic is not meeting your needs, ask for an outside referral
  - The National Suicide Prevention Lifeline offers 24/7 suicide prevention and emotional distress support online and/or by telephone, 1-800-273-8255

o When observing a friend or roommate's early warning signs of mental distress such as suicidal comments or menacing threats, you should immediately notify school administrators, your dorm RA and police; ask for your parents' help if the school is slow to respond

CHAPTER 13:
Drugs, Alcohol, and Smoking

This chapter may seem that it is veering off from guiding you in your goal to graduate from college. Many teens and young adults get side-tracked by drugs, alcohol and smoking. Each substance can ruin your health and life when their use becomes excessive or addictive habits. I am not preaching to you but I do have your best interest at heart in bringing up these topics. You may choose to skip the chapter; however, I suggest that you come back and take a few minutes to read it at some point. Each section has no-nonsense advice for the young person who is thinking about experimenting for the first time or those currently at risk.

Ultimately, a drug habit or alcoholism will stop you in your tracks. Under these influences, you will only care about getting your next fix or drink. College and career ambitions will take a back seat. In addition, your continued use of these substances can lead to arrests, mental distress, health problems especially liver disease and death due to overdose. I want you to live in the moment without clouding your mind with foreign substances. Drugs and alcohol can make you forget what happened an hour ago. You may rationalize your drug or extreme alcohol use because you use them recreationally or for escapism. Well, find another hobby.

Instead of drugs and alcohol, you should get high on life. Use your money to buy experiences. For example, buy the boxed set of HBO's "Breaking Bad." You can spend time with your friends, hanging out, eating popcorn, and watching the last season. That is a great way to enjoy life. I want you to notice the irony of "only" watching a series about Methamphetamine (Meth) dealers instead of using meth. In the same way as drugs and alcohol, a smoking addiction wastes your money and affects your health. Nicotine stained hands and teeth are only attractive to other smokers. Also, many colleges ban smokers from smoking in or near campus buildings. People who smoke outside in the dead of winter or the pouring rain have nicotine dependence. Drug usage, alcoholism, and smoking are addictions. Instead, you ought to live your life with a sound, uncontaminated body and mind. First Lady Eleanor Roosevelt famously said, "Life was meant to be lived." Take heed because you have so many dreams to fulfill.

In my personal example, I have had a full life: working, traveling and acquiring experiences while drug, alcohol and smoking free. In your future, you can eat a great meal at a quaint restaurant outside the Louvre museum in Paris, France (oh wait, that was me). You should try kayaking down the Potomac River as the sun rises over the Key Bridge (me, again). Then, there is tandem parachuting over the Ocean City shoreline (yep, me). Or, you can observe the vistas of St. Louis from the Gateway Arch (I loved it). A possibility could be trekking up the Great Wall of China or across the rim of the Grand Canyon (the views were great). Another experience is driving your car down San Francisco's Lombard Street, which is one of the steepest, most winding streets in North America, as the car's bottom makes sparks (That was fun, but not so great for my car). Or, run the 5K portion of the Chicago Marathon (I had a blast). Perhaps, you can ride an elephant in Thailand (I have pictures). Maybe, you would like to see the fireworks on New Year's Eve in South Beach, Florida (been there, done that). Or, you can surf the waves in Lima, Peru (on my bucket list). My adventures don't have to sound so unique; they are accessible to any healthy, driven young person.

Without drugs, alcohol, and smoking, you can find awe, challenge, victory, joy, and entertainment in experiencing life. Incidentally, when you spend copious hours "following" celebrities on television and social media, you are consuming those celebrities' lives like drugs. You are forgetting to live your own life. Frequently, you should put down the smartphone/tablet in order to experience the people and situations in your immediate environment.

Section A: Drugs

I am climbing up on my soapbox and making an impassioned plea for you to stay away from drugs. In 1982, Nancy Reagan, the former First Lady, sponsored a campaign against drugs with the tagline, "Just say 'No.'" At the time, I thought it was the stupidest thing I had ever heard. Drugs were sweeping across the inner cities and dragging down countless lives. Her call was so simple. With time and life experience, I realize that she was right. Substance abuse and addiction are horrible. Numerous people become addicted to prescribed and illegal drugs after the first use. Yet, taking drugs is an individual responsibility. No one can force you to take drugs or prevent you from getting help. In actuality, countless television ads warn people about the negative consequences of using drugs. Parents, the police, politicians, and educators constantly tell young adults to stay away. Still, countless young people embrace and live the drug lifestyle. Unless it is under a doctor's care for pain or any other medical issue, you should not put your future in jeopardy experimenting/using drugs. You have been warned!

If you are of sound mind and body, you should not pollute your system. The number of illegal/synthetic drugs are staggering, including Sizzurp (cough syrup containing Codeine), 25I/N-Bomb (25I-NBoMe), 2C-E, Molly, Salvia, Fentanyl, Heroin, Marijuana, Methamphetamine, Ecstasy, Bath Salts, and DXM.[272] In addition, some users abuse prescription medication namely Oxycotin, Codeine, Methadone, Amphetamines, or Adderall. Some young people also get high using over-the-counter-medication particularly cold medicine. In *The 2012 National Survey on Drug Use and Health*, 23.9 million Americans aged 12 or older used illicit drugs namely hashish, cocaine, crack, or heroin.[273] The same 2012 survey also noted that about 18.9 million Americans used marijuana. In high school and college, drugs typically are available on campus. Teens and young adults may try them out especially in social situations. Your friends may be encouraging or pressuring you to use drugs. I hope that you realize you need to find new friends. These people are trying to turn you into a loser too. Remember, drugs affect each individual differently. Some people have a higher tolerance for drugs based on repeated use over time. A drug may not readily affect one person but may be extremely addictive for another. Do not fall for it.

I want you to know that smart people do not use drugs. Studies have shown that a person's level of education has an impact on rates of substance abuse. According to *The 2012 National Survey on Drug Use and Health*, among adults aged 18 or older, high school dropouts, high school graduates and those with some college typically had higher substance dependency rates than college graduates.[274] The statistics show that informed people stay away from drugs. In fact, the drug sellers/dealers are opportunists who are trying to make money off of you. These people are living and paying their bills while you descend into addiction and despair. If individuals do not use drugs, the cartels will lose their customer base.

Don't live your life in a cloudy haze of drugs. You may convince yourself that you can handle using Ecstasy, Crazy Clown, Bath Salts, Molly, airplane glue, Crack, Meth, Cocaine, Heroin, or whatever poison. The graveyard is full of people who thought they could handle drugs. Let me name a few: Prince, Philip Seymour Hoffman, Whitney Houston, Heath Ledger, Janis Joplin, Corey Montieth, Jimmy Hendrix, and so many others who are not rich or famous. When I see news stories about these talented people, I think "God rest his/her soul, what a waste!" He/she wasted the gifts of talent and life. These people usually combine multiple types of drugs together. Their bodies become so tolerant to their drug of choice that they must use more and more of the drug, which leads to deadly overdoses. As a result, the addicted person is in and out of rehab before he/she can distance himself/herself from drugs. If they survive, they may take years of treatment to get their life back on track. The drug experience is similar to prison in that these addicted people become separated from parents, other family members, and friends. Drug addiction takes work, time, money and commitment. You ought to find something else to do.

Today, Methamphetamine (Meth) and Heroin are poisons of choice for many young people to get high. Both drugs destroy communities because they are cheap and readily accessible on the street. Meth and Heroin consume addicts until they do not care about anything but getting more of these drugs. For instance, Meth wreaks havoc on a person's mind and body. Rehab.com showcases a montage of time-lapse pictures, featuring men and women who were addicted to Meth.[275] If you don't believe me about the ravages of drugs, these pictures do not lie. Zombies do exist. The pictures highlight the horrific transformation of people during their

Meth addicted years. Glassy eyes, acne, sallow skin, yellow/discolored teeth, premature aging, and gaunt features illustrate lives wasted and futures gone wrong. Using Heroin, you will have a similar loss of ambition, physical health, and mental acuity. When you get hooked on either drug, you will throw your college plans and life down the toilet unless you finally seek/obtain medical treatment and counseling.

Additionally, society's mores are changing about marijuana usage. The mixed message is discordant to young people. You should not fall prey to the hype about marijuana. Some people claim that marijuana is no worse than alcohol. In contrast, the U.S. Food and Drug Administration (FDA) has only approved marijuana medications in pill form.[276] Nonetheless, the FDA does not have enough data from long-term scientific study to approve the whole or partial use of the marijuana plant for recreational purposes. Despite the unknowns, thousands of people, including some state legislators, want to decriminalize marijuana usage. These state legislators want the enormous tax revenues from sanctioned marijuana businesses. Dealers/sellers, however, constantly mix ingredients into marijuana, increasing its addictive properties and potency to alter reality. Sadly, marijuana users are inhaling foreign substances into their perfectly healthy lungs or eating marijuana-infused baked goods with the potential for harm. In addition, the distribution and sale of marijuana is a federal crime with mandatory minimum sentencing and fines. Moreover, you may face a felony conviction and jail if the police find that you are in possession of marijuana. Marijuana usage has health concerns and a currently enforced federal law. Thus, you should not fall into the cause célèbre of marijuana.

Any affiliation with drugs can destroy your future if law enforcement catches you in possession of illegal drugs or controlled substances. According to the Bureau of Prisons and the Bureau of Justice Statistics, in 2015, 48.6% of those people in federal prisons and 16% of the people in state prisons were incarcerated for drug offenses.[277] Frequently, low income and minority groups receive harsher and longer sentences in prison for drug offenses due to inadequate legal representation. Furthermore, individuals who are convicted of a drug-related offense or incarcerated in federal/state prison might have federal financial aid suspended or be limited in eligibility for federal student loans or Pell Grants.[278] Thus, a drug felony may side-track many people's dreams of financing their future college education. In reality, the U.S. spends more money on the incarceration of drug offenders than sending young people to college. In one 2013 estimate, the U.S. spent $1 trillion over four decades on the drug war or $51 billion per year at the state and local level.[279] Jail and prison are cruel and often violent places. When you stay away from drugs, you are taking the opportunity to live in a dorm room instead of a prison cell. Unlike college, jails are more likely to teach prisoners how to be better criminals than citizens.

In some states, individuals who are arrested may be charged and convicted of a felony for drug possession/distribution. Often, these parolees experience high unemployment rates after a felony conviction. Depending on the state, government agency, or business, a felony may prevent obtaining licensing/certification in certain career fields in particular security, law enforcement, health care, child care and pharmaceuticals. Some states also prohibit felony offenders from voting. Lastly, the time served in prison separates people from family, friends, and everything that they know.

At this point, you might be applying for a military scholarship or want to join the military. You are putting your goals at risk by using drugs. Many government agencies notably the military and private companies require their personnel to take annual or semi-annual drug tests. If you are caught with illegal substances in your system, you will be fired or never hired. Drug use will put roadblocks in your future. Plus, you should avoid hanging out with drug users. My mother used to say "When you lie down with dogs, you are going to get fleas." In other words, you may be caught up in a police bust because you are with your "friend(s)" who are using/dealing/in possession of drugs. The consequences may include your arrest, your car impounded, your home raided, fines, paying thousands of dollars to a lawyer in order to clear your name, or a felony drug charge/conviction. Your life's goals will be stopped while you fix the mess.

This moment, you may be in the grip of drug addiction. You should seek help from your campus mental health services. They often sponsor counseling and treatment options. Or, the campus mental health center can refer you to off-campus drug addiction rehabilitation programs. Drug addiction is not a character flaw but a treatable disease. Seeking help is the first step toward recovery. Otherwise, you may spiral into a hell of substance abuse, stealing, betrayal of trust, loss of friends/family, jail, mental/physical deterioration, homelessness, despair, loss of dreams, and possibly death. Thus, I am hijacking Nancy Reagan's call to action about substance abuse, "Just say 'No.'"

Section B: Alcohol

People drink alcohol all the time. Often, drinking alcohol and socializing are not problems. When you drink responsibly, you should be able to keep your wits about you and your environment.

Your drinking can become a concern when your alcohol consumption affects other aspects of your life. In college, alcohol abuse can cause issues academically and socially for you. For instance, you can jeopardize your graduation with foolish behavior in particular binge drinking, underage drinking, or driving under the influence of alcohol. In the movies, binge drinking is celebrated as a rite of passage for college students. Binge drinkers consume huge amounts of liquor in a short period of time. On college campuses, numerous students attempt to recreate their nightly or weekly version of the movie "Animal House." In *The 2012 National Survey on Drug Use and Health,* full-time college students between 18 to 22 years old engaged in binge drinking at a rate of 40.1 percent while part-time college students engaged in binge drinking at a rate of 35.0 percent.[280] Additionally, Spring Break Youtube.com videos are a testament to college drinking excesses. These young college students drink until they are sloppy, incoherent, impaired, or passed out. The same 2012 survey claimed "male full-time college students aged 18 to 22 were more likely than their female counterparts to be binge drinkers (45.5 vs. 35.3 percent)."[281] This behavior is reckless regardless of gender or age. Depending on a person's weight, alcohol consumption and duration of intake, he/she could quickly drink beyond intoxication. The result is unconsciousness, alcohol withdrawal, a coma, or possibly death. Other impacts of alcohol abuse are traffic-related accidents and alcohol poisoning. The consequences outweigh the temporary highs of binge drinking.

Danger lurks for the unsuspecting at parties on or off campus. The National Institute on Alcohol Abuse and Alcoholism (NIAAA) cited that "696,000 students between the ages of 18 and 24 are assaulted by another student who has been drinking."[282] While some students are drinking to excess, they are likely to fight or assault others as the alcohol flows. Hopefully, while attending such a party, you will not get caught in the snare of flying fists or the dragnet of the police. The same NIAAA statistics also claimed that between the ages of 18 and 24 years old, "97,000 students reported experiencing alcohol-related sexual assault or date rape."[283] While drunk, you might get into a fight, catch an STI, have an unplanned pregnancy, or be the victim of sexual assault/rape. You need to be aware of and avoid the dangers of excessive/binge drinking or associating with those who do.

In many states, college students under the legal limit of 21 years of age are minors and cannot drink legally.[284] Alas, college parties or fraternities engaged in hazing are notorious for the free flow of alcohol and underage drinking. If you are under age and drinking, you can receive punishment, including revocation of your driver's license, fines, or enrollment in an alcohol education program. With a few statutory exceptions, when you permit or encourage underage drinking, you can be subject to fines, arrest, and imprisonment. The consequences of condoning or participating in underage drinking are enormous. During a party at a frat house, Dustin Starks, a University of North Texas student, fell to his death from a balcony after a night of excessive drinking.[285] He was 20 years old. The campus police issued arrest warrants for seven people for allegedly furnishing alcohol to Stark. Underage drinking ruined eight lives, which was senseless and avoidable.

When you drink or are otherwise impaired, you must not get behind the wheel of a car. As a licensed driver, you are responsible for your car's safe operation, protecting yourself, your passengers and other drivers. When driving, you must be focused and not be distracted by calls, texts, other occupants, or impaired with alcohol. I also implore you to reconsider riding in a car with a driver who has been drinking or is otherwise distracted. In fact, driving is a privilege that can be suspended or revoked. Unfortunately, the NIAAA estimated that "1,825 college students between the ages of 18 and 24 died from alcohol-related unintentional injuries, including motor vehicle crashes."[286] When you drive drunk, you may encounter several scenarios. While you sit in a pool of your own puke, the police will cordon off the scene of your wrecked car accident to gather evidence. Hopefully, you only hurt yourself. More than likely, you may have killed others in your car, other people in another car, or someone walking/bicycling along the road which equates to lives destroyed. Do not do this to yourself, the other people, or your family. Your parent(s) will not be attending your college graduation because you may be recuperating in a hospital from alcohol-related injuries, in jail, or dead.

Your eyes are probably glazing over or you have started to skim. You are probably saying to yourself, "I'm young and can handle my drinking." Drinking alcohol excessively can sneak up on you. Alcohol-impaired people take chances with their safety and reputation because they rationalize unwise behavior especially unprotected sex, binge drinking, going home with strangers, reckless driving, walking down the center-lane in traffic, or vandalism. If your drunken friends are puking or peeing behind the closest building, do you really want to follow their lead? Besides the mess, you and your friends will probably get arrested for disorderly conduct and indecent exposure. Since many college campuses also have cameras almost everywhere, your mayhem might be featured in a continuous loop on Youtube.com. How do you want to define yourself? You may feel that drinking gives you courage, acceptance from your peers, or independence as an adult. Excessive drinking only instigates uncharacteristic behavior.

Now is the time to ask for help. If drinking is affecting your personality, your grades, and your life, you should seek treatment at your on-campus or off-campus mental health center. The trained professionals can offer recommendations for your return to sobriety. You are smart, attractive, and unique. You are destined for so many wonderful experiences and accomplishments in the future as you graduate, work, travel, play, and live. Be yourself; so, people will come to know and appreciate the real you. You should enjoy your youth without excessive alcohol consumption, underage drinking or driving while impaired. You can still be the life of the party.

Section C: Smoking

When you smoke, you are sucking into your lungs at least 7000 chemicals in particular ammonia, carbon monoxide, nicotine, acetone, arsenic, tar, and formaldehyde of which at least 69 of these ingredients cause cancer.[287] You may think that smoking or chew makes you look cool or helps relieve stress. Those reasons are illusions. By smoking, you are putting your health at risk. A person's smoking habit is also a risk to others who inhale the second-hand smoke. Many colleges and universities ban smoking on campus mainly in classrooms and dorms. Cigarettes, cigars, hookahs, smokeless cigarettes, e-cigarettes, Juuls, chewing tobacco, or snuff have no health benefits. Tobacco usage only has disadvantages. The cosmetic issues consist of bad breath, persistent coughing, a raspy voice, smelly hair, yellowed teeth, and nicotine stained hands. Non-smokers typically do not want to kiss smokers. As a smoker, you have already decreased your dating pool. Also, smoking seriously cuts down your life expectancy due to cancer of the jaw, lungs, lip, esophagus, larynx (voice box), mouth, throat, kidney, bladder, pancreas, stomach, and cervix.[288] Other medical issues abound namely heart disease, infertility, stroke, gum disease, and asthma. None of these health problems sound sexy or cool.

Another shortcoming of smoking cigarettes is the cost. Cigarette sales and taxes are a great way for states to generate revenue from addicted smokers. Cigarette smokers are willing to pay anything to get their hit of nicotine. In 2017, for example, the state of New York proposed taxes that would increase the cost of a pack to about $13.[289] If a New Yorker smokes a pack a day, he/she will pay $4,745 over the course of a year. You can spend that kind of money on a trip to Disney World, paying for a semester in college, or throwing a party for a bunch of your friends. Smoking is an addiction that will empty your pockets while killing you. Although you are exercising and eating right, you are wasting your efforts by smoking. You also are making the state, the tobacco company, its shareholders, the cancer doctor, and the dentist very rich. Smokes and chew are for chumps.

Granted, nicotine is an addictive drug, which makes smoking very hard to quit. The Centers for Disease Control and Prevention (CDC) analyzed smoking cessation data from a survey conducted over a 10-year period. In 2010, the CDC claimed about 68.8% of adult smokers wanted to quit smoking but only approximately 6.2% actually stopped smoking.[290] To help students kick the habit, colleges' student health clinics typically offer free smoking cessation programs. These programs may include nicotine replacement or counseling. If you want or have tried to stop, you ought to check out your campus' smoking cessation resources. You will increase your life expectancy, improve your lung function and reduce the risk of smoking-related cancer. In college, you want to run to your classes and breathe freely instead of carrying an oxygen tank with you due to smoking. With help, if needed, you should completely sever your ties with smoking products.

Life lessons – Chapter 13: Drugs, Alcohol and Smoking
- Drug addiction wastes your money and adversely affects your health
  - Just say "No!"
  - Drugs affect people differently and can lead to addiction for some
  - Numerous famous and ordinary people populate the graveyard due to drugs
  - Marijuana usage can negatively impact your health, freedom, job prospects and future
  - Drug addiction takes work, time, money and commitment; so, find another pastime and get help
- Excessive drinking breeds poor judgment and behavior
  - You can jeopardize your graduation with binge drinking, underage drinking and driving under the influence
  - Binge drinking can lead to withdrawal, coma or even death
  - Underage drinking can lead to revocation of your license, fines or enrollment in an alcohol education program
  - Driving under the influence can lead to your death, others in another car, or a friend in your car
  - Drunk people are not cute but dangerous to themselves and others
  - Get help for alcohol addiction from your campus' student health clinic or off-campus referral
- Smoking products are health risks
  - Tobacco smoke releases at least 7000 chemicals into your lungs
  - Get help for your smoking addiction from your campus' student health clinic

CHAPTER 14:
Graduation

Wow, you are almost there. Graduation is weeks away. With your college diploma, you will be one of approximately 30% of the population that has earned a bachelor's degree or higher. You should be proud of yourself and your accomplishment! You are graduating in your major and on your scheduled timetable. Think about the many hours that you spent studying, researching, reading and writing. Take a moment and reflect on the countless course papers, exams, projects and presentations that you turned in. Then, consider every extracurricular activity and sports games that you attended. In addition, you have made many friends who you will miss or hope to see again. As you look back, hopefully, you will remember an exciting and truly wonderful college experience. You have done everything right and cannot wait to get into the real world. Surely, you can sit back and soak in the achievement of being a college graduate. Not yet! You have a few actions to finish before your graduation.

Section A: Exit Counseling

To ensure students are eligible to graduate, colleges may require that graduating seniors complete an administrative checklist also known as an exit counseling checklist. Filling out the checklist, you are ensuring that your college student records, account balances and other administrative obligations are completely satisfied. In contrast, some colleges host an online web portal for students to check their graduation clearance status. As a student checks in, each department/office administrator will check-off a "completed" status if everything is in order. When the graduating student finishes each department's requirements, he/she will see a final completed status. Then, he/she is ready to graduate and march down the aisle at the commencement ceremony. Such a portal may be an option for you. You then will update your status frequently until you have a fully cleared status. Through your student online portal, you also should print a copy of your unofficial transcript for your records. Your transcript is important because it displays your completed classes and semester GPAs. Your college might not require exit counseling but you may have issues that will prevent you from graduating on time. So, you should perform your own exit counseling. At a minimum, you should meet with your academic advisor, a bursar's office representative and an agent of the Registrar's Office.

At least the semester prior to graduation, you should visit your old friend, your academic advisor. You and your academic advisor will review your two or four-year graduation plan. With him/her, you should verify that you will have the correct number of credits to graduate and ensure your graduation timeline is correct. You should alert him/her if you are having any academic problems in your final few classes. He/she will make sure that you have developed a plan to fix the issues. Some graduating seniors extend past their original graduation date due to a failed class or late submission of an assignment. You should not be one of them because you have obtained academic help early, as necessary, to pass your classes.

At the bursar/financial aid office or online, you must check your college student account and billing statements. You should verify if you have any outstanding fees/bills. These would include unpaid tuition, late fees, outstanding parking tickets, or delinquent health service payments. Normally, your college's bursar/financial aid office should notify you of your debts at the start of each semester. You ought to know and satisfy your college financial obligations as they accrue. Your school will not release your official transcript or diploma until your student account balance is cleared. You might be thinking "So, what?" Graduate schools, internships, or even employers will not accept your application without an official transcript. The official transcript shows your grades and confirms that you graduated. They will not accept your unofficial copy as proof. You also will be unsuccessful in skating out from college without paying. Despite a grace period, your college may even turn over your debt to a collection agency.

If you borrowed federal or private student loans, you should meet with a bursar/financial aid office representative. He/she will conduct a loan exit counseling session to ensure that you understand your repayment responsibilities and requirements. To prevent future problems, you also ought to make certain that your federal and private student loan lenders have your contact information, including a working telephone number. By the end of the meeting, you must know the total loan amount, when your payments start, the monthly repayment amount, and where to send payment. This is also your time to ask questions, take notes and obtain copies of your loan paperwork. Additionally, to assist borrowers, the Federal Student Aid website offers the National Student Loan Data System (NSLDS) student access.[291] NSLDS is the U.S. Department of Education's central database that tracks the number, type and total amount of an individual's federal financial aid including federal student loans and grants. The NSLDS system also alerts a student if he/she is reaching his/her lifetime limits in federal student loan amounts or "maximum eligibility period." In contrast, your college may not have handled your private student loans. Then, you should contact your lender or loan servicer to confirm your loan repayment requirements prior to graduation. Although it will not stop your graduation, you must take steps to stay on top of your federal or private student loans. Otherwise, you will adversely impact yourself or your co-signer's credit and financial well-being for failure to make repayment.

Your next contact will be with the Registrar's Office to confirm your graduation eligibility. Otherwise, the Registrar's Office will notify graduating seniors that they must apply for graduation at least the semester prior to graduation. If you miss the deadline to apply, you may have to wait until the next available graduation date. When you apply for graduation, you will indicate your expected graduation semester and request a verification of your graduation eligibility. You will also verify your permanent address for diploma delivery and the spelling of your name. When the Registrar's Office receives your application, a representative will assess whether you have tentatively earned enough college credits and completed all degree requirements. When the review is satisfactory, the Registrar's Office will confirm your current graduation date or notify you of a change. After final course grades are posted, the Registrar's Office will conduct a final review of your student record and notify you of your degree completion. At the commencement ceremony, you and your fellow graduates will receive empty diploma folder jackets. You are probably shocked by this tidbit. Some students sign-up for commencement and walk but do not graduate. They falter in their last semester due to incomplete academic requirements or unpaid student accounts. After the commencement ceremony, colleges normally will mail diplomas to cleared graduates. In summary, you must meet/contact your academic advisor, a financial office representative, and Registrar's Office agent to confirm your graduation status. Failure to do so will prevent your goal of graduating on time. Take the initiative and get it done.

<u>Section B: Graduation Costs</u>

Graduation costs money. Your high school graduation was only two or four-years ago. Yet, your college will require you again to purchase your regalia, which include the cap and gown, departmental hood and tassel, in order to participate in the commencement ceremony. You do not have to attend; however, you should because you worked hard and earned that graduation walk. If money is a concern, you ought to budget a practical amount to spend on optional items namely a class ring, official announcements, invitations, graduation photos and a diploma frame. Typically, college-sponsored vendors sell them. Thus, you should check your finances to determine if you can and should buy:

- The class ring signifies your membership as a college graduate of your school. Since only 30% of the U.S. population has a bachelor's degree or higher, a college ring is similar to a Super Bowl ring. They can be expensive depending on the stones and metal used. A class ring purchase is strictly voluntary but holds special significance for a graduating student who buys it.
- Announcements and invitations can be expensive based on fancy paper, tissue inserts, envelope seals and other accessories. Often, students buy huge amounts to send to

friends and family. After graduation, these students may have dozens of unused announcements/invitations. Instead, you might purchase the minimum amount of invitations then send out announcements that you create in MS Word or MS PowerPoint.

- Official graduation photos capture the student walking across the commencement stage, receiving his/her diploma envelope, and shaking hands with the college dean/chancellor/ provost. The cost of graduation photos vary based on the sizes and quantities purchased.

- A diploma frame makes your diploma look official, signifying that you met all degree requirements to graduate. You ought to decide on a budget and research frame vendors in particular local and online vendors. They may be cheaper than the college-sponsored vendor. NOTE: You earned your college diploma; so, you ought to frame and display it.

Section C: Graduation Day

On graduation day, you do not want to be stressed and anxious. The day should be a culmination of your great academic work. Some students mar the day by getting the commencement ceremony's details wrong. You should pay attention to your college's graduation announcements. Many colleges have a graduation "frequently asked question" website, spelling out procedures and policies. Or, most schools post information about graduation on their websites at least one to two months ahead of the date. They will provide the date, the location, driving directions, parking information, the commencement ceremony start time, the graduate line-up time, and other vital details. You should read this information carefully. You do not want to be one of those students who come running up lost, dazed, and confused with their family in tow to the information booth on graduation day. Although graduation is your day, you should think about your invited guests. For the ceremony, you and your guests ought to arrive on time. On time means you should show up at least one hour to an hour and a half before the ceremony begins. Otherwise, there is no way that you can park, seat your guests and get to the line-up location. Many colleges will not allow students to march if they are late. Before you leave your guests to line-up, you should coordinate an after-graduation meeting location or distribute your cell phone number to them.

Your school may have a commencement practice. You should use the chance to scope out where your parents and friends will sit. You ought to locate the wheelchair accessible areas especially elevators or ramps designated for guests with wheelchairs or guest unable to navigate stairs. As the graduate, you also are responsible for e-mailing or mailing graduation information (who, what, where, etc.) to all of your invitees. Other things to include would be a schematic of the graduation venue, hotel accommodations and the closest airport for guests flying from out of town. This prior planning will reduce the chaos and confusion on the special day.

Regarding graduation day, this moment should not be the first time that you have put on your cap and gown. Previously, you should have made sure all of the items are in the regalia bag. Also, you should shake out your gown and (sigh) iron it. You ought to consider attaching two or three safety pins to the inside of your gown in case something comes loose. Although the cap and gown will cover your clothes, you may take pictures or go out with your guests later. Your best bet is dress nicely with appropriate shoes (no flip-flops or tennis shoes). In addition, you probably should consider wearing comfortable, broken-in shoes. You and your classmates will be standing for quite a long time before the graduation procession. You will be hating life if your feet are in pain. In addition, you should eat a quick breakfast or lunch because some ceremonies can last two to three hours. Also, you might put a few small snacks such as packaged peanut butter crackers, cheese crackers, or trail mix in a pocket. The snacks will fill any hunger pangs during the ceremony.

At the end of the main campus-wide ceremony, your biggest feat will be to meet with your guests for congratulations, photos, and maybe even a celebratory dinner at a local restaurant. Your family and friends will envelop you in congratulatory hugs and kisses. Hopefully, they have provided encouragement, love, and advice over the course of your college journey. You may have done the work but you did not accomplish the feat alone. You ought to give your thanks and praise to them as well as any higher power that guides you. If you are at graduation alone, you still have the support of those who could not attend. In either case, you should be proud of yourself because you have reached your goal. You can take a breath and absorb this moment. You are a college graduate! Congratulations, you have made it to the finish line of this chapter in your life.

Section D: After Graduation

Now that you have graduated on time, you hopefully are gainfully employed in a fantastic new career that pays well. Your job should challenge you and exercise the key knowledge and skills earned from getting your college degree. If you have not started before, you should begin saving at least six months worth of living expenses. After graduation, you probably had to pay the security deposit and rent for your first apartment; pay for gas or transportation; and, other essential expenses as appropriate. Still, unexpected emergencies may happen. A medical crisis, sustained unemployment or other events can prevent you from earning income to pay your college tuition, student loans, and bills. Your savings can help you to ride out these types of hardships. When you have accumulated a savings cushion, your next course of action is to invest your money as early as possible. When you invest, you will understand the vital distinction between accumulating financial assets for financial freedom versus amassing liabilities especially high-end clothes/shoes, expensive cars, and restaurant receipts. Investing encompasses wealth builders such as contributing to a Traditional/ROTH Individual Retirement Account, putting money in an index fund, having a portfolio of individual stocks and bonds, or owning an income producing rental property. You have to do your homework on the best investments for your situation. Similar to saving, investing is a systematic process that should occur over time.

At this point, you may feel that you don't have enough money to invest. Then, if possible, you ought to consider decreasing your expenses, earning more, and/or obtaining a part-time job in order to use that extra money solely for investment. Your money decisions today will positively or negatively impact your future financial picture. Yet, you do not want to deny yourself completely or live like a pauper. Instead, you want to live a sensible financial life. Thus, you are not saving and investing for the sake of counting your money in your old age. You are acquiring wealth; so that, you can live the life you want, including traveling, taking classes, spending time with friends, working at your dream job, volunteering, or spending time with your grandchildren (hopefully, you have no kids yet). In 2018, Social Security's average payout is about $1,400 in monthly income or $16,800 annually. That amount is virtually nothing in today's economy especially as the costs of housing, goods, and services continue to soar. For numerous retirees, this amount is their *only* source of income because they failed to save or invest. Therefore, investing is a hedge against inflation (rising costs) as well as poverty in retirement.

As you invest, you ought to be leery of financial scammers and charlatans who will try to part you from your money. They do not have formal financial training or professional certifications. If an investment opportunity sounds too good to be true, it probably is a scam. I caution you to be very critical and cautious. You should question, investigate, and verify anyone or any financial vehicle that promises outrageous returns. The burden is on you to perform your due diligence. Do not invest in something that you do not fully understand. Also, you ought to discuss the pros and cons of any investment with a trusted friend, mentor, or relative to prevent making a decision in isolation. When you do business with any company, especially an investment firm, I suggest that you search the appropriate regulatory board's website as well as Google or Yelp the firm's representative and/or company for any complaints or poor reviews. If you seek financial advice, you should interview a few fee-based certified financial planners (CFPs). A CFP is a fiduciary who counsels clients about investment management and puts their clients' interests first.[292] He/she does not work on commission. Each CFP has passed rigorous exams to obtain the CFP certification. You ought to ensure the selected CFP has a pristine reputation, at least eight years of experience and will work with you toward reaching your financial goals.

Financial gurus including Michelle Singletary (National Public Radio financial contributor), Clark Howard (consumer expert and host of the Clark Howard Show), Mellody Hobson (CBS financial contributor), Dave Ramsey (financial author and radio personality) and Jill Schlesinger (CBS financial contributor) provide practical advice about personal finance. They explain the benefits of saving and investing, dollar cost averaging, dividends, diversification, and other solid monetary principles through their podcasts, books, blogs, websites, and appearances. Their books are usually available in public libraries for check out or download as e-Books. Or, you can read these gurus' online articles. Another good source is CNN's Money 101 Guide to Financial Freedom website.[293] It discusses budgeting, banking basics, investing, and other useful topics. In addition, apps like Robinhood, Wealthfront, and Acorns put investing at your fingertips with a smartphone download.[294] Lastly, feedthepig.org educates on financial subjects in interactive and fun ways.[295] Savings and investments are means to future wealth and financial health. Yet again, money is a tool that you must learn to use effectively in order to have a level of comfort, health, and security in everyday life. Since you have increased your financial literacy as you obtained your college degree, you are financially ready to conquer the brave new world of working (or starting a business), earning an income, and living independently.

Section E: Conclusion

Your college degree is important for a better salary, lower unemployment, and long-term stability. As a high school drop-out or high school graduate, you will find it difficult to obtain high lifetime earnings and thrive in the job market. Otherwise, you will need marketable specialized skills, talent and/or knowledge. For some, a technical program or apprenticeship will provide licensing and certification to become blue collar workers. For others, they will need to earn two-year degrees depending on their career fields. A four-year college is a launching pad to a college graduate's professional career. Since the world is a big place, there are unlimited paths to success. Hopefully, your path will help fuel your desire to be a life-long learner. In today's globalized world, the U.S. needs individuals who are innovative, imaginative, and technically skilled. With your certification/licensing or college degree, you should use your newly earned knowledge and skills to positively impact your community and the country.

If you attend college, your goal is to graduate on time within your two or four-year degree program. When feasible, you want to graduate with the least amount of debt. You cannot survive on a hope and a prayer when it comes to attending and paying for college. You and your parent(s) must make college preparation and financial decisions as early as your ninth grade year in high school. Although high school guidance counselors and teachers can offer input, you must take the initiative to research potential colleges and their costs. You should be realistic about what you can afford to pay after your parents have provided how much they can and will pay for your degree. You and your parents also must seek out the means to fund college namely scholarships, grants, tuition assistance and working. The decision to attend a particular college has to be thoughtful and detailed. In addition, you must take the appropriate rigorous high school classes that will prepare you for college coursework particularly in math, English and the sciences. You must study and hone these skills and knowledge while in high school.

On the first day of class, the clock starts ticking. In high school, hopefully, you researched various interests and career fields. Your college exposure should solidify if a particular major/degree is right for you. As soon as possible, you must select a major and attend those college courses that fulfill your degree requirements. At college, you will read a lot, write endlessly and engage in critical thinking. Additionally, you are obligated to attend classes, take notes, complete assignments on time, and contribute to the discussion. You might need help at any time during your journey to graduation. You must be proactive. Your academic advisor is your guide. Your two or four-year academic plan is your roadmap to keep you on track toward graduation. You also have other resources namely qualified, inspiring teachers (O.K, not all), TAs, your academic department and online resources. Ask for academic help as early as possible. Despite all of the help provided to you, your major may not be a good fit. You have to make an informed decision about switching majors. Yet again, you should obtain input from your academic and financial office advisors.

College is not studying 24 hours/7 days a week. You must connect with your classmates and the college community. Your fun, however, needs to be tempered with safety. To make it to graduation, you must take responsibility for prudent decisions and actions primarily concerning drugs, alcohol and relationships/sex. From starting college to the end, the goal should remain constant: graduate on time and obtain your degree.

Sadly, we are at the end of the road. If you are in high school, college bound, or currently in college, you have the smarts, desire and now the knowledge to obtain your college degree. If you are graduating college, I hope this book has helped you along the way to overcome some of the obstacles that many college students face.

When you graduate from college, you will join a select group that represents a small fraction of the U.S. population. Take a bow. College is just one chapter in your life; so, turn the page to a brighter future. Do not let distractions, other people, or fear stop you from your dream. You can do it!

Life lessons – Chapter 14: Graduation
- Conduct an exit counseling at your college with your academic advisor, the financial aid office and the Office of the Registrar to ensure that you have satisfied graduation requirements
  - Apply for graduation
  - Pay any outstanding balances on your student account
  - Obtain all information on repayment terms, concerning your federal and/or private student loans
  - Make sure the registrar has your correct future contact information
- Budget funds to pay for your regalia at a minimum because you earned the honor to walk down that commencement aisle
- Save yourself and your guests grief by showing up on time and at the right location for the commencement ceremony
  - Notify guests in advance of who, what, why, etc.
  - Shake out your regalia and make sure everything is there
- Frame your diploma and proudly hang it up on a wall
- You graduated on time with the least amount of debt – Take a bow!
- Save and invest for today and tomorrow
- I enjoyed taking the college graduation journey with you. Congratulations and my best hopes for your continued success and accomplishments.

Acronyms

Advancement Placement (AP)

American Association of Community Colleges (AACC)

Bureau of Justice Statistics (BJS)

Centers for Disease Control and Prevention (CDC)

Certified Financial Planners (CFPs)

Consumer Financial Protection Bureau (CFPB)

Chief Executive Officer (CEO)

Enterprise Learning Management System (ELMS)

Fair Isaac Credit Organization (FICO)

Federal Bureau of Investigation (FBI)

Free Application for Federal Student Aid (FAFSA)

Grade Point Average (GPA)

Institute for College Access & Success (TICAS)

International Baccalaureate (IB)

Massive Open Online Courses (MOOCs)

Methamphetamine (Meth)

Montgomery College (MC)

National Center for Education Statistics (NCES)

National Collegiate Honors Council (NCHC)

National Institute on Alcohol Abuse and Alcoholism (NIAAA)

National Student Loan Data System (NSLDS)

Office of Multi-Ethnic Student Education (OMSE)

Public Broadcasting Service (PBS)

Reserve Officers Training Corps (ROTC)

Resident Assistant (RA)

Science, Technology, Engineering, or Math (STEM)

Sexually Transmitted Infections (STIs)

Teaching Assistants (TAs)

UMCP Office of the Registrar (TESTUDO)

University of Maryland-College Park (UMCP)

University of Wisconsin-Milwaukee (UWM)

United States Military Academy (USMA)

List of Figures

Index

Bibliography

"10 Very Successful People Without A College Degree." BuzzFeed, Inc. January 17, 2013. Accessed June 2015. http://www.buzzfeed.com/suits/very-successful-people-without-a-college-degree.

"2016 NCIC Missing Person and Unidentified Person Statistics." FBI. gov. January 20, 2017. Accessed November 26, 2017. https://www.fbi.gov/file-repository/2016-ncic-missing-person-and-unidentified-person-statistics.pdf/view.

"25 Colleges and Universities Ranked by Their OpenCourseWare." Learn.org. 2003-2017. Accessed November 25, 2017. https://learn.org/articles/25_Colleges_and_Universities_Ranked_by_Their_OpenCourseWare.html.

"A Stronger Nation 2016 ©2016." Lumina Foundation for Education, Inc. April 2016. Accessed November 2017. http://strongernation.luminafoundation.org/report/2016/.

"About MC." Montgomery College. 2016. Accessed July 2016. http://www.montgomerycollege.edu/.

Academic Catalogue 2013-2014. Volume XXXI: U.S. Edition, DeVry Institute of Technology, 2013. July 29, 2013. Accessed December 2013. https://www.devry.edu/d/US_Catalog.pdf.

"Academic Scholarships and Merit Scholarships." *Scholarships.com*. 2018. Accessed August 19, 2018. https://www.scholarships.com/financial-aid/college-scholarships/scholarships-by-type/academic-scholarships-and-merit-scholarships/.

"Academies of Louisville." *Jefferson County Public Schools*. 2017. Accessed June 8, 2018. https://www.jefferson.kyschools.us/academies-louisville.

"Access Your Full File Disclosure." LexisNexis Personal Reports. 2017. Accessed November 16, 2017. https://personalreports.lexisnexis.com/access_your_full_file_disclosure.jsp.

"Accreditation - Institution Search, U.S. Department of Education Database of Accredited Postsecondary Institutions and Programs." Office of Post Secondary Education, U.S. Department of Education. 2017. Accessed November 09, 2017. http://ope.ed.gov/accreditation/Search.aspx.

"Accreditation: What does Accreditation Mean?" Digital Properties, LLC. 2013. Accessed March 2015. https://www.50states.com/college-resources/accreditation.htm.

"Add a citation and create a bibliography: Word." Microsoft. 2017. Accessed November 22, 2017. https://support.office.com/en-us/article/Add-a-citation-and-create-a-bibliography-17686589-4824-4940-9c69-342c289fa2a5.

"Advising Policies, Undergraduate Computer Science at UMD." University of Maryland, College Park. Accessed November 17, 2013. http://undergrad.cs.umd.edu/advising-policies.

Alcohol Facts and Statistics." National Institute on Alcohol Abuse and Alcoholism, U.S. Department of Health and Human Services. June 2017. Accessed November 29, 2017. https://www.niaaa.nih.gov/alcohol-health/overview-alcohol-consumption/alcohol-facts-and-statistics.

"Alcohol Policy Information System - Underage Drinking Maps & Charts." National Institute on Alcohol Abuse and Alcoholism, U.S. Department of Health and Human Services. 2016. Accessed November 29, 2017. http://alcoholpolicy.niaaa.nih.gov/Underage_Drinking_Maps_and_Charts.html.

American Civil Liberties Union. *Know Your Rights and Your College's Responsibilities: Title IX and Sexual Assault.* Women's Rights Project. Accessed December 13, 2017. https://www.aclu.org/files/pdfs/womensrights/titleixandsexualassaultknowyourrightsandyourcollege%27sresponsibilities.pdf.

"America's Top Colleges." Forbes. 2014. Accessed April 2014. http://www.forbes.com/top-colleges/list/.

"America's Top Colleges - United States Military Academy." Forbes. 2013. Accessed May 2015. http://www.forbes.com/colleges/united-states-military-academy/.

"America's Top Colleges - University of Maryland, College Park." Forbes. 2013. Accessed March 2015. http://www.forbes.com/colleges/university-of-maryland-college-park/.

"America's Top Colleges - University of Maryland, College Park." Forbes. 2016. Accessed October 22, 2016. http://www.forbes.com/colleges/university-of-maryland-college-park/.

"America's Top Colleges - University of Wisconsin, Milwaukee." Forbes. 2013. Accessed July 2013. http://www.forbes.com/colleges/university-of-wisconsin-milwaukee/.

"America's Top Colleges - University of Wisconsin, Milwaukee." Forbes. 2016.
    Accessed October 22, 2016. http://www.forbes.com/colleges/university-of-
    wisconsin-milwaukee/.

Andrews, Linda Landis. *How to Choose a College Major*. New York, NY: McGraw-Hill,
    2006.

"AP Course Ledger." The College Board, University of Oregon. 2002-2016. Accessed
    February 13, 2015. https://apcourseaudit.epiconline.org/ledger/.

"Application Deadlines." The Campus Commons, University Language Services. 1998-
    2017. Accessed November 09, 2017.
    http://www.universitylanguage.com/guides/us-university-and-us-college-
    application-deadlines/.

"*Annual Credit Report.com*." Central Source, LLC. 2018. Accessed May 5, 2018.
    https://www.annualcreditreport.com/index.action.

"Associate Degree Programs Online & Classroom - DeVry." DeVry Institute of
    Technology. 2013. Accessed March 2014. http://www.DeVry.edu/degree-
    programs/associate-degree.html.

"Avoiding Scams." *Federal Student Aid, U.S. Department of Education*. 2018. Accessed
    August 8, 2018. https://studentaid.ed.gov/sa/types/scams.

"Back to School Statistics." Fast Facts - National Center for Education Statistics, U.S.
    Department of Education. January 1, 2014. Accessed February 6, 2015.
    http://nces.ed.gov/fastfacts/display.asp?id=372.

Bader, John B. *Dean's list: eleven habits of highly successful college students*. Baltimore,
    MD: The Johns Hopkins University Press, 2011.

"Bankrate.com Credit Card Minimum Payment Calculator -- How long will it take to pay
    off credit cards?" Bankrate.com. 2017. Accessed November 17, 2017.
    https://www.bankrate.com/calculators/credit-cards/credit-card-minimum-
    payment.aspx.

"Before & After Drugs: The Horrors of Methamphetamines - Infographic." Rehabs.com.
    2012. Accessed May 2014. https://www.rehabs.com/explore/meth-before-and-
    after-drugs/infographic.php#.WhMkFyaWzIU.

"Best Colleges - University of Maryland, College Park." U.S. News & World Report L.P.
    November 2017. Accessed November 09, 2017. https://www.usnews.com/best-
    colleges/university-of-maryland-2103.

"Best Colleges - United States Military Academy." U.S. News & World Report L.P.
    2013. Accessed May 2015.

http://colleges.usnews.rankingsandreviews.com/best-colleges/united-states-military-academy-2893.

"Best Colleges - United States Military Academy." Map. U.S. News & World Report L.P. 2013. Accessed May 2015. http://colleges.usnews.rankingsandreviews.com/best-colleges/united-states-military-academy-2893/map?int=c6b9e3

"Best Colleges - University of Maryland, College Park." Map. U.S. News & World Reports L.P. 2013. Accessed June 2015. http://colleges.usnews.rankingsandreviews.com/best-colleges/university-of-maryland-college-park-2103/map?int=c6b9e3.

"BibMe: Free Bibliography & Citation Maker - MLA, APA, Chicago, Harvard." BibMe, a Chegg Service. 2017. Accessed November 22, 2017. http://www.bibme.org/.

"Birth Control Methods." Bedsider. 2013. Accessed March 13, 2014. http://bedsider.org/methods.

"Browse Student Organizations - OrgSync at UMD." University of Maryland, College Park. 2013. Accessed July 2015. http://orgsync.umd.edu/browse_student_organizations.

Byrne, Richard. "7 Resources for Detecting and Preventing Plagiarism." Free Technology for Teachers. August 24, 2010. Accessed November 22, 2017. http://www.freetech4teachers.com/2010/08/7-resources-for-detecting-and.html.

"Camp Information." Maryland Athletics, University of Maryland, College Park. March 22, 2016. Accessed November 2016. http://www.umterps.com/ViewArticle.dbml?DB_OEM_ID=29700&ATCLID=208130407.

"Campus Safety and Security." U.S. Department of Education. 2017. Accessed November 28, 2017. https://ope.ed.gov/campussafety/#/institution/search.

Caplinger, Dan. "Graduates Keep Struggling With Private Student Loans." Daily Finance, AOL.com. September 1, 2014. Accessed November 14, 2017. http://www.dailyfinance.com/2013/09/01/students-still-struggle-private-loan-college-debt/.

Carnevale, Anthony P., Stephen J. Rose, and Ban Cheah. "The College Pay Off: Education, Occupations, Lifetime Earnings." *Center on Education and the Workforce: Georgetown University.* 2014. Accessed May 8, 2018. https://cew.georgetown.edu/wp-content/uploads/2014/11/collegepayoff-complete.pdf.

"Certificates: Gateway to Gainful Employment and College Degrees." Chart. McCourt School of Public Policy, Center on Education and the Workforce, Georgetown

University. June 5, 2012. Accessed November 13, 2017.
http://cew.georgetown.edu/certificates/.

"CFPB Ombudsman." *Consumer Financial Protection Bureau.* 2018. Accessed August
19, 2018. https://www.consumerfinance.gov/.

Choy, Susan P. "Students Whose Parents Did Not Go to College: Postsecondary Access,
Persistence, and Attainment, NCES 2001–126." National Center for Education
Statistics, U.S. Department of Education. December 2001. Accessed November
7, 2017. http://nces.ed.gov/pubs2001/2001126.pdf.

"Choose the Federal Student Loan Repayment Plan That's Best for You." *Federal
Student Aid, U.S. Department of Education.* 2018. Accessed July 14, 2018.
https://studentaid.ed.gov/sa/repay-loans/understand/plans.

"Circle of 6." Tech 4 Good Inc. 2015. Accessed June 26, 2016.
http://www.circleof6app.com/.

"*City-data.com: Crime Rate in Washington, D.C.*" Advameg, Inc. 2018. Accessed May 5,
2018. http://www.city-data.com/crime/crime-Washington-District-of-
Columbia.html.

Clark, Kim. "Community college: How to choose the right school." CNNMoney. June 7,
2012. Accessed July 2015.
http://money.cnn.com/2012/06/07/pf/college/community-college/index.htm.

Clark, Kim. "6 tips to help you pick the best community college." CNNMoney. June 7,
2012. Accessed November 13, 2017.
http://money.cnn.com/2012/06/06/pf/college/best-community-
college/index.htm.

"Closure of ITT Technical Institutes." Federal Student Aid. May 11, 2017. Accessed
November 09, 2017. https://studentaid.ed.gov/sa/about/announcements/itt.

"College Affordability and Transparency Center." U.S. Department of Education. 2015.
Accessed November 17, 2017. http://collegecost.ed.gov/catc/#.

"College Affordability and Transparency Center." U.S. Department of Education. 2018.
Accessed August 10, 2018. https://collegecost.ed.gov/index.aspx.

"*College and University Food Bank Alliance.*" CUFBA National. 2018. Accessed May 7,
2018. https://sites.temple.edu/cufba/about-us/.

"College Data, College Profile - University of Wisconsin - Milwaukee." 1st Financial
Bank, USA. 2013. Accessed October 22, 2016.
http://www.collegedata.com/cs/data/college/college_pg01_tmpl.jhtml?schoolId
=1702.

"College Navigator." National Center for Education Statistics, U.S. Department of Education. 2013. Accessed August 2015. http://nces.ed.gov/collegenavigator/.

"College Navigator - DeVry University-Virginia." National Center for Education Statistics, U.S. Department of Education. 2018. Accessed April 2018. https://nces.ed.gov/collegenavigator/?q=DeVry+university&s=VA&id=482653#expenses.

"College Navigator - Montgomery College." National Center for Education Statistics, U.S. Department of Education. 2016. Accessed April 2016. https://nces.ed.gov/collegenavigator/?q=montgomery%20college&s=MD&id=163426#general.

"College Navigator – Sarah Lawrence College." National Center for Education Statistics, U.S. Department of Education. 2018. Accessed June 2018. https://nces.ed.gov/collegenavigator/?id=195304#expenses.

"College Navigator - University of Maryland-College Park." National Center for Education Statistics, U.S. Department of Education. 2018. Accessed April 2018. https://nces.ed.gov/collegenavigator/?q=University+of+Maryland+College+Park&s=MD+VA&id=163286#expenses.

College Navigator: Find the School to Match any Interest from Archery to Zoology. New York, NY: Random House, 2007.

"College Rankings - Top 500 Ranked Community Colleges." StateUniversity.com. 2013. Accessed July 2015. http://www.stateuniversity.com/rank/score_rank_by_commc.html.

"College Transfer Simplified." AcademyOne, Inc. 2017. Accessed November 13, 2017. http://www.collegetransfer.net/Home/tabid/976/Default.aspx.

"College Video Tours." It's Nacho, YOUniversityTV. 2017. Accessed November 08, 2017. https://www.youniversitytv.com/category/college/.

"Compare Schools." *Consumer Financial Protection Bureau.* 2018. Accessed August 9, 2018. https://www.consumerfinance.gov/paying-for-college/compare-financial-aid-and-college-cost/.

"Compiling the Forbes/CCAP Rankings." Center for College Affordability and Productivity. Accessed August 2015. http://centerforcollegeaffordability.org/uploads/2012_Methodology.pdf.

Colley, Angela. "Credit Unions vs. Banks - Differences, Pros & Cons." Money Crashers. July 13, 2011. Accessed November 17, 2017. http://www.moneycrashers.com/why-credit-unions-are-better-than-banks/.

"Costs." University of Maryland, College Park. 2016. Accessed October 22, 2016. https://admissions.umd.edu/finance/costs.

"Cost to Attend University of Wisconsin Milwaukee: Annual Costs." CollegeCalc.org. 2018. Accessed May 19, 2018. http://www.cite.com/bibliography.html?id=5b007c70b9aa8fef618b4571.

Cotner, Herb. "Ask a Cop: What Should I Say When I Call 911 for a Loved One?" National Alliance on Mental Illness. January 31, 2014. Accessed November 28, 2017. https://www.nami.org/About-NAMI/NAMI-News/Ask-a-Cop-What-Should-I-Say-When-I-Call-911-for-a.

Couch, Christina. "Six Things to Know About Private Student Loans | Fox Business." Personal Finance, Fox Business/Bankrate, Inc. August 2, 2012. Accessed November 15, 2017. http://www.foxbusiness.com/features/2012/08/02/6-things-to-know-about-private-student-loans.html.

"Council for Higher Education Accreditation." Council for Higher Education Accreditation. 2013. Accessed March 2015. http://www.chea.org/.

"Coursera - Courses." Coursera Inc. 2017. Accessed November 25, 2017. https://www.coursera.org/courses?languages=en.

"Credit vs. debit: Get the most from your cards." Better Money Habits, Bank of America Corporation. 2017. Accessed November 17, 2017. https://bettermoneyhabits.bankofamerica.com/en/personal-banking/difference-between-debit-and-credit?cm_mmc=EBZ-CorpRep-_-Taboola-_-text_link_creditvsdebit-_-Taboola_Desktop_Textlink_CPC_CC_CreditVsDebit%25252525252520-%25252525252520fbid#fbid=REEvu9JkTe5.

Csiszar, John. "12 Best Apps for First-Time Investors." GOBankingRates. July 26, 2017. Accessed November 17, 2017. https://www.gobankingrates.com/investing/10-apps-timid-first-time-investors/.

Curry, Colleen. "Natalee Holloway Is Dead, Judge Decides." ABC News. January 12, 2012. Accessed November 26, 2017. http://abcnews.go.com/News/judge-pronounces-natalee-holloway-dead/story?id=15346993.

"Deferment and Forbearance." Federal Student Aid, U.S. Department of Education. 2017. Accessed November 17, 2017. https://studentaid.ed.gov/sa/repay-loans/deferment-forbearance.

"Degree Mill and Accreditation Mills - Video." Council for Higher Education Accreditation/CHEA International Quality Group. 2013. Accessed March 2015. http://www.chea.org/4DCGI/cms/review.html?Action=CMS_Document&DocID=208&MenuKey=main.

"Department of Mathematics - Testbank." University of Maryland, College Park. 2016. Accessed November 22, 2017. https://www-math.umd.edu/testbank.html.

"Digest of Education Statistics: 2011 - Undergraduate Prices." National Center for Education Statistics, U.S. Department of Education. May 2012. Accessed October 2014. https://nces.ed.gov/programs/digest/d11/.

"Directorate of Cadet Activities." United States Military Academy, West Point. 2013. Accessed May 2016. http://www.usma.edu/dca/SitePages/Home.aspx.

"Directory of Accredited Institutions." Accrediting Commission of Career Schools and Colleges. 2013. Accessed March 2015. http://www.accsc.org/Directory/index.aspx.

"Educational attainment of the labor force age 25 and older by race and Hispanic or Latino ethnicity, 2014 annual averages." Chart. TED: The Economics Daily - U.S. Bureau of Labor Statistics. November 18, 2015. Accessed November 26, 2016. http://www.bls.gov/opub/ted/2015/educational-attainment-and-occupation-groups-by-race-and-ethnicity-in-2014.htm.

"Educational Attainment: 2012 - 2016 American Community Survey 5 - Year Estimates." American FactFinder - U.S. Census Bureau. 2016. Accessed April 19, 2018. https://factfinder.census.gov/faces/tableservices/jsf/pages/productview.xhtml?pid=ACS_16_5YR_S1501&src=pt. Educational Attainment of the Population 25 Years and Over data.

Edwards, Halle. "SAT / ACT Prep Online Guides and Tips." What's Better for You: IB or AP? College Expert Guide: PrepScholar. 2013-2018. Accessed April 23, 2018. https://blog.prepscholar.com/whats-better-for-you-ib-or-ap.

"ELMS." Division of Information Technology, University of Maryland, College Park. 2016. Accessed October 27, 2016. http://www.elms.umd.edu/.

Executive Summary – Mid-Year snapshot of private student loan complaints. Report. Consumer Financial Protection Bureau. July 2013. Accessed November 14, 2017. http://files.consumerfinance.gov/f/201308_cfpb_complaint-snapshot.pdf.

"FAFSA4caster." Federal Student Aid, U.S. Department of Education. 2018. Accessed August 7, 2018. https://fafsa.ed.gov/FAFSA/app/f4cForm?execution=e1s1.

Fain, Paul. "Graduate, Transfer, Graduate." Inside Higher Ed. November 8, 2012. Accessed July 2015. http://www.insidehighered.com/news/2012/11/08/high-graduation-rates-community-college-transfers.

"FAQ on Textbooks." National Association of College Stores. January 2014. Accessed June 10, 2015. https://www.nacs.org/advocacynewsmedia/faqs/faqontextbooks.aspx.

"Fast Facts - AACC." American Association of Community Colleges. 2017. Accessed November 10, 2017. https://www.aacc.nche.edu/research-trends/fast-facts/.

"Federal Pell Grant Program – Federal Student Aid." U.S. Department of Education. 2018. Accessed May 1, 2018. https://studentaid.ed.gov/sa/types/grants-scholarships/pell.

"Federal Student Loan Portfolio by Volume ($), September 2011 (source Federal Student Aid - Outstanding Principal Balance)." Chart. New York Times. December 9, 2011. Accessed July 7, 2015. http://graphics8.nytimes.com/news/business/piecharts.pdf.

"Federal Student Loans for College or Career School Are an Investment in Your Future." *Federal Student Aid, U.S. Department of Education.* 2018. Accessed August 14, 2018. https://studentaid.ed.gov/sa/types/loans.

"Federal Work-Study Jobs Help Students Earn Money to Pay for College or Career School." *Federal Student Aid, U.S. Department of Education.* 2018. Accessed August 17, 2018. https://studentaid.ed.gov/sa/types/work-study.

"Feed The Pig: Tools to Invest, Save and Budget Your Money." Feed the Pig, American Institute of CPAs. 2006-2013. Accessed November 17, 2017. https://www.feedthepig.org/.

"Find a college that's right for you! - College Search." Peterson's, A Nelnet Company. 2017. Accessed November 08, 2017. http://www.petersons.com/college-search.aspx.

"Find Support, National Alliance on Mental Illness (NAMI)." NAMI. 2014. Accessed November 28, 2017. https://www.nami.org/Find-Support/NAMI-Programs/NAMI-Family-to-Family.

"Find Your College - College Search." The Princeton Review: TPR Education IP Holdings, LLC. 2013. Accessed February 2015. https://www.princetonreview.com/college-search?ceid=cp-1023919.

Fiske, Edward B., and Shawn Logue. *Fiske guide to colleges, 2013.* Naperville, IL: Sourcebooks, 2012.

"For-profit Colleges and Universities." National Conference of State Legislatures. July 3, 2013. Accessed October 2013. http://www.ncsl.org/research/education/for-profit-colleges-and-universities.aspx.

"Forgiveness, Cancellation, and Discharge." Federal Student Aid, U.S. Department of Education. 2017. Accessed November 15, 2017. https://studentaid.ed.gov/sa/repay-loans/forgiveness-cancellation.

"Four Year Plans." College of Computer, Mathematical, and Natural Sciences, University of Maryland, College Park. October 12, 2012. Accessed November 17, 2013. https://cmns.umd.edu/undergraduate/advising-academic-planning/academic-planning/four-year-plans.

"Four-year Curriculum: Bachelor of Science in Computer Science (BSCS)." Chart. Department of Electrical Engineering and Computer Science, The Catholic University of America. 2017. Accessed November 18, 2017. http://eecs.cua.edu/res/docs/CS-General-Track-Fall-2017.pdf.

"Free English Tests and Exercises Online for ESL, TOEFL, TOEIC, GRE, SAT, GMAT." EnglishTestStore. 2005-2016. Accessed November 07, 2017. http://englishteststore.net/index.php?option=com_content&view=featured&Itemid=344.

"Free Online Proofreader: Grammar Check, Plagiarism Detection, and more." Paper Rater. 2014. Accessed November 10, 2015. http://www.paperrater.com/.

"FAQs for the Media: 'When Reporting a Crime, Who Should Students and Residents Located on Campus Call?'" *International Association of Campus Law Enforcement Administrators*. 2018. Accessed August 18, 2018. https://www.iaclea.org/faqs-for-the-media.

"Freshman Application Checklist." University of Maryland, College Park. Accessed November 09, 2017. https://www.admissions.umd.edu/apply/freshmanchecklist.php.

"Friend Radar." Not Exactly Software LLC. 2009 - 2013. Accessed October 10, 2015. http://www.notexactlysoftware.com/FriendRadar.

"General Education Courses at MC and at UMCP." Montgomery College. 2013. Accessed August 2015. http://cms.montgomerycollege.edu/EDU/Department2.aspx?id=26608.

"General Education Program." University of Maryland, College Park. 2013. Accessed September 24, 2015. http://www.gened.umd.edu/.

Giang, Vivian. "The 40 Highest-Paying Jobs You Can Get Without A Bachelor's Degree." Business Insider. August 07, 2012. Accessed June 2015. http://www.businessinsider.com/the-40-highest-paying-jobs-you-can-get-without-a-bachelors-degree-2012-8.

Gould, Jon B. *How to Succeed in College (While Really Trying): A Professor's Inside Advice*. Chicago, IL: The University of Chicago Press, 2012.

"Grants and Scholarships Are Free Money to Help Pay for College or Career School." *Federal Student Aid, U.S. Department of Education*. 2018. Accessed August 7, 2018. https://studentaid.ed.gov/sa/types/grants-scholarships.

Gray, Meghan, and Rachel Mehlhaff. "UNT bans alcohol at fraternity events following student's fall." Dallas News. February 07, 2013. Accessed November 29, 2017. https://www.dallasnews.com/news/denton/2013/02/07/unt-bans-alcohol-at-fraternity-events-following-students-fall.

Grove, Allen. "Why Do College Textbooks Cost So Much Money?" ThoughtCo. January 1, 2017. Accessed November 21, 2017. http://collegeapps.about.com/od/payingforcollege/f/college-books-cost.htm.

Guo, Jeff. "*Attention college students: You may have earned a degree without knowing it.*" Washington Post.com. Feb 10, 2018. Accessed May 7, 2018. https://www.washingtonpost.com/blogs/govbeat/wp/2015/02/10/attention-college-students-you-may-have-earned-a-degree-without-knowing-it/?noredirect=on&utm_term=.0dbea3f4d454.

"Harms of Cigarette Smoking and Health Benefits of Quitting." National Cancer Institute. December 3, 2014. Accessed November 29, 2017. https://www.cancer.gov/about-cancer/causes-prevention/risk/tobacco/cessation-fact-sheet.

Helhoski, Anna. "2 extra years in college could cost you almost $300,000." USA Today. June 21, 2016. Accessed June 21, 2016. https://www.usatoday.com/story/money/personalfinance/2016/06/21/2-extra-years-college-could-cost-you-almost-300000/86148832/.

Helmenstine, Anne Marie. "Get Facts Rohypnol or Roofies." ThoughtCo. March 7, 2017. Accessed November 26, 2017. https://www.thoughtco.com/rohypnol-or-roofies-fast-facts-606394.

"Helping Victims with Safety. Helping States with Implementation." Cynthia L. Bischof Memorial Foundation. March 03, 2015. Accessed November 27, 2017. http://www.cindysmemorial.org/.

Hershbein, Brad, and Melissa S. Kearney. "Major Decisions: What Graduates Earn over Their Lifetimes." The Hamilton Project: Brookings Institution. September 29, 2015. Accessed October 2017. http://www.hamiltonproject.org/papers/major_decisions_what_graduates_earn_over_their_lifetimes.

Hicken, Melanie. "Average cost to raise a kid: $241,080." CNNMoney. August 14, 2013. Accessed November 26, 2017. http://money.cnn.com/2013/08/14/pf/cost-children/.

"High Hopes, Big Debts." The Project on Student Debt. May 2010. Accessed November 9, 2017. https://ticas.org/files/pub/High_Hopes_Big_Debts_2008.pdf.

"High School Students and Teachers." American Mathematical Society. 2014. Accessed July 2015. http://www.ams.org/programs/students/high-school/high-school.

"Highest Educational Attainment Levels Since 1940: Adults 25 Years and Older with a Bachelor's Degree or Higher." U.S. Census Bureau. March 30, 2017. Accessed April 19, 2018. https://www.census.gov/library/visualizations/2017/comm/cb17-51_educational_attainment.html.

"How does your community college stack up?" CNNMoney. Accessed September 2015. http://money.cnn.com/pf/college/community-colleges/.

"How FICO Credit Score is calculated." Fair Isaac Corporation. 2001-2017. Accessed November 18, 2017. http://www.myfico.com/crediteducation/whatsinyourscore.aspx.

"How to Choose a Financial Planner." The Wall Street Journal, Dow Jones & Company. 2017. Accessed December 13, 2017. http://guides.wsj.com/personal-finance/managing-your-money/how-to-choose-a-financial-planner/.

"How to Write a Thesis Statement." Writing Guides: Writing Tutorial Services, Indiana University, Bloomington. April 7, 2014. Accessed November 24, 2017. http://www.indiana.edu/~wts/pamphlets/thesis_statement.shtml.

"Illiteracy Statistics." STATS, Statisticsbrain.com. July 22, 2017. Accessed November 22, 2017. https://www.statisticbrain.com/number-of-american-adults-who-cant-read/.

"Interest Rates and Fees." Federal Student Aid, U.S. Department of Education. 2017. Accessed November 15, 2017. https://studentaid.ed.gov/sa/types/loans/interest-rates.

"Is Taking a Gap Year Before College Right For You?" *The Princeton Review*. 2018. Accessed August 23, 2018. https://www.princetonreview.com/college-advice/deferred-admission.

"Intuit Mint: It's All Coming Together." *Intuit, Inc.* 2018. Accessed August 18, 2018. https://www.mint.com/.

Kannel, Susan. "A Consumer's Guide to Going to School: Types of colleges and universities." Chart. Chicago, IL: Council for Experiential Learning. 2013. Accessed October 25, 2017. http://www.cael.org/pdfs/a_consumer-s_guide_to_going_to_school_-_cael.

"Khan Academy." Khan Academy. 2017. Accessed November 25, 2017. http://www.khanacademy.org/.

Kimbro, Dennis Paul. *The Wealth Choice: Success Secrets of Black Millionaires*. The Napoleon Hill Foundation, 2013.

Latimer, Leah Y. *Higher Ground: Preparing African-American children for College*. New York, NY: Avon Books, Inc., 1999.

Leadership21 Committee. "Campus Mental Health: Know Your Rights." The Judge David L. Bazelon Center for Mental Health Law. 2008. Accessed March 7, 2015. http://www.bazelon.org/wp-content/uploads/2017/01/YourMind-YourRights.pdf.

"Leanna's Essentials - All Natural Products." Leanna's Essentials - All Natural Products. 2016. Accessed October 3, 2016. http://www.leannasessentials.com/.

"Learning Assistance Service." Counseling Center, University of Maryland, College Park. 2015. Accessed March 11, 2015. https://www.counseling.umd.edu/las/.

"Learning Links." Grays Harbor College. 2017. Accessed November 07, 2017. https://www.ghc.edu/content/learning-center-learning-links.

Lewin, Tamar. "Unwed Fathers Fight for Babies Placed for Adoption by Mothers." The New York Times. March 19, 2006. Accessed March 7, 2015. http://www.nytimes.com/2006/03/19/us/unwed-fathers-fight-for-babies-placed-for-adoption-by-mothers.html.

Lewis, Darcy. "Consider a College With a Focus on Minority Students." *U.S. News & World Report*. September 21, 2016. Accessed August 18, 2018. https://www.usnews.com/education/best-colleges/articles/2016-09-21/consider-a-college-with-a-focus-on-minority-students.

Lino, Mark. "*The Cost of Raising a Child.*" U.S. Department of Agriculture. Jan 13, 2017. Accessed May 6, 2018, https://www.usda.gov/media/blog/2017/01/13/cost-raising-child.

Lobosco, Katie. "Too Poor to Pay for College, Too Rich for Financial Aid." *CNNMoney, Cable News Network, A WarnerMedia Company*. April 29, 2018. Accessed August 17, 2018. https://money.cnn.com/2016/04/28/pf/college/college-financial-aid/index.html.

Ma, Jennifer, Matea Pender, and Meredith Welch. "Education Pays 2016 © 2016: The Benefits of Higher Education for Individuals and Society." The College Board. 2016. Accessed June 2018. https://trends.collegeboard.org/sites/default/files/education-pays-2016-full-report.pdf.

MacDonald, Jay. "Debt Payoff Debate: Pay Smallest Balance 1st? Or Highest Rate?." *CreditCards.com*. January 23, 2013. Accessed June 22, 2018. https://www.creditcards.com/credit-card-news/paying-off-debt-study-smallest_balance-financially-wrong-1276.php.

Macionis, John J., and Vincent N. Parrillo. *Cities and urban life*. 6th ed. New Jersey: Pearson Education Inc, 2013.

"Majors by College." University of Maryland, College Park. 2017. Accessed November 18, 2017. https://www.admissions.umd.edu/explore/majors/majors-college.

Malone, Michael S. *The Everything College Survival Book: From Social Life to Study Skills—All You Need to Know to Fit Right In*. 2nd ed. Avon, MA: Adams Media, 2005.

Marcus, Lilit. "Fundraising helps teen go from homeless to Howard U." Today, NBC News. August 19, 2013. Accessed June 13, 2015. https://www.today.com/news/fundraising-helps-teen-go-homeless-howard-u-6C10945702.

"Marijuana as Medicine." National Institute of Drug Abuse. April 2017. Accessed November 28, 2017. https://www.drugabuse.gov/publications/drugfacts/marijuana-medicine.

Martin, Andrew, and Andrew W. Lehren. "Student Loans Weighing Down a Generation with Heavy Debt." The New York Times. May 12, 2012. Accessed November 17, 2017. http://www.nytimes.com/2012/05/13/business/student-loans-weighing-down-a-generation-with-heavy-debt.html?pagewanted=all&_r=0.

Marus, John. "Stopping the clock on credits that don't count." The Hechinger Report, Teachers College at Columbia University. April 22, 2013. Accessed February 10, 2015. http://hechingerreport.org/stopping-the-clock-on-credits-that-dont-count/.

"Maryland at a Glance: Maryland Community Colleges." Maryland State Archives. June 2, 2017. Accessed November 08, 2017. http://msa.maryland.gov/msa/mdmanual/01glance/html/colcom.html.

"Maryland at a Glance: Maryland Higher Education, Colleges, Universities." Maryland State Archives. October 24, 2017. Accessed November 08, 2017. http://msa.maryland.gov/msa/mdmanual/01glance/html/edhigh.html.

"Maryland Community Colleges." *Maryland Association of Community Colleges*. 2018. Accessed August 20, 2018. https://mdacc.org/.

"Maryland Junior College Athletic Conference." Maryland Junior College Athletic Conference. 2017. Accessed November 14, 2017. http://www.mdjuco.org/landing/index.

"Maryland Transfer Advantage Program (MTAP) - Science, Engineering and Technology (SET)." Montgomery College. 2013. Accessed July 2015. http://cms.montgomerycollege.edu/EDU/Department2.aspx?id=24851.

"Massive Open Online Courses (MOOCs)." edX Inc. 2016. Accessed November 25, 2017. http://mooc.org/.

"Matching Careers to Degrees." Chart. Big Future, The College Board. October 20, 2017. Accessed October 20, 2017. https://bigfuture.collegeboard.org/explore-careers/careers/matching-careers-to-degrees.

"Math Success Program, Frequently Asked Questions." Department of Resident Life, University of Maryland, College Park. 2016. Accessed October 27, 2016. http://reslife.umd.edu/programs/math_success/faq/.

"Mathematics Placement Test Information." Department of Mathematics, University of Maryland, College Park. 2013. Accessed February 2015. http://www-math.umd.edu/placement-test-information.html.

McGurran, Brianna. "When to Refinance Student Loans." *Nerdwallet.com*. July 26, 2018. Accessed 2018. https://www.nerdwallet.com/blog/loans/student-loans/student-loan-refinancing-faq/.

Meyer, Cathy. "4 Things You Need to Know about Restraining Orders." LiveAbout. July 14, 2017. Accessed November 27, 2017. http://divorcesupport.about.com/od/abusiverelationships/a/restrain_order.htm.

"Michelle Obama." Biography.com. 2016. Accessed October 3, 2016. http://www.biography.com/people/michelle-obama-307592.

"Middle States Commission on Higher Education." Middle States Commission on Higher Education. 2017. Accessed November 09, 2017. http://www.msche.org/?Nav1=ABOUT&Nav2=MISSION.

"Money 101: Personal Finance, Investing, Retirement, Saving." Time, Inc. 2017. Accessed November 17, 2017. http://time.com/money/collection/money-101/.

"National Junior College Athletic Association." National Junior College Athletic Association. 2017. Accessed November 14, 2017. http://www.njcaa.org/.

"National Suicide Prevention Lifeline." *Substance Abuse and Mental Health Services Administration, Mental Health Association of New York City*. 2018. Accessed June 8, 2018. https://suicidepreventionlifeline.org/.

"Naviance by Hobsons." *Hobsons - Naviance.com*. 2016. Accessed May 8, 2018. <https://www.naviance.com/>.

"NCHC Online Guide." National Collegiate Honors Council. 2017. Accessed November 14, 2017. http://www.nchcguide.com/nchc-directory/#more-52.

Nichols, James. "Kids React to Gay Marriage." YouTube. November 03, 2013. Accessed November 28, 2017. http://www.youtube.com/watch?v=8TJxnYgP6D8.

"NSLDS Student Access: National Student Loan Data System." *Federal Student Aid, U.S. Department of Education.* 2018. Accessed July 14, 2018. https://www.nslds.ed.gov/nslds/nslds_SA/.

"Nutrition Services." University Health Center, University of Maryland, College Park. 2009. Accessed November 28, 2017. http://www.health.umd.edu/nutritionservices.

O'shaungnessy, Lynn. "Why freshmen retention rates matter | Unigo." Unigo. June 1, 2015. Accessed July 13, 2016. https://www.unigo.com/get-to-college/college-search/why-freshmen-retention-rates-matter.

Olefson, Shari B. *Financial Fresh Start: your five-step plan for adapting and prospering in the new economy.* New York, NY: American Management Association, 2013.

"Oral Communications Center." *Excellence from planning to practice* (web log). Department of Communications, University of Maryland, College Park. 2014. Accessed September 24, 2015. http://umdocc.wixsite.com/blog.

"Parents - Helping your child with the College Planning Process." The College Board. 2013. Accessed July 2015. https://bigfuture.collegeboard.org/get-started/for-parents.

Paul, Annie Murphy. "What We Can Learn from First-Generation College Students." Time, Inc. April 11, 2012. Accessed November 07, 2017. http://ideas.time.com/2012/04/11/what-we-can-learn-from-first-generation-college-students/.

"PCC Compass Placement Test Review Packet." Portland Community College. Accessed November 7, 2017. https://www.pcc.edu/resources/tutoring/sylvania/student-success/documents/total.pdf.

Petrecca, Laura. "In tight job market, some teens start their businesses." USA Today. May 22, 2009. Accessed October 2016. http://usatoday30.usatoday.com/money/smallbusiness/2009-05-18-teen-entrepreneurs-start-businesses_N.htm.

"Phi Beta Kappa National Honor Society." Phi Theta Kappa. 2017. Accessed November 14, 2017. https://www.ptk.org/default.aspx.

"PLUS Loans." Federal Student Aid, U.S. Department of Education. 2015. Accessed February 17, 2015. https://studentaid.ed.gov/sa/types/loans/plus.

"Practice and Be Prepared for ACCUPLACER." The College Board. 2017. Accessed November 07, 2017. https://accuplacer.collegeboard.org/student/practice.

"Pre-Transfer Advising." Office of Undergraduate Studies, University of Maryland, College Park. Accessed November 10, 2017. http://www.transferadvising.umd.edu/.

Private Loans: Facts and Trends. Report. The Institute for College Access & Success. June 2016. Accessed November 14, 2017. https://ticas.org/sites/default/files/pub_files/private_loan_facts_trends.pdf.

"Program Requirements, Aerospace Engineering." University of Maryland, College Park. 2017. Accessed November 18, 2017. http://www.aero.umd.edu/undergrad/program-req.

"Prosecutors: Theater shooting suspect told classmate he wanted to kill people." CNN. August 24, 2012. Accessed November 28, 2017. http://www.cnn.com/2012/08/24/justice/colorado-shooting/index.html.

"Public Service Loan Forgiveness." Federal Student Aid, U.S. Department of Education. 2017. Accessed November 15, 2017. http://studentaid.ed.gov/repay-loans/forgiveness-cancellation/charts/public-service#what-is-the-public.

"Quick Facts about Financial Aid and Community Colleges, 2007-08." Institute for College Access & Success. March 2009. Accessed July 2013. https://eric.ed.gov/?id=ED540078.

"Quick Guide: College Costs." Chart. The College Board. 2017. Accessed November 15, 2017. https://bigfuture.collegeboard.org/pay-for-college/college-costs/quick-guide-college-costs.

"Quitting Smoking Among Adults --- United States, 2001--2010." Centers for Disease Control and Prevention. November 11, 2011. Accessed November 30, 2017. https://www.cdc.gov/mmwr/preview/mmwrhtml/mm6044a2.htm?s_cid=mm6044a2_w.

"Rate My Professors - Review Teachers and Professors, School Reviews, College Campus Ratings." Ratemyprofessors.com. 2013. Accessed June 21, 2015. http://www.ratemyprofessors.com/.

Roeder, Oliver. "Releasing Drug Offenders Won't End Mass Incarceration." *FiveThirtyEight, ABC News Internet Ventures.* 2018. Accessed August 17, 2018. https://fivethirtyeight.com/features/releasing-drug-offenders-wont-end-mass-incarceration/.

"Reporting to Law Enforcement ." RAINN. 2016. Accessed November 27, 2017. https://www.rainn.org/articles/reporting-law-enforcement.

"Requirements for a Bachelors Degree." College of Liberal Arts & Sciences, The University of Iowa. July 18, 2016. Accessed July 2016. https://clas.uiowa.edu/students/handbook/requirements-bachelors-degree.

Substance Abuse and Mental Health Services Administration. *Results from the 2012 National Survey on Drug Use and Health: summary of national findings.* NSDUH Series H-46, HHS Publication No. (SMA) 13-4795. Rockville, MD: U.S. Dept. of Health and Human Services, Substance Abuse and Mental Health Services Administration, Center for Behavioral Health Statistics and Quality, 2013. https://archive.samhsa.gov/data/NSDUH/2012SummNatFindDetTables/Nation alFindings/NSDUHresults2012.htm#ch2.2

Sullivan, Bob. "Know Your Rights on Bank Account Fraud." *NBCNews.com.* August 12, 2005. Accessed September 6, 2018. http://www.nbcnews.com/id/8915217/ns/technology_and_science-security/t/know-your-rights-bank-account-fraud/#.W5EwpyaWxjo.

"Salted Caramel Mocha Frappuccino® Blended Beverage." Starbucks Corporation. 2016. Accessed November 28, 2017. https://www.starbucks.com/menu/drinks/frappuccino-blended-beverages/salted-caramel-mocha-frappuccino-blended-beverage.

Schneider, Zola Dincin, and Norman G. Schneider. *Campus Visits & College Interviews: A Complete Guide for College-bound Students and their Families.* 3rd ed. New York, NY: College Board, 2012.

Scholarship America. "Get Money for College Through ROTC Programs." U.S. News & World Report. July 25, 2013. Accessed April 29, 2018. https://www.usnews.com/education/blogs/the-scholarship-coach/2013/07/25/get-money-for-college-through-rotc-programs.

Scott, Amy. "First generation college students go viral." Marketplace - Minnesota Public Radio. November 21, 2013. Accessed July 2015. http://www.marketplace.org/topics/wealth-poverty/first-family/first-generation-college-students-go-viral.

Shakespeare, William. *The Tragedy of Macbeth.* The Harvard Classics. Vol. XLVI, Part 4. New York, NY: P.F. Collier & Son, 1909–14. Bartleby.com, 2001. Accessed November 11, 2015. www.bartleby.com/46/4/.

Shakespeare, William. *Macbeth.* SparkNotes, LLC. 2013. Accessed November 24, 2017. http://www.sparknotes.com/shakespeare/macbeth/canalysis.html.

Sinozich, Sofi, and Lynn Langton. *Rape and Sexual Assault Victimization Among College-Age Females, 1995–2013.* Report no. NCJ 248471. Bureau of Justice Statistics, U.S. Department of Justice. December 2014. Accessed November 27, 2017. https://www.bjs.gov/content/pub/pdf/rsavcaf9513.pdf.

Sledge, Matt. "The Drug War And Mass Incarceration By The Numbers." The Huffington Post. April 08, 2013. Accessed November 28, 2017.

https://www.huffingtonpost.com/2013/04/08/drug-war-mass-incarceration_n_3034310.html.

"Stafford Loans @ 2013." Chart. Scholarships.com. 2013. Accessed November 15, 2017. http://www.scholarships.com/financial-aid/student-loans/stafford-loans/.

Stalter, Kate. "8 Common Misconceptions About 529 Plans." U.S. News & World Report. November 24, 2014. Accessed April 29, 2018. https://money.usnews.com/money/personal-finance/mutual-funds/articles/2014/11/24/8-common-misconceptions-about-529-plans.

Stalter, Kate. "Everything You Need to Know About 529 College Savings Plans." U.S. News & World Report. August 28, 2017. Accessed November 17, 2017. https://money.usnews.com/529s.

"Steps to Admissions: The West Point Application Process." West Point Admissions, United States Military Academy, West Point. October 2016. Accessed October 29, 2016. https://www.usma.edu/admissions/SitePages/Steps.aspx.

Stewart, Anna M., Keith Bowman, Mitchell Graves, Catherine Landis, Neil Patterson, Yazmin Rivera, and Nicole Werner. "A Research Guide for Students and Teachers - SUNY-ESF." State University of New York, College of Environmental Science and Forestry. 2009. Accessed November 22, 2017. http://www.esf.edu/outreach/sciencecorps/documents/ResearchGuide_NSFGK 12.pdf.

"Student Aid Deadlines." Federal Student Aid, U.S. Department of Education. 2018. Accessed May 19, 2018. https://fafsa.ed.gov/deadlines.htm.

"Student Loan Calculator." *Bankrate.com*. 2018. Accessed August 16, 2018. https://www.bankrate.com/calculators/college-planning/loan-calculator.aspx.

"Students with Criminal Convictions Have Limited Eligibility for Federal Student Aid." *Federal Student Aid, U.S. Department of Education*. 2018. Accessed August 17, 2018. https://studentaid.ed.gov/sa/eligibility/criminal-convictions.

"Study Abroad Vs Exchange." *Study Abroad Center, The University of Hawai'i at Manoa*. 2018. Accessed June 24, 2018. http://www.studyabroad.hawaii.edu/students/study-abroad-vs-exchange/.

"Subsidized and Unsubsidized Loans." Federal Student Aid, U.S. Department of Education. 2015. Accessed February 15, 2015. https://studentaid.ed.gov/sa/types/loans/subsidized-unsubsidized.

"Sugars, Added Sugars and Sweeteners." American Heart Association Inc. 2013. Accessed July 17, 2015. http://www.heart.org/HEARTORG/GettingHealthy/NutritionCenter/HealthyDi etGoals/Sugars-and-Carbohydrates_UCM_303296_Article.jsp.

"Table A-4. Employment status of the civilian population 25 years and over by educational attainment." U.S. Bureau of Labor Statistics. November 03, 2017. Accessed November 07, 2017. http://www.bls.gov/news.release/empsit.t04.htm.

"TESTUDO, Office of the Registrar." University of Maryland, College Park. 2017. Accessed November 18, 2017. http://www.testudo.umd.edu/.

"Testudo, Schedule of Classes, Deadlines." University of Maryland, College Park. 2013. Accessed June 10, 2015. http://www.testudo.umd.edu/acad_deadlines/fall_2013.html.

"Textbook Rentals." Amazon.com Help. 1996-2017. Accessed November 22, 2017. http://www.amazon.com/gp/help/customer/display.html/?nodeId=200974570.

"The 50 Most Innovative Computer Science Departments in the U.S." Computer Science Degree Hub. 2017. Accessed November 26, 2017. http://www.computersciencedegreehub.com/50-innovative-computer-science-departments/.

"The Articulation System for Maryland Colleges and Universities." Sunrise Software Arts, Inc. 1996-2017. Accessed November 13, 2017. http://www.acaff.usmh.usmd.edu/artweb/chgri.cgi.

"The Best Colleges in America, Ranked." U.S. News & World Report L.P. November 8, 2017. Accessed November 08, 2017. http://colleges.usnews.rankingsandreviews.com/best-colleges.

"The Honor Program - The Simon Center for Professional Military Ethic." United States Military Academy, West Point. 2014. Accessed November 10, 2015. https://www.usma.edu/scpme/SitePages/Honor.aspx.

"The Office of Extended Studies." Office of Extended Studies, University of Maryland, College Park. March 20, 2013. Accessed September 2015. http://oes.umd.edu/.

"The Pros and Cons of AP Classes." College Foundation of West Virginia. 2009. Accessed February 13, 2015. https://secure.cfwv.com/Home/Article.aspx?level=3XAP2FPAX6J7I3kztATGu YyXAP2BPAXDahIQXAP3DPAXXAP3DPAX&articleId=VTv0Iu2AvHXAP 2FPAXqUmR2EHLZXgXAP3DPAXXAP3DPAX.

"The Purdue OWL: Citation Chart." The Purdue OWL. October 2014. Accessed November 10, 2015. https://owl.english.purdue.edu/media/pdf/20110928111055_949.pdf.

"The Smart Student Guide to Financial Aid - Calculators." FinAid - Financial Aid
Advice, Fastweb LLC. 2017. Accessed November 15, 2017.
http://www.finaid.org/calculators/.

"The U.S. Department of Education Offers Low-interest Loans to Eligible Students to
Help Cover the Cost of College or Career School." *Federal Student Aid, U.S.
Department of Education.* 2018. Accessed August 17, 2018.
https://studentaid.ed.gov/sa/types/loans/subsidized-unsubsidized#eligibility-
time-limit.

Tilus, Grant. "100 Celebrities with College Degrees." Rasmussen College. May 9, 2012.
Accessed November 26, 2016. http://www.rasmussen.edu/student-
life/blogs/main/100-celebrities-with-college-degrees/.

Tilus, Grant. "Semester Vs. Quarter: What You Need to Know When Transferring
Credits." *Rasmussen College.* September 27, 2012. Accessed August 28, 2018.
https://www.rasmussen.edu/student-life/blogs/main/semester-vs-quarter-need-
to-know-when-transferring-credits/.

"Time to degree: Table 3." Chart. Fast Facts - National Center for Education Statistics,
U.S. Department of Education. 2011. Accessed June 2015.
http://nces.ed.gov/fastfacts/display.asp?id=569.

Tizon, Christian. "Signature Report 6: Completing College: A National View of Student
Attainment Rates – Fall 2007 Cohort." National Student Clearinghouse
Research Center. December 15, 2013. Accessed November 21, 2016.
http://nscresearchcenter.org/signaturereport6/#prettyPhoto.

"Transfer Agreements." Montgomery College. 2017. Accessed November 13, 2017.
http://cms.montgomerycollege.edu/agreements/.

"Transfer Course Database." Transfer Credit Services, University of Maryland, College
Park. 2013. Accessed November 2013. https://ntst.umd.edu/tce/.

"Transfer Course Database: Devry University-Arlington." Transfer Credit Services,
University of Maryland, College Park. 2018. Accessed May 5, 2018.
https://app.transfercredit.umd.edu/inst-
select.html?searchType=master&searchString=devry&countryCode=US&state
Code=.

"Transfer Equivalency Databases." Montgomery College. 2017. Accessed November 13,
2017. http://cms.montgomerycollege.edu/EDU/Plain.aspx?id=50742.

Tretina, Kat. "5 Common Myths About Student Loan Consolidation." *Student Loan
Hero.* May 16, 2017. Accessed August 21, 2018.
https://studentloanhero.com/featured/student-loan-debt-consolidation-myths/.

Tuttle, Brad. "Cigarettes Taxes: States with Highest, Cheapest Prices." Money, Time Inc. April 20, 2017. Accessed November 29, 2017. http://time.com/money/4748310/smoking-costs-cigarette-taxes-expensive/.

"Types of Aid." Federal Student Aid, U.S. Department of Education. June 19, 2017. Accessed November 14, 2017. https://studentaid.ed.gov/sa/types.

"U.S. and World Population Clock." U.S. Census Bureau. January 1, 2014. Accessed November 2016. https://www.census.gov/popclock/.

"U.S. Department of Education Database of Accredited Postsecondary Institutions and Programs." Office of Postsecondary Education, U.S. Department of Education. 2017. Accessed November 09, 2017. http://ope.ed.gov/accreditation/.

"UMD Undergraduate Admissions." University of Maryland, College Park. 2017. Accessed November 09, 2017. https://www.admissions.umd.edu/.

"UMD Undergraduate Admissions - Student Organizations." University of Maryland, College Park. 2013. Accessed July 2015. http://www.admissions.umd.edu/student/ClubsAndOrganizations.php.

"Undergraduate Admissions." University of Wisconsin-Milwaukee. 2017. Accessed November 09, 2017. https://www4.uwm.edu/admission/new-freshmen.cfm.

"Undergraduate Catalog - Limited Enrollment Programs." Brigham Young University. 2017. Accessed November 21, 2017. https://catalog.byu.edu/about-byu/limited-enrollment-programs.

"Undergraduate Catalog 2016/2017 - Limited Enrollment Programs." University of Maryland, College Park, 2016-2017. 2016-2017. Accessed November 21, 2017. https://catalogundergraduate.umd.edu/files/2016-2017_Undergraduate_catalog.pdf.

"Unemployment rates by educational attainment in April 2015: The Economics Daily." U.S. Bureau of Labor Statistics. April 2015. Accessed November 23, 2016. http://www.bls.gov/opub/ted/2015/unemployment-rates-by-educational-attainment-in-april-2015.htm.

"*University of Maryland - College Park: Student Life – Crime.*" College Factual, Media Factual. 2018. Accessed May 6, 2018. https://www.collegefactual.com/colleges/university-of-maryland-college-park/student-life/crime/.

"University of Maryland TV." Montgomery County Government. 2016. Accessed November 2016. http://www.montgomerycountymd.gov/PEG/UMDTV/UniversityofMarylandTV.html.

Varsity Tutors. "Should I Join My College's Honors Program?." USA Today College. September 5, 2015. Accessed May 1, 2018, http://college.usatoday.com/2015/09/05/college-honors-program/.

Vazifdar, Lena. "Top Ten Poorest States in America 2012." TravelersToday. September 25, 2012. Accessed June 2015. http://www.travelerstoday.com/articles/3150/20120925/top-ten-poorest.htm.

Venable, Melissa A. "Mental Health Guide for College Students." OnlineColleges.net. October 22, 2013. Accessed March 7, 2015. http://www.onlinecolleges.net/for-students/mental-health-resources/.

"Victims of Sexual Violence: Statistics." RAINN. 2016. Accessed November 27, 2017. https://www.rainn.org/statistics/victims-sexual-violence.

"Virginia Tech Shootings Fast Facts." CNN. April 03, 2017. Accessed November 28, 2017. http://www.cnn.com/2013/10/31/us/virginia-tech-shootings-fast-facts/index.html.

"Visit Maryland Day." University of Maryland, College Park. 2017. Accessed November 09, 2017. https://www.admissions.umd.edu/visit/vmd.php.

Walsh, Dustin. "College credit transfer system examined." Crain's Detroit Business. April 06, 2011. Accessed October 26, 2016. http://www.crainsdetroit.com/article/20110403/SUB01/110409981/college-credit-transfer-system-examined.

"Welcome to Tutoring." Tutoring @ UMD, University of Maryland, College Park. 2016. Accessed October 27, 2016. http://tutoring.umd.edu/.

"What courses should I take? - FAQ: Admissions." The United States Military Academy – West Point®. 2013. Accessed July 2015. http://www.westpoint.edu/admissions/SitePages/FAQ_Admission.aspx.

"What is a credit score?" Bankrate.com April 22, 2010. Accessed November 18, 2017. http://www.bankrate.com/finance/credit-cards/what-is-a-credit-score.aspx.

"What Is an Associate's Degree?" *GetEducated.com*. 2018. Accessed September 2, 2018. https://www.geteducated.com/career-center/detail/what-is-an-associate-degree.

"What is profession? Definition and meaning." BusinessDictionary.com. 2013. Accessed July 2015. http://www.businessdictionary.com/definition/profession.html.

"What's Your Plan? College with a Mental Health Disorder." Mental Health America. February 04, 2016. Accessed October 27, 2016. http://www.mentalhealthamerica.net/whats-your-plan-college-mental-health-disorder.

"When it comes to paying for college, career school, or graduate school, federal student loans offer several advantages over private student loans - Summary of Federal and Private Loan Differences." Chart. Federal Student Aid, U.S. Department of Education. 2017. Accessed November 13, 2017. https://studentaid.ed.gov/sa/types/loans/federal-vs-private.

White, Martha C. "Students with private debt left out by Obama plan." NBCNews.com. October 28, 2011. Accessed November 14, 2017. http://business.nbcnews.com/_news/2011/10/28/8507854-students-with-private-debt-left-out-by-obama-plan.

Willsey, Marie. "How Stafford Loans Work." HowStuffWorks. 2013. Accessed February 13, 2015. https://money.howstuffworks.com/personal-finance/college-planning/financial-aid/stafford-loans.htm.

Winerip, Michael. "How to Assess a College's Mental Health Offerings." The New York Times. January 28, 2011. Accessed October 2, 2016. https://thechoice.blogs.nytimes.com/2011/01/28/mental-health/?_r=0 Web.

"Wolfram Alpha: Computational Knowledge Engine." Wolfram. 2017. Accessed November 25, 2017. http://www.wolframalpha.com/.

"Work Ethic Scholarship Program." *mikeroweWorks Foundation*. 2018. Accessed August 19, 2018. http://profoundlydisconnected.com/.

"Working In Groups - Writing and Speaking, Composing Processes: Drafting, Designing, and Revising." Writing@CSU, Colorado State University. 1993-2017. Accessed November 24, 2017. https://writing.colostate.edu/guides/guide.cfm?guideid=42.

"World of Math Online." Math.com. Accessed November 2016. http://www.math.com/.

"World Population Prospects: The 2017 Revision | Multimedia Library - United Nations Department of Economic and Social Affairs." United Nations. June 21, 2017. Accessed November 28, 2017. https://www.un.org/development/desa/publications/world-population-prospects-the-2017-revision.html.

"Writing Center." English Department, University of Maryland, College Park. 2013. Accessed September 24, 2014. http://www.english.umd.edu/academics/writingcenter.

"YouTube." YouTube LLC. 2017. Accessed November 25, 2017. http://www.youtube.com/.

Zelkadis, Elvi. "Just Explain It: Is America's Middle Class Recovering?" Yahoo! Finance. June 05, 2013. Accessed June 2015. http://finance.yahoo.com/blogs/just-explain-it/just-explain-america-middle-class-recovering-202502943.html?vp=1.

Notes

1. Three good books among others that provide specific actions about staying in college are John B. Bader, *Dean's List: Eleven Habits of Highly Successful College Students* (Baltimore: The Johns Hopkins University Press, 2011), Jon B. Gould, *How to Succeed in College (while Really Trying): A Professor's Inside Advice* (Chicago, IL: The University of Chicago Press, 2012), and Michael S. Malone, *The Everything College Survival Book: From Social Life to Study Skills—All You Need to Know to Fit Right In*, 2nd ed. (Avon, MA: Adams Media, 2005).

2. "Back to School Statistics," Fast Facts - National Center for Education Statistics, U.S. Department of Education, January 1, 2014, accessed February 6, 2015, http://nces.ed.gov/fastfacts/display.asp?id=372.

3. "Educational Attainment: 2012 - 2016 American Community Survey 5 - Year Estimates," American FactFinder - U.S. Census Bureau, 2016, accessed April 19, 2018, https://factfinder.census.gov/faces/tableservices/jsf/pages/productview.xhtml?pid=ACS_16_5YR_S1501&src=pt.

4. "Highest Educational Attainment Levels Since 1940: Adults 25 Years and Older with a Bachelor's Degree or Higher," US Census Bureau, March 30, 2017, accessed April 19, 2018, https://www.census.gov/library/visualizations/2017/comm/cb17-51_educational_attainment.html.

5. "A Stronger Nation 2016 ©2016," Lumina Foundation for Education, Inc., April 2016, accessed November 2017, http://strongernation.luminafoundation.org/report/2016/.

6. "Educational attainment of the labor force age 25 and older by race and Hispanic or Latino ethnicity, 2014 annual averages," chart, TED: The Economics Daily - U.S. Bureau of Labor Statistics, November 18, 2015, accessed November 26, 2016, http://www.bls.gov/opub/ted/2015/educational-attainment-and-occupation-groups-by-race-and-ethnicity-in-2014.htm.

7. "Quick Guide: College Costs," Chart, The College Board, 2017, accessed November 15, 2017, https://bigfuture.collegeboard.org/pay-for-college/college-costs/quick-guide-college-costs.

8. Elvi Zelkadis, "Just Explain It: Is America's Middle Class Recovering?" Yahoo! Finance, June 05, 2013, accessed June 2015, http://finance.yahoo.com/blogs/just-explain-it/just-explain-america-middle-class-recovering-202502943.html?vp=1.

9. Andrew Martin and Andrew W. Lehren, "Student Loans Weighing Down a Generation with Heavy Debt," The New York Times, May 12, 2012, accessed November 17, 2017. http://www.nytimes.com/2012/05/13/business/student-loans-weighing-down-a-generation-with-heavy-debt.html?pagewanted=all&_r=0.

10. Lena Vazifdar, "Top Ten Poorest States in America 2012," TravelersToday, September 25, 2012, accessed June 2015, http://www.travelerstoday.com/articles/3150/20120925/top-ten-poorest.htm

11. Annie Murphy Paul, "What We Can Learn from First-Generation College Students," Time, Inc., April 11, 2012, accessed November 07, 2017, http://ideas.time.com/2012/04/11/what-we-can-learn-from-first-generation-college-students/.

12. Ibid.

13. Amy Scott, "First generation college students go viral," Marketplace - Minnesota Public Radio. November 21, 2013, accessed July 2015, http://www.marketplace.org/topics/wealth-poverty/first-family/first-generation-college-students-go-viral.

14. "10 Very Successful People without A College Degree," BuzzFeed, Inc., January 17, 2013, accessed June 2015, http://www.buzzfeed.com/suits/very-successful-people-without-a-college-degree.

15. "Academies of Louisville," *Jefferson County Public Schools*, 2017, accessed June 8, 2018, https://www.jefferson.kyschools.us/academies-louisville.

16. "Work Ethic Scholarship Program," *mikeroweWorks Foundation,* 2018, accessed August 19, 2018, http://profoundlydisconnected.com/.

17. Vivian Giang, "The 40 Highest-Paying Jobs You Can Get Without A Bachelor's Degree," Business Insider, August 07, 2012, accessed June 2015, http://www.businessinsider.com/the-40-highest-paying-jobs-you-can-get-without-a-bachelors-degree-2012-8.

18. "Leanna's Essentials - All Natural Products," Leanna's Essentials - All Natural Products, 2016, accessed October 3, 2016, http://www.leannasessentials.com/.

19. Laura Petrecca, "In tight job market, some teens start their businesses," USA Today, May 22, 2009, accessed October 2016, http://usatoday30.usatoday.com/money/smallbusiness/2009-05-18-teen-entrepreneurs-start-businesses_N.htm.

20. "Unemployment rates by educational attainment in April 2015: The Economics Daily," U.S. Bureau of Labor Statistics, April 2015, accessed November 23, 2016, http://www.bls.gov/opub/ted/2015/unemployment-rates-by-educational-attainment-in-april-2015.htm.

21. "Table A-4, Employment status of the civilian population 25 years and over by educational attainment," U.S. Bureau of Labor Statistics, November 03, 2017, accessed November 07, 2017, http://www.bls.gov/news.release/empsit.t04.htm.

22. Jennifer Ma, Matea Pender and Meredith Welch, "Education Pays 2016 © 2016: The Benefits of Higher Education for Individuals and Society." The College Board, 2016, 17, accessed June 2018, https://trends.collegeboard.org/sites/default/files/education-pays-2016-full-report.pdf.

23. Brad Hershbein and Melissa S. Kearney, "Major Decisions: What Graduates Earn over Their Lifetimes," The Hamilton Project: Brookings Institution, September 29, 2015, accessed October 2017, http://www.hamiltonproject.org/papers/major_decisions_what_graduates_earn_over_thei r_lifetimes.

24. Anthony P. Carnevale, Stephen J. Rose, and Ban Cheah, "The College Pay Off: Education, Occupations, Lifetime Earnings," *Center on Education and the Workforce: Georgetown University,* 2014, 16-18, accessed May 8, 2018, https://cew.georgetown.edu/wp-content/uploads/2014/11/collegepayoff-complete.pdf.

25. "What is profession? Definition and meaning," BusinessDictionary.com, 2013, accessed July 2015, http://www.businessdictionary.com/definition/profession.html.

26. "What courses should I take? - FAQ: Admissions," The United States Military Academy – West Point, 2013, accessed July 2015, http://www.westpoint.edu/admissions/SitePages/FAQ_Admission.aspx.

27. Halle Edwards, "SAT / ACT Prep Online Guides and Tips," What's Better for You: IB or AP? College Expert Guide: PrepScholar, 2013-2018, accessed April 23, 2018, https://blog.prepscholar.com/whats-better-for-you-ib-or-ap.

28. "AP Course Ledger," The College Board, University of Oregon, 2002-2016, accessed February 13, 2015, https://apcourseaudit.epiconline.org/ledger/.

29. Edwards.

30. "The Pros and Cons of AP Classes," College Foundation of West Virginia, 2009, accessed February 13, 2015, https://secure.cfwv.com/Home/Article.aspx?level=3XAP2FPAX6J7I3kztATGuYyXAP2 BPAXDahIQXAP3DPAXXAP3DPAX&articleId=VTv0Iu2AvHXAP2FPAXqUmR2EH LZXgXAP3DPAXXAP3DPAX

31. Edwards.

32. "Practice and Be Prepared for ACCUPLACER," The College Board, 2017, accessed November 07, 2017, https://accuplacer.collegeboard.org/student/practice.

33. "PCC Compass Placement Test Review Packet," Portland Community College, accessed November 7, 2017, https://www.pcc.edu/resources/tutoring/sylvania/student-success/documents/total.pdf.

34. "Learning Links," Grays Harbor College, 2017, accessed November 07, 2017, https://www.ghc.edu/content/learning-center-learning-links.

35. "Free English Tests and Exercises Online for ESL, TOEFL, TOEIC, GRE, SAT, GMAT," EnglishTestStore, 2005-2016, accessed November 07, 2017, http://englishteststore.net/index.php?option=com_content&view=featured&Itemid=344.

36. "World of Math Online," Math.com, accessed November 2016, http://www.math.com/.

37. "High School Students and Teachers," American Mathematical Society, 2014, accessed July 2015, http://www.ams.org/programs/students/high-school/high-school.

38. Leah Y. Latimer, *Higher Ground: Preparing African-American children for College* (New York, NY: Avon Books, Inc., 1999), 267.

39. "Mathematics Placement Test Information," Department of Mathematics, University of Maryland, College Park, 2013, accessed February 2015, http://www-math.umd.edu/placement-test-information.html.

40. "Application Deadlines," The Campus Commons, University Language Services, 1998-2017, accessed November 09, 2017, http://www.universitylanguage.com/guides/us-university-and-us-college-application-deadlines/.

41. Susan Kannel, "A Consumer's Guide to Going to School: Types of colleges and universities," chart, Chicago, IL: Council for Experiential Learning, 2013, accessed October 25, 2017, http://www.cael.org/pdfs/a_consumer-s_guide_to_going_to_school_-_cael.

42. Darcy Lewis, "Consider a College With a Focus on Minority Students," *U.S. News & World Report,* September 21, 2016, accessed August 18, 2018, https://www.usnews.com/education/best-colleges/articles/2016-09-21/consider-a-college-with-a-focus-on-minority-students.

43. "College Navigator," National Center for Education Statistics, U.S. Department of Education, 2013, accessed August 2015, http://nces.ed.gov/collegenavigator/.

44. "Find Your College - College Search," The Princeton Review: TPR Education IP Holdings, LLC, 2013, accessed February 2015, https://www.princetonreview.com/college-search?ceid=cp-1023919.

45. "Naviance by Hobsons," *Hobsons - Naviance.com,* 2016, accessed May 8, 2018, https://www.naviance.com/.
46. "America's Top Colleges," Forbes, 2014, accessed April 2014, http://www.forbes.com/top-colleges/list/.

47. "Compiling the Forbes/CCAP Rankings," Center for College Affordability and Productivity, accessed August 2015, http://centerforcollegeaffordability.org/uploads/2012_Methodology.pdf.

48. "The Best Colleges in America, Ranked," U.S. News & World Report L.P., November 8, 2017, accessed November 08, 2017, http://colleges.usnews.rankingsandreviews.com/best-colleges.

49. "Find a college that's right for you! - College Search," Peterson's, A Nelnet Company, 2017, accessed November 08, 2017, http://www.petersons.com/college-search.aspx.

50. "College Video Tours," It's Nacho, YOUniversityTV, 2017, accessed November 08, 2017, https://www.youniversitytv.com/category/college/.

51. "Accreditation: What does Accreditation Mean?" Digital Properties, LLC, 2013, accessed March 2015, https://www.50states.com/college-resources/accreditation.htm.

52. "Council for Higher Education Accreditation," Council for Higher Education Accreditation, 2013, accessed March 2015, http://www.chea.org/.
53. "U.S. Department of Education Database of Accredited Postsecondary Institutions and Programs," Office of Postsecondary Education, U.S. Department of Education, 2017, accessed November 09, 2017, http://ope.ed.gov/accreditation/.

54. "Accreditation - Institution Search, U.S. Department of Education Database of Accredited Postsecondary Institutions and Programs," Office of Post Secondary Education, U.S. Department of Education, 2017, accessed November 09, 2017, http://ope.ed.gov/accreditation/Search.aspx.

55. "Degree Mill and Accreditation Mills - Video," Council for Higher Education Accreditation/CHEA International Quality Group, 2013, accessed March 2015, http://www.chea.org/4DCGI/cms/review.html?Action=CMS_Document&DocID=208&MenuKey=main.
56. "Maryland Community Colleges," *Maryland Association of Community Colleges,* 2018, accessed August 20, 2018, https://mdacc.org/.

57. "Work Ethic Scholarship Program," *mikeroweWorks Foundation.*

58. "General Education Courses at MC and at UMCP," Montgomery College, 2013, accessed August 2015, http://cms.montgomerycollege.edu/EDU/Department2.aspx?id=26608.

59. Ibid.

60. "Transfer Equivalency Databases," Montgomery College, 2017, accessed November 13, 2017, http://cms.montgomerycollege.edu/EDU/Plain.aspx?id=50742.

61. "Transfer Agreements," Montgomery College, 2017, accessed November 13, 2017, http://cms.montgomerycollege.edu/agreements/.

62. Paul Fain, "Graduate, Transfer, Graduate," Inside Higher Ed., November 8, 2012, accessed July 2015, http://www.insidehighered.com/news/2012/11/08/high-graduation-rates-community-college-transfers.

63. Dustin Walsh, "College credit transfer system examined," Crain's Detroit Business, April 06, 2011, accessed October 26, 2016, http://www.crainsdetroit.com/article/20110403/SUB01/110409981/college-credit-transfer-system-examined.

64. Jeff Guo, "*Attention college students: You may have earned a degree without knowing it,*" Washington Post.com, Feb 10, 2015, accessed May 7, 2018, https://www.washingtonpost.com/blogs/govbeat/wp/2015/02/10/attention-college-students-you-may-have-earned-a-degree-without-knowing-it/?noredirect=on&utm_term=.0dbea3f4d454.

65. "Requirements for a Bachelors Degree," College of Liberal Arts & Sciences, The University of Iowa, July 18, 2016, accessed July 2016, https://clas.uiowa.edu/students/handbook/requirements-bachelors-degree.

66. "College Transfer Simplified," AcademyOne, Inc., 2017, accessed November 13, 2017, http://www.collegetransfer.net/Home/tabid/976/Default.aspx.

67. "College Transfer Timeline," Campus Explorer, 2015, accessed June 26, 2016, http://www.campusexplorer.com/college-advice-tips/0DF8B2E9/College-Transfer-Timeline/.

68. "Fast Facts - AACC," American Association of Community Colleges, 2017, accessed November 10, 2017, https://www.aacc.nche.edu/research-trends/fast-facts/.

69. Ibid.

70. Christian Tizon, "Signature Report 6: Completing College: A National View of Student Attainment Rates – Fall 2007 Cohort," Six-Year Outcomes by Starting Institution Type, National Student Clearinghouse Research Center, December 15, 2013, 5, accessed November 21, 2016, http://nscresearchcenter.org/signaturereport6/#prettyPhoto. The total cohort was 2,397,524 students.

71. Ibid.

72. Ibid.

73. "About MC," Montgomery College, 2016, accessed July 2016, http://www.montgomerycollege.edu/.

74. "College Navigator - Montgomery College," National Center for Education Statistics, U.S. Department of Education, 2016, accessed April 2016, https://nces.ed.gov/collegenavigator/?q=montgomery%20college&s=MD&id=163426#ge neral.

75. Ibid. "Total Enrollment (All Undergraduates)."

76. "Work Ethic Scholarship Program," *mikeroweWorks Foundation.*

77. "What Is an Associate's Degree?," *GetEducated.com*, 2018, accessed September 2, 2018, https://www.geteducated.com/career-center/detail/what-is-an-associate-degree.

78. John Marus, "Stopping the clock on credits that don't count," The Hechinger Report, Teachers College at Columbia University, April 22, 2013, accessed February 10, 2015, http://hechingerreport.org/stopping-the-clock-on-credits-that-dont-count/.

79. "What Is an Associate's Degree?," *GetEducated.com.*

80. Kim Clark, "Community college: How to choose the right school," CNNMoney. June 7, 2012, accessed July 2015, http://money.cnn.com/2012/06/07/pf/college/community-college/index.htm.

81. "College Navigator," National Center for Education Statistics, U.S. Department of Education.

82. "How does your community college stack up?" CNNMoney, accessed September 2015, http://money.cnn.com/pf/college/community-colleges/.

83. "College Rankings - Top 500 Ranked Community Colleges," StateUniversity.com, 2013, accessed July 2015, http://www.stateuniversity.com/rank/score_rank_by_commc.html.

84. Martin.

85. Kannel.

86. Marus.

87. "For-profit Colleges and Universities," National Conference of State Legislatures, July 3, 2013, accessed October 2013, http://www.ncsl.org/research/education/for-profit-colleges-and-universities.aspx.

88. Ibid.

89. "Closure of ITT Technical Institutes," Federal Student Aid, May 11, 2017, accessed November 09, 2017, https://studentaid.ed.gov/sa/about/announcements/itt.

90. Martha C. White, "Students with private debt left out by Obama plan," NBCNews.com, October 28, 2011, 3, accessed November 14, 2017, http://business.nbcnews.com/_news/2011/10/28/8507854-students-with-private-debt-left-out-by-obama-plan.

91. "High Hopes, Big Debts," The Project on Student Debt, May 2010, 2, accessed November 9, 2017, https://ticas.org/files/pub/High_Hopes_Big_Debts_2008.pdf.

92. Ibid.

93. Martin.

94. "High Hopes, Big Debts."

95. "College Navigator - DeVry University-Virginia," National Center for Education Statistics, U.S. Department of Education, 2018, accessed August 2018, https://nces.ed.gov/collegenavigator/?q=DeVry+university&s=VA&id=482653#expenses

96. Ibid, "Multiyear Tuition Calculator."

97. "College Navigator - University of Maryland-College Park," National Center for Education Statistics, U.S. Department of Education, 2018, accessed August 2018, https://nces.ed.gov/collegenavigator/?q=University+of+Maryland+College+Park&s=MD+VA&id=163286#expenses.

98. "College Navigator - DeVry University-Virginia," Cohort Default Rates – Fiscal Year 2014.

99. "College Navigator - University of Maryland-College Park," Cohort Default Rates – Fiscal Year 2014.

100. "College Navigator - DeVry University-Virginia."

101. "College Navigator - University of Maryland-College Park."

102. "Transfer Course Database: Devry University-Arlington," Transfer Credit Services, University of Maryland, College Park, 2018, accessed May 5, 2018, https://app.transfercredit.umd.edu/inst-select.html?searchType=master&searchString=devry&countryCode=US&stateCode=.

103. Zola Dincin. Schneider and Norman G. Schneider, *Campus Visits & College Interviews: A Complete Guide for College-bound Students and their Families, 3rd ed.* (New York, NY: College Board, 2012).

104. Ibid.

105. "Visit Maryland Day," University of Maryland, College Park, 2017, accessed November 09, 2017, https://www.admissions.umd.edu/visit/vmd.php.

106. "Quick Facts about Financial Aid and Community Colleges, 2007-08," Institute for College Access & Success, March 2009, accessed July 2013, https://eric.ed.gov/?id=ED540078.

107. "College Affordability and Transparency Center," U.S. Department of Education, 2015, accessed November 17, 2017, http://collegecost.ed.gov/catc/#. The website provides a method to generate reports about tuition and fees by school.

108. "College Navigator – Sarah Lawrence College," National Center for Education Statistics, U.S. Department of Education, 2018, accessed June 2018. https://nces.ed.gov/collegenavigator/?id=195304#expenses.

109. Ibid, "Multiyear Tuition Calculator."

110. "The Smart Student Guide to Financial Aid - Calculators," FinAid - Financial Aid Advice, Fastweb LLC, 2017, accessed November 15, 2017, http://www.finaid.org/calculators/.

111. "FAFSA4caster," Federal Student Aid, U.S. Department of Education, 2018, accessed August 7, 2018, https://fafsa.ed.gov/FAFSA/app/f4cForm?execution=e1s1.

112. "America's Top Colleges - University of Maryland, College Park," Forbes, 2016, accessed October 22, 2016, http://www.forbes.com/colleges/university-of-maryland-college-park/.

113. Ibid.

114. "College Data, College Profile - University of Wisconsin - Milwaukee," 1st Financial Bank, USA, 2013, Accessed October 22, 2016. http://www.collegedata.com/cs/data/college/college_pg01_tmpl.jhtml?schoolId=1702.

115. "College Affordability and Transparency Center," U.S. Department of Education, 2018, accessed August 10, 2018, https://collegecost.ed.gov/index.aspx.

116. "Costs," University of Maryland, College Park, 2016, accessed October 22, 2016, https://admissions.umd.edu/finance/costs.

117. "America's Top Colleges - University of Maryland, College Park," Forbes, 2016.

118. "Cost to Attend University of Wisconsin Milwaukee: Annual Costs," *CollegeCalc.org*, 2018, accessed May 19, 2018, http://www.cite.com/bibliography.html?id=5b007c70b9aa8fef618b4571.

119. "America's Top Colleges - University of Wisconsin, Milwaukee," Forbes, 2016, accessed October 22, 2016, http://www.forbes.com/colleges/university-of-wisconsin-milwaukee/.

120. "The Smart Student Guide to Financial Aid - Calculators," FinAid - Financial Aid Advice, Fastweb LLC, 2017, accessed November 15, 2017, http://www.finaid.org/calculators/.

121. "Compare Schools," *Consumer Financial Protection Bureau,* 2018, accessed August 2018, https://www.consumerfinance.gov/paying-for-college/compare-financial-aid-and-college-cost/.

122. Latimer, 241.

123. "Academic Scholarships and Merit Scholarships," *Scholarships.com*, 2018, accessed August 19, 2018, https://www.scholarships.com/financial-aid/college-scholarships/scholarships-by-type/academic-scholarships-and-merit-scholarships/. Scholarships.com is one such source for scholarship information.

124. "Avoiding Scams," Federal Student Aid, U.S. Department of Education, 2018, accessed August 8, 2018, https://studentaid.ed.gov/sa/types/scams.

125. Scholarship America, "Get Money for College Through ROTC Programs," U.S. News & World Report, July 25, 2013, accessed April 29, 2018, https://www.usnews.com/education/blogs/the-scholarship-coach/2013/07/25/get-money-for-college-through-rotc-programs.

126. Ibid.

127. Latimer, 74.

128. Kate Stalter, "Everything You Need to Know about 529 College Savings Plans," U.S. News & World Report, August 28, 2017, accessed November 17, 2017, https://money.usnews.com/529s.

129. Kate Stalter, "8 Common Misconceptions about 529 Plans," U.S. News & World Report, November 24, 2014, accessed April 29, 2018, https://money.usnews.com/money/personal-finance/mutual-funds/articles/2014/11/24/8-common-misconceptions-about-529-plans.

130. Microsoft Office has features to print out thank you notes, and announcements on plain bond or colored paper. You can send high school graduation announcements via regular mail, e-mail, or using on-line free e-cards and e-invitations. Using a digital camera, you can take acceptable pictures of the graduate that you can attach or enclose with announcements and thank you notes.

131. Lilit Marcus, "Fundraising helps teen go from homeless to Howard U.," Today, NBCNews, August 19, 2013, accessed June 13, 2015, https://www.today.com/news/fundraising-helps-teen-go-homeless-howard-u-6C10945702.

132. Ibid.

133. "Quick Guide: College Costs," Chart.

134. Ibid.

135. "Types of Aid," Federal Student Aid, U.S. Department of Education, June 19, 2017, accessed November 14, 2017, https://studentaid.ed.gov/sa/types.

136. "Federal Work-Study Jobs Help Students Earn Money to Pay for College or Career School," *Federal Student Aid, U.S. Department of Education,* 2018, accessed August 17, 2018, https://studentaid.ed.gov/sa/types/work-study.

137. "Student Aid Deadlines," Federal Student Aid, U.S. Department of Education, 2018, accessed May 19, 2018, https://fafsa.ed.gov/deadlines.htm.

138. Katie Lobosco, "Too Poor to Pay for College, Too Rich for Financial Aid," *CNNMoney, Cable News Network, A WarnerMedia Company,* April 29, 2018, accessed August 17, 2018. https://money.cnn.com/2016/04/28/pf/college/college-financial-aid/index.html.

139. "Grants and Scholarships Are Free Money to Help Pay for College or Career School," Federal Student Aid, U.S. Department of Education, 2018, Accessed August 7, 2018, https://studentaid.ed.gov/sa/types/grants-scholarships, Other federal grants include the Federal Supplemental Educational Opportunity Grants, Teacher Education Assistance for College and Higher Education (TEACH) Grants, and Iraq and Afghanistan Service Grants.

140. "Federal Pell Grant Program – Federal Student Aid," U.S. Department of Education, 2018, accessed May 1, 2018, https://studentaid.ed.gov/sa/types/grants-scholarships/pell.

141. "New College Board Report Finds Millions in Financial Aid Go Unclaimed at Community Colleges," May 19th, 2010, The College Board, accessed November 2017, http://press.collegeboard.org/releases/2010/new-college-board-report-finds-millions-financial-aid-go-unclaimed-community-colleges

142. Ibid.

143. Ibid.

144. "When it comes to paying for college, career school, or graduate school, federal student loans offer several advantages over private student loans - Summary of Federal and Private Loan Differences," chart, Federal Student Aid, U.S. Department of

Education, 2017, accessed November 13, 2017, https://studentaid.ed.gov/sa/types/loans/federal-vs-private.

145. "Federal Student Loans for College or Career School Are an Investment in Your Future," *Federal Student Aid, U.S. Department of Education*, 2018, accessed August 14, 2018, https://studentaid.ed.gov/sa/types/loans.

146. "Choose the Federal Student Loan Repayment Plan That's Best for You," *Federal Student Aid, U.S. Department of Education*, 2018, accessed July 14, 2018, https://studentaid.ed.gov/sa/repay-loans/understand/plans.

147. Kat Tretina, "5 Common Myths About Student Loan Consolidation," *Student Loan Hero,* May 16, 2017, accessed August 21, 2018, https://studentloanhero.com/featured/student-loan-debt-consolidation-myths/.

148. "Federal Student Loans for College or Career School Are an Investment in Your Future," *Federal Student Aid, U.S. Department of Education.*

149. Marie Willsey, "How Stafford Loans Work," HowStuffWorks, 2013, accessed February 13, 2015, https://money.howstuffworks.com/personal-finance/college-planning/financial-aid/stafford-loans.htm.

150. "Subsidized and Unsubsidized Loans," Federal Student Aid, U.S. Department of Education, 2015, accessed February 15, 2015, https://studentaid.ed.gov/sa/types/loans/subsidized-unsubsidized.

151. "Stafford Loans @ 2013," chart, Scholarships.com, 2013, accessed November 15, 2017, http://www.scholarships.com/financial-aid/student-loans/stafford-loans/.

152. "Interest Rates and Fees," Federal Student Aid, U.S. Department of Education, 2017, accessed November 17, 2017, https://studentaid.ed.gov/sa/types/loans/interest-rates.

153. "Deferment and Forbearance," Federal Student Aid, U.S. Department of Education, 2017, accessed November 17, 2017, https://studentaid.ed.gov/sa/repay-loans/deferment-forbearance.

154. *Private Loans: Facts and Trends,* report, The Institute for College Access & Success, June 2016, 2, accessed November 14, 2017, https://ticas.org/sites/default/files/pub_files/private_loan_facts_trends.pdf.

155. "The U.S. Department of Education Offers Low-interest Loans to Eligible Students to Help Cover the Cost of College or Career School," *Federal Student Aid, U.S. Department of Education,* 2018, accessed August 17, 2018, https://studentaid.ed.gov/sa/types/loans/subsidized-unsubsidized#eligibility-time-limit.

156. Ibid.

157. Dan Caplinger, "Graduates Keep Struggling With Private Student Loans," Daily Finance, AOL.com, September 1, 2014, accessed November 14, 2017, http://www.dailyfinance.com/2013/09/01/students-still-struggle-private-loan-college-debt/.

158. *Executive Summary – Mid-Year snapshot of private student loan complaints,* report, Consumer Financial Protection Bureau, July 2013, 1, accessed November 14, 2017, http://files.consumerfinance.gov/f/201308_cfpb_complaint-snapshot.pdf.

159. Christina Couch, "Six Things to Know About Private Student Loans | Fox Business," Personal Finance, Fox Business/Bankrate, Inc., August 2, 2012, accessed November 15, 2017, http://www.foxbusiness.com/features/2012/08/02/6-things-to-know-about-private-student-loans.html.

160. *Private Loans: Facts and Trends,* report.

161. *Executive Summary – Mid-Year snapshot of private student loan complaints*, 5.

162. "CFPB Ombudsman," *Consumer Financial Protection Bureau,* 2018, accessed August 19, 2018, https://www.consumerfinance.gov/.

163. "The Smart Student Guide to Financial Aid - Calculators," FinAid - Financial Aid Advice, Fastweb LLC, 2017, accessed November 15, 2017, http://www.finaid.org/calculators/.

164. "Student Loan Calculator," *Bankrate.com,* 2018, accessed August 16, 2018, https://www.bankrate.com/calculators/college-planning/loan-calculator.aspx.

165. Brianna McGurran, "When to Refinance Student Loans," *Nerdwallet.com,* July 26, 2018, accessed 2018. https://www.nerdwallet.com/blog/loans/student-loans/student-loan-refinancing-faq/.

166. Ibid.

167. Jay MacDonald, "Debt Payoff Debate: Pay Smallest Balance 1st? Or Highest Rate?" *CreditCards.com,* January 23, 2013, accessed June 22, 2018. https://www.creditcards.com/credit-card-news/paying-off-debt-study-smallest_balance-financially-wrong-1276.php.

168. Radhika Bodapati, "Overview of Military Education Benefits," Military.com, a Monster Company, 2017, accessed November 17, 2017, http://www.military.com/education/money-for-school/education-benefits-in-the-military.html.

169. "The U.S. Department of Education Offers Low-interest Loans to Eligible Students to Help Cover the Cost of College or Career School," *Federal Student Aid, U.S. Department of Education.*

170. Angela Colley, "Credit Unions vs. Banks - Differences, Pros & Cons," Money Crashers, July 13, 2011, accessed November 17, 2017, http://www.moneycrashers.com/why-credit-unions-are-better-than-banks/.

171. Dennis Paul Kimbro, *The Wealth Choice: Success Secrets of Black Millionaires* (The Napoleon Hill Foundation, 2013), 252.

172. "Credit vs. debit: Get the most from your cards," Better Money Habits, Bank of America Corporation, 2017, accessed November 17, 2017, https://bettermoneyhabits.bankofamerica.com/en/personal-banking/difference-between-debit-and-credit?cm_mmc=EBZ-CorpRep-_-Taboola-_-text_link_creditvsdebit-_-Taboola_Desktop_Textlink_CPC_CC_CreditVsDebit%25252525252520-%25252525252520fbid#fbid=REEvu9JkTe5.

173. Bob Sullivan, "Know Your Rights on Bank Account Fraud," *NBCNews.com,* August 12, 2005, accessed September 6, 2018, http://www.nbcnews.com/id/8915217/ns/technology_and_science-security/t/know-your-rights-bank-account-fraud/#.W5EwpyaWxjo.

174. "What is a credit score?" Bankrate, April 22, 2010, accessed November 18, 2017, http://www.bankrate.com/finance/credit-cards/what-is-a-credit-score.aspx.

175. Ibid.

176. Shari B. Olefson, *Financial Fresh Start: your five-step plan for adapting and prospering in the new economy* (New York, NY: American Management Association, 2013), 91.

177. "*Annual Credit Report.com*," Central Source, LLC, 2018, accessed May 5, 2018, https://www.annualcreditreport.com/index.action.

178. Ibid.

179. " Bankrate.com Credit Card Minimum Payment Calculator -- How long will it take to pay off credit cards?" Bankrate.com, 2017, accessed November 17, 2017, https://www.bankrate.com/calculators/credit-cards/credit-card-minimum-payment.aspx.

180. "Intuit Mint: It's All Coming Together," *Intuit, Inc.,* 2018, accessed August 18, 2018, https://www.mint.com/.

181. Linda Landis Andrews, *How to Choose a College Major* (New York, NY: McGraw-Hill, 2006), 4.

182. Andrews, 16.

183. "Matching Careers to Degrees," chart, Big Future, The College Board, October 20, 2017, accessed October 20, 2017, https://bigfuture.collegeboard.org/explore-careers/careers/matching-careers-to-degrees.

184. Andrews, 197.

185. "Is Taking a Gap Year Before College Right For You?" *The Princeton Review,* 2018, accessed August 23, 2018, https://www.princetonreview.com/college-advice/deferred-admission.

186. "UMD Undergraduate Admissions," University of Maryland, College Park, 2017, accessed November 09, 2017, https://www.admissions.umd.edu/.

187. "Majors by College," University of Maryland, College Park, 2017, accessed November 18, 2017, https://www.admissions.umd.edu/explore/majors/majors-college.

188. "Program Requirements, Aerospace Engineering," University of Maryland, College Park, 2017, accessed November 18, 2017, http://www.aero.umd.edu/undergrad/program-req.

189. "TESTUDO, Office of the Registrar," University of Maryland, College Park, 2017, accessed November 18, 2017, http://www.testudo.umd.edu/.

190. "Advising Policies, Undergraduate Computer Science at UMD," University of Maryland, College Park, accessed November 17, 2013, http://undergrad.cs.umd.edu/advising-policies.

191. "Four Year Plans," College of Computer, Mathematical, and Natural Sciences, University of Maryland, College Park, October 12, 2012, accessed November 17, 2013, https://cmns.umd.edu/undergraduate/advising-academic-planning/academic-planning/four-year-plans.

192. Grant Tilus, "Semester Vs. Quarter: What You Need to Know When Transferring Credits," *Rasmussen College,* September 27, 2012, accessed August 28, 2018, https://www.rasmussen.edu/student-life/blogs/main/semester-vs-quarter-need-to-know-when-transferring-credits/.

193. "NCHC Online Guide," National Collegiate Honors Council, 2017, accessed November 14, 2017, http://www.nchcguide.com/nchc-directory/#more-52.

194. Varsity Tutors, "Should I Join My College's Honors Program?," USA Today College, September 5, 2015, Accessed May 1, 2018, http://college.usatoday.com/2015/09/05/college-honors-program/.

195. Kim Clark, "6 tips to help you pick the best community college," CNNMoney, June 7, 2012, Accessed November 13, 2017, http://money.cnn.com/2012/06/06/pf/college/best-community-college/index.htm.

196. "Phi Beta Kappa National Honor Society," Phi Theta Kappa, 2017, accessed November 14, 2017, https://www.ptk.org/default.aspx.

197. "Study Abroad Vs Exchange," *Study Abroad Center, The University of Hawai'i at Manoa*, 2018, accessed June 24, 2018. http://www.studyabroad.hawaii.edu/students/study-abroad-vs-exchange/.

198. "Testudo, Schedule of Classes, Deadlines," University of Maryland, College Park, 2013, accessed June 10, 2015, http://www.testudo.umd.edu/acad_deadlines/fall_2013.html

199. "The U.S. Department of Education Offers Low-interest Loans to Eligible Students to Help Cover the Cost of College or Career School," *Federal Student Aid, U.S. Department of Education.*

200. "Rate My Professors - Review Teachers and Professors, School Reviews, College Campus Ratings," Ratemyprofessors.com, 2013, accessed June 21, 2015, http://www.ratemyprofessors.com/

201. "General Education Program," University of Maryland, College Park, 2013, accessed September 24, 2015, http://www.gened.umd.edu/.

202. "Illiteracy Statistics," STATS, Statisticsbrain.com, July 22, 2017, accessed November 22, 2017, https://www.statisticbrain.com/number-of-american-adults-who-cant-read/.

203. Ibid.

204. "FAQ on Textbooks," National Association of College Stores, January 2014, accessed June 10, 2015, https://www.nacs.org/advocacynewsmedia/faqs/faqontextbooks.aspx.

205. "Department of Mathematics - Testbank," University of Maryland, College Park, 2016, accessed November 22, 2017, https://www-math.umd.edu/testbank.html.

206. "The Honor Program - The Simon Center for Professional Military Ethic," United States Military Academy, West Point, 2014, accessed November 10, 2015, https://www.usma.edu/scpme/SitePages/Honor.aspx.

207. Richard Byrne, "7 Resources for Detecting and Preventing Plagiarism," Free Technology for Teachers, August 24, 2010, accessed November 22, 2017, http://www.freetech4teachers.com/2010/08/7-resources-for-detecting-and.html.

208. "Free Online Proofreader: Grammar Check, Plagiarism Detection, and more," Paper Rater, 2014, accessed November 10, 2015, http://www.paperrater.com/.

209. "BibMe: Free Bibliography & Citation Maker - MLA, APA, Chicago, Harvard," BibMe, a Chegg Service, 2017, accessed November 22, 2017, http://www.bibme.org/.

210. "The Purdue OWL: Citation Chart," The Purdue OWL, October 2014, accessed November 10, 2015, https://owl.english.purdue.edu/media/pdf/20110928111055_949.pdf. The Citation Chart provides explanations to illustrate the different styles.

211. "Add a citation and create a bibliography: Word," Microsoft, 2017, accessed November 22, 2017, https://support.office.com/en-us/article/Add-a-citation-and-create-a-bibliography-17686589-4824-4940-9c69-342c289fa2a5.

212. William Shakespeare, *The Tragedy of Macbeth*, The Harvard Classics, vol. XLVI, Part 4, New York, NY: P.F. Collier & Son, 1909–14, Bartleby.com, 2001, accessed November 11, 2015, www.bartleby.com/46/4/.

213. Anna M. Stewart et al., "A Research Guide for Students and Teachers - SUNY-ESF," State University of New York, College of Environmental Science and Forestry, 2009, accessed November 22, 2017, http://www.esf.edu/outreach/sciencecorps/documents/ResearchGuide_NSFGK12.pdf. The pamphlet is a guide for conducting scientific research, which can be used by any new college student who has to write a research paper.

214. William Shakespeare, *Macbeth*, SparkNotes, LLC, 2013, accessed November 24, 2017, http://www.sparknotes.com/shakespeare/macbeth/canalysis.html. SparkNotes do not take the place of reading the book or play.

215. "How to Write a Thesis Statement," Writing Guides: Writing Tutorial Services, Indiana University, Bloomington, April 7, 2014, accessed November 24, 2017, http://www.indiana.edu/~wts/pamphlets/thesis_statement.shtml.

216. "Writing Center," English Department, University of Maryland, College Park, 2013, accessed September 24, 2014, http://www.english.umd.edu/academics/writingcenter.

217. "ELMS," Division of information Technology, University of Maryland, College Park, 2016, accessed October 27, 2016, http://www.elms.umd.edu/.

218. "Math Success Program, Frequently Asked Questions," Department of Resident Life, University of Maryland, College Park, 2016, accessed October 27, 2016, http://reslife.umd.edu/programs/math_success/faq/.

219. "Welcome to Tutoring," Tutoring @ UMD, University of Maryland, College Park, 2016, accessed October 27, 2016, http://tutoring.umd.edu/.

220. "Learning Assistance Service," Counseling Center, University of Maryland, College Park, 2015, accessed March 11, 2015, https://www.counseling.umd.edu/las/.

221. "Khan Academy," Khan Academy, 2017, accessed November 25, 2017, http://www.khanacademy.org/.

222. "Wolfram Alpha: Computational Knowledge Engine," Wolfram, 2017, accessed November 25, 2017, http://www.wolframalpha.com/.

223. "YouTube," YouTube LLC, 2017, accessed November 25, 2017, http://www.youtube.com/.

224. "Massive Open Online Courses (MOOCs)," EdX Inc, 2016, accessed November 25, 2017, http://mooc.org/.

225. "25 Colleges and Universities Ranked by Their OpenCourseWare," Learn.org, 2003-2017, accessed November 25, 2017, https://learn.org/articles/25_Colleges_and_Universities_Ranked_by_Their_OpenCourse Ware.html

226. "Coursera - Courses," Coursera Inc, 2017, accessed November 25, 2017, https://www.coursera.org/courses?languages=en.

227. "The 50 Most Innovative Computer Science Departments in the U.S.," Computer Science Degree Hub, 2017, accessed November 26, 2017, http://www.computersciencedegreehub.com/50-innovative-computer-science-departments/.

228. Ibid.

229. "*University of Maryland - College Park: Student Life – Crime,*" College Factual, Media Factual, 2018, accessed May 6, 2018, https://www.collegefactual.com/colleges/university-of-maryland-college-park/student-life/crime/.

230. "Campus Safety and Security," U.S. Department of Education, 2017, accessed November 28, 2017, https://ope.ed.gov/campussafety/#/institution/search.

231. "*City-data.com: Crime Rate in Washington, D.C.,*" Advameg, Inc., 2018, accessed May 5, 2018, http://www.city-data.com/crime/crime-Washington-District-of-Columbia.html.

232. Ibid.

233. "Circle of 6," Tech 4 Good Inc, 2015, accessed June 26, 2016, http://www.circleof6app.com/.

234. "Friend Radar," Not Exactly Software LLC, 2009 - 2013, accessed October 10, 2015, http://www.notexactlysoftware.com/FriendRadar.

235. Colleen Curry, "Natalee Holloway Is Dead, Judge Decides," ABC News, January 12, 2012, accessed November 26, 2017, http://abcnews.go.com/News/judge-pronounces-natalee-holloway-dead/story?id=15346993.

236. Ibid.

237. "2016 NCIC Missing Person and Unidentified Person Statistics," FBI. gov, January 20, 2017, accessed November 26, 2017, https://www.fbi.gov/file-repository/2016-ncic-missing-person-and-unidentified-person-statistics.pdf/view.

238. Anne Marie Helmenstine, "Get Facts Rohypnol or Roofies," ThoughtCo, March 7, 2017, accessed November 26, 2017, https://www.thoughtco.com/rohypnol-or-roofies-fast-facts-606394.

239. Ibid.

240. "Birth Control Methods," Bedsider, 2013, accessed March 13, 2014, http://bedsider.org/methods.

241. John J. Macionis and Vincent N. Parrillo, *Cities and Urban Life*, 6th ed. (New Jersey: Pearson Education Inc, 2013), 282.

242. Mark Lino, "*The Cost of Raising a Child,*" U.S. Department of Agriculture, Jan 13, 2017, accessed May 6, 2018, https://www.usda.gov/media/blog/2017/01/13/cost-raising-child.

243. Tamar Lewin, "Unwed Fathers Fight for Babies Placed for Adoption by Mothers," The New York Times, March 19, 2006, accessed March 7, 2015, http://www.nytimes.com/2006/03/19/us/unwed-fathers-fight-for-babies-placed-for-adoption-by-mothers.html.

244. Kevin Dolak, "Yeardley Love's Family Worried About George Huguely's Violent Past," ABC News, September 20, 2012, accessed October 15, 2014, http://abcnews.go.com/US/yeardley-loves-family-worried-george-huguelys-violent-past/story?id=17278322.

245. American Civil Liberties Union, *Know Your Rights and Your College's Responsibilities: Title IX and Sexual Assault* (Women's Rights Project), accessed December 13, 2017, https://www.aclu.org/files/pdfs/womensrights/titleixandsexualassaultknowyourrightsandyourcollege%27sresponsibilities.pdf.

246. Cathy Meyer, "4 Things You Need to Know about Restraining Orders," LiveAbout, July 14, 2017, accessed November 27, 2017, http://divorcesupport.about.com/od/abusiverelationships/a/restrain_order.htm.

247. "Helping Victims with Safety. Helping States with Implementation," Cynthia L. Bischof Memorial Foundation, March 03, 2015, accessed November 27, 2017, http://www.cindysmemorial.org/.

248. "Victims of Sexual Violence: Statistics," RAINN, 2016, accessed November 27, 2017, https://www.rainn.org/statistics/victims-sexual-violence.

249. Sofi Sinozich and Lynn Langton, *Rape and Sexual Assault Victimization Among College-Age Females, 1995–2013,* report no. NCJ 248471, Bureau of Justice Statistics, U.S. Department of Justice, December 2014, 1, accessed November 27, 2017, https://www.bjs.gov/content/pub/pdf/rsavcaf9513.pdf.

250. Sinozich.

251. "FAQs for the Media: 'When Reporting a Crime, Who Should Students and Residents Located on Campus Call?'" *International Association of Campus Law Enforcement Administrators,* 2018, accessed August 18, 2018, https://www.iaclea.org/faqs-for-the-media.

252. Ibid.

253. Ibid.

254. "Reporting to Law Enforcement," RAINN, 2016, accessed November 27, 2017, https://www.rainn.org/articles/reporting-law-enforcement.

255. Ibid.

256. American Civil Liberties Union, *Know Your Rights and Your College's Responsibilities: Title IX and Sexual Assault* (Women's Rights Project).

257. Sinozich.

258. "National Junior College Athletic Association," National Junior College Athletic Association, 2017, accessed November 14, 2017, http://www.njcaa.org/.

259. "World Population Prospects: The 2017 Revision | Multimedia Library - United Nations Department of Economic and Social Affairs," United Nations, June 21, 2017, accessed November 28, 2017, https://www.un.org/development/desa/publications/world-population-prospects-the-2017-revision.html.

260. James Nichols, "Kids React to Gay Marriage," YouTube, November 03, 2013, accessed November 28, 2017, http://www.youtube.com/watch?v=8TJxnYgP6D8.

261. "Nutrition Services," University Health Center, University of Maryland, College Park, 2009, accessed November 28, 2017, http://www.health.umd.edu/nutritionservices.
262. *College and University Food Bank Alliance,*" CUFBA National, 2018, accessed May 7, 2018, https://sites.temple.edu/cufba/about-us/.

263. "Salted Caramel Mocha Frappuccino® Blended Beverage," Starbucks Corporation, 2016, accessed November 28, 2017, https://www.starbucks.com/menu/drinks/frappuccino-blended-beverages/salted-caramel-mocha-frappuccino-blended-beverage.

264. "Sugars, Added Sugars and Sweeteners," American Heart Association Inc, 2013, accessed July 17, 2015, http://www.heart.org/HEARTORG/GettingHealthy/NutritionCenter/HealthyDietGoals/Sugars-and-Carbohydrates_UCM_303296_Article.jsp.

265. "What's Your Plan? College with a Mental Health Disorder," Mental Health America, February 04, 2016, accessed October 27, 2016, http://www.mentalhealthamerica.net/whats-your-plan-college-mental-health-disorder.

266. Michael Winerip, "How to Assess a College's Mental Health Offerings," The New York Times, January 28, 2011, accessed October 2, 2016, https://thechoice.blogs.nytimes.com/2011/01/28/mental-health/?_r=0 Web. The article addresses questions that parents and students should ask about prospective colleges' mental health services.

267. Leadership21 Committee, "Campus Mental Health: Know Your Rights," The Judge David L. Bazelon Center for Mental Health Law, 2008, 13, accessed March 7, 2015, http://www.bazelon.org/wp-content/uploads/2017/01/YourMind-YourRights.pdf.

268. "National Suicide Prevention Lifeline," *Substance Abuse and Mental Health Services Administration, Mental Health Association of New York City*, 2018, accessed June 8, 2018. https://suicidepreventionlifeline.org/.

269. Melissa A. Venable, "Mental Health Guide for College Students," OnlineColleges.net, October 22, 2013, accessed March 7, 2015, http://www.onlinecolleges.net/for-students/mental-health-resources/.

270. Leadership21 Committee, "Campus Mental Health: Know Your Rights."

271. "Prosecutors: Theater shooting suspect told classmate he wanted to kill people," CNN, August 24, 2012, accessed November 28, 2017, http://www.cnn.com/2012/08/24/justice/colorado-shooting/index.html.

272. "Commonly Abused Drugs Charts," National Institute on Drug Abuse, March 2011, accessed August 28, 2015, http://www.drugabuse.gov/drugs-abuse/commonly-abused-drugs/commonly-abused-drugs-chart.

273. Substance Abuse and Mental Health Services Administration, *Results from the 2012 National Survey on Drug Use and Health: summary of national findings*, NSDUH Series H-46, HHS Publication No. (SMA) 13-4795 (Rockville, MD: U.S. Dept. of Health and Human Services, Substance Abuse and Mental Health Services Administration, Center for Behavioral Health Statistics and Quality, 2013), 5, https://archive.samhsa.gov/data/NSDUH/2012SummNatFindDetTables/NationalFindings/NSDUHresults2012.htm#ch2.2.

274. Ibid.

275. "Before & After Drugs: The Horrors of Methamphetamines - Infographic," Rehabs.com, 2012, accessed May 2014, https://www.rehabs.com/explore/meth-before-and-after-drugs/infographic.php#.WhMkFyaWzIU.

276. "Marijuana as Medicine," National Institute of Drug Abuse, April 2017, accessed November 28, 2017, https://www.drugabuse.gov/publications/drugfacts/marijuana-medicine.

277. Oliver Roeder, "Releasing Drug Offenders Won't End Mass Incarceration," *FiveThirtyEight, ABC News Internet Ventures*, 2018, accessed August 17, 2018, https://fivethirtyeight.com/features/releasing-drug-offenders-wont-end-mass-incarceration/.

278. "Students with Criminal Convictions Have Limited Eligibility for Federal Student Aid," *Federal Student Aid, U.S. Department of Education*, 2018, accessed August 17, 2018, https://studentaid.ed.gov/sa/eligibility/criminal-convictions.

279. Matt Sledge, "The Drug War and Mass Incarceration by the Numbers," The Huffington Post, April 08, 2013, accessed November 28, 2017, https://www.huffingtonpost.com/2013/04/08/drug-war-mass-incarceration_n_3034310.html.

280. "Substance Abuse and Mental Health Services Administration, *Results from the 2012 National Survey on Drug Use and Health,* Illicit Drugs.

281. Ibid.

282. "Alcohol Facts and Statistics," National Institute on Alcohol Abuse and Alcoholism, U.S. Department of Health and Human Services, June 2017, 3, accessed November 29, 2017, https://www.niaaa.nih.gov/alcohol-health/overview-alcohol-consumption/alcohol-facts-and-statistics.

283. Ibid.

284. "Alcohol Policy Information System - Underage Drinking Maps & Charts," National Institute on Alcohol Abuse and Alcoholism, U.S. Department of Health and Human Services, 2016, accessed November 29, 2017, http://alcoholpolicy.niaaa.nih.gov/Underage_Drinking_Maps_and_Charts.html.

285. Meghan Gray and Rachel Mehlhaff, "UNT bans alcohol at fraternity events following student's fall," Dallas News, February 07, 2013, accessed November 29, 2017, https://www.dallasnews.com/news/denton/2013/02/07/unt-bans-alcohol-at-fraternity-events-following-students-fall.

286. "Alcohol Facts and Statistics," National Institute on Alcohol Abuse and Alcoholism.

287. "Harms of Cigarette Smoking and Health Benefits of Quitting," National Cancer Institute, December 3, 2014, accessed November 29, 2017, https://www.cancer.gov/about-cancer/causes-prevention/risk/tobacco/cessation-fact-sheet.

288. Ibid.

289. Brad Tuttle, "Cigarettes Taxes: States with Highest, Cheapest Prices," Money, Time Inc, April 20, 2017, accessed November 29, 2017, http://time.com/money/4748310/smoking-costs-cigarette-taxes-expensive/.

290. "Quitting Smoking Among Adults --- United States, 2001--2010," Centers for Disease Control and Prevention, November 11, 2011, 60(44); 1513-1519, accessed November 30, 2017, https://www.cdc.gov/mmwr/preview/mmwrhtml/mm6044a2.htm?s_cid=mm6044a2_w.

291. "NSLDS Student Access: National Student Loan Data System," *Federal Student Aid, U.S. Department of Education,* 2018, accessed July 14, 2018, https://www.nslds.ed.gov/nslds/nslds_SA/.

292. "How to Choose a Financial Planner," The Wall Street Journal, Dow Jones & Company, 2017, accessed December 13, 2017, http://guides.wsj.com/personal-finance/managing-your-money/how-to-choose-a-financial-planner/.

293. "Money 101: Personal Finance, Investing, Retirement, Saving," Time, Inc., 2017, accessed November 17, 2017, http://time.com/money/collection/money-101/.

294. John Csiszar, "12 Best Apps for First-Time Investors," GOBankingRates, July 26, 2017, accessed November 17, 2017, https://www.gobankingrates.com/investing/10-apps-timid-first-time-investors/.

295. "Feed The Pig: Tools to Invest, Save and Budget Your Money," Feed the Pig, American Institute of CPAs, 2006-2013, accessed November 17, 2017, https://www.feedthepig.org/.